Undocumented Immigrants in an Era of Arbitrary Law

This book describes the experiences of undocumented migrants, all around the world, bringing to life the challenges they face from the moment they consider leaving their country of origin, until the time they are deported back to it. Drawing on a broad array of academic studies in areas including law, literature and law, interpretation and translation studies, border studies, human rights, communication, critical discourse analysis and sociology, Robert Barsky argues that many of the actions that are taken against undocumented migrants are often arbitrary, and exercised by an array of officials who can and do exercise considerable discretion, both positive and negative.

Employing insights from a decade-long research project, Barsky also finds that every stop along the migrant's pathway into, and inside of, the host country is strewn with language issues, relating to intercultural communication, interpretation, gossip, hearsay, and the challenges of peddling linguistic wares in the social discourse marketplace. These language issues are almost always impediments to anodyne or productive interactions with host country officials, particularly on the "front lines" where migrants encounter border patrol and law enforcement officers without adequate means of communicating their situation or understanding their rights. Since undocumented people are categorized as "illegal", they can be subjected to abuse and exploitation by host country officials, who can choose to either tolerate or punish them on the basis of unpredictable, changeable and even illusory or "arbitrary" laws and regulations.

Citing experts at every level of the undocumented immigrant apparatuses worldwide, from public defenders to interpreters, Barsky concludes that the only viable policy to address prevailing abuses and inequalities is to move towards open borders, an approach that would address prevailing issues and, surprisingly, provide security and economic benefits to both host and home countries.

Robert F. Barsky is a Professor at Vanderbilt University. He has published widely in areas relating to language theory, Convention refugee adjudication and border studies, and he is the author of a trilogy of books about the milieus of Noam Chomsky and Zellig Harris.

Undocumented Immigrants in an Era of Arbitrary Law

The Flight and the Plight of People Deemed "Illegal"

Robert F. Barsky

Routledge
Taylor & Francis Group
LONDON AND NEW YORK

First published 2016
by Routledge
2 Park Square, Milton Park, Abingdon, Oxfordshire OX14 4RN

and by Routledge
711 Third Avenue, New York, NY 10017

First issued in paperback 2016

Routledge is an imprint of the Taylor & Francis Group, an informa business

British Library Cataloguing in Publication Data
A catalogue record for this book is available from the British Library

Library of Congress Cataloging-in-Publication Data
A catalog record has been requested for this title

ISBN: 978-1-138-63499-2 (pbk)
ISBN: 978-1-138-84948-8 (hbk)

Typeset in Garamond by
Servis Filmsetting Ltd, Stockport, Cheshire

This book is dedicated to public defenders and other advocates who work on the front lines, fighting the good fight on behalf of vulnerable populations everywhere.

Contents

Acknowledgements

The debts I owe for this book are so vast that it would require another preface to enumerate them, and so I'll simply say to those people who assisted me over the decade it took to complete this project: *Thank you*! I can't name the interviewees because I'm bound by Institutional Review Board (IRB) regulations set forth in the first chapter, but I would like to thank them. First and foremost. Routledge has been a joy to work with, thanks to the many wonderful people who work therein, and I'd like to especially thank Colin Perrin, Laura Muir and Ashlie Jackman for their constant guidance and support, Mathew Willis for the cover design, Sue Cope for copy-editing and Heather Jones for proof-reading the manuscript. I am also deeply grateful to the institution that has supported me from the day when I arrived, which, as it turns out, is also the day when this research started. Vanderbilt University has been my workplace and my home, literally, and a host of colleagues here have actively supported and inspired this project. The list is long, but I'd single out: Frank Bloch, Jody Combs, Kevin Davis, Daniel Gervais, Susan Kay, Andrea Mirabile, Letizia Modena, Lynn Ramey, Martin Rapisarda, Ed Rubin and Virginia Scott, who all provided significant intellectual support. The administration and various directors of research units provided funding and institutional support, and for this I'd like to thank, most notably: Carolyn Dever, Mona Fredrick, Gordon Gee, Dennis Hall, Richard McCarty, John Sloop, Susan Wente and Nick Zeppos. I was fortunate to work closely on these issues with the Migration and Diversity group at the VU Amsterdam Law School, and with members of the Amsterdam Critical Discourse Community (ACDC), thanks to a Visiting Professorship funded by the Dutch Royal Academy. I was also very glad to spend precious research time at the Institute for Advanced Studies in Toulouse, for which I'm especially grateful to Patrick Bolton and Paul Seabright. Students from Vanderbilt offered precious time and inspiration, and I owe special debts of thanks to Mallory Hope, Fabrice Picon, Alex Scavone and Alham Usman and the students of West House on the Vanderbilt Commons. I would also like to thank Debbie Anker, François Crépeau, Guy Goodwin-Gill, Julius Grey, Michael Hawes, Barbara Harrell-Bond, Jim Silk and Thomas Spijkeboer for inspiration and guidance all along the way in this and many other projects. Regular visits to Switzerland to teach Maymesters has provided me with precious occasions to learn from a vast array of devoted individuals, including Guido Ambroso, Jeff Crisp, George Höfflin, Mark Mason, Dominique Oliva Höfflin, Kristina Touzenis, Dorine Q. Da Re-Van Der Wal, and Mohammad Taghi Yasamy. I am grateful for mentors who over the years have become my dearest friends: Marc Angenot, Noam Chomsky, Michael Holquist, Michel Pierssens, Elise Snyder and George Szanto. And finally, to my family, Marsha, Tristan, Ben and Kai, for whom each of my very best efforts are directed, with love and passion.

Permissions: Some of the material in this book was discussed in preliminary form at conferences, and I have published work that includes early articulations of themes included herein. I would like to thank the publishers for having granted me the right to elaborate upon them for this book: "Accessing Contextual Assumptions in Dialogue Interpreting", in *Text and Context: Essays On Translation and Interpreting*, eds. Mona Baker et al. (Manchester: St. Jerome Press), 2010, pp. 288–302; "Activist Translation in an Era of Fictional Law", for a special issue called *Translation and Social Activism*, ed. Sherry Simon, *Traduction, Terminologie, Rédaction* XVIII.2 (2007), pp. 17–48; "From Discretional to Fictional Law", SubStance 35.1, pp. 1–52; "Methodological Issues for the Study of Migrant incarceration in an Era of Discretion in Law in the Southern USA", eds. Ilse van Liempt and Veronika Bilger; *The Ethics of Migration Research Methodology: Processes, Policy and Legislation in Dealing with Vulnerable Immigrants*. Eastbourne: Sussex Academic Press, 2009, pp. 25–48.

Preface

> I find borders sort of arbitrary and bizarre. I find the whole idea morally repugnant.
>
> (A public defender interviewed for the project)[1]

This book describes the high levels of unpredictability, discretion, fickleness and arbitrariness that in my opinion pervade dealings with undocumented migrants at all levels of interaction between them and officials from host countries, all around the world. The consequence of this treatment, which is often reflected in language and communication concerns that I will outline in detail, is to render a population of predominantly poor and marginalized people even more vulnerable, and it opens the door to extreme levels of abuse. In order to capture an adequately descriptive image of the lives of irregular migrants, I have organized this book in a roughly chronological fashion, beginning with the underlying issues, moving to the push and pull factors that lure people away from their countries of origin, and then following the terrifying process that begins with front-line interactions between people from the home and host countries, and continues all the way to the incarceration and eventual deportation of the migrant back to his/her country of origin. Many of the examples provided are from a decade-long research project undertaken in the United States, but since the general presuppositions that underlie national borders, illegality and foreignness are similar from one state system to another, I think it fair to say that this book describes the challenges that any undocumented person endures in host countries all around the world. And since the root issue is the criminalization of foreigners who cross national borders without proper documentation, I propose that the root answer to how to address the problem is to take aim at the borders themselves, and ask ourselves whether it is legitimate that the state system has as part of its underlying character the idea of restricting the right, deemed in international law to be fundamental and unalienable, to free movement. This doesn't mean that states cannot police their borders in the exercise of legitimate law enforcement, it means that restricting the flow of people across borders as undertaken in most countries of the world creates an underclass of people who are rendered vulnerable, alien and criminal, a process that is antithetical to fostering the promotion and protection of basic human rights amongst those who are most affected by state violence.

The perspective from which this book is written is highly descriptive, but also deeply critical of the current systems by which undocumented immigrants are treated. I rely heavily upon interviews with migrants and parties to the enforcement system, as well as secondary literatures from a broad array of disciplines, especially law and language studies writ large. But this book neither references nor promotes obscure models or defers to vague theories because the first can have the effect of providing false solutions for complex issues, and the second provides a level of obscurity that is anything other than constructive in a realm that is of great and growing concern. I don't think that researchers in this realm should hide behind either of these so-called objective or so-called theoretical walls in order to claim objectivity because there's no such thing as a purely scientific analysis of a process like this one that is so deeply saturated in the subjectivity of each actor. Furthermore, I'm not unbiased with regards to this issue because I am an advocate for the humane treatment of people, and I believe that special efforts should be exerted to protect those who are most vulnerable.

Despite considerable evidence to the contrary, I would like to think that a perspective rooted in decency and that favors the respectful treatment of vulnerable people is uncontroversial, and that if the public was made aware of the injustices of the current system, then individuals and policy makers would be more likely to advocate for fundamental human rights, including the rights to free movement and freedom from illegitimate authority. I argue from this perspective because in almost any situation we might imagine, undocumented people are subjected to a range of abuses, both unofficial and official, that many people don't even realize exist. This occurs despite valiant efforts on the part of advocates, attorneys and academics because the very logic of exclusion and segregation on the basis of class, race, country of origin and gender inevitably produce persecution, and the ambiguity, discretion and arbitrariness of the legal processes that have been set up to adjudicate irregular migrants can provide the grounds for its execution. I will build a case to suggest that these endemic processes can only be challenged if borders between states allow for free or freer movement of people, and if countries facilitate mechanisms to regularize undocumented migrants. Only then will the current crapshoot that determines whether the host country official will exercise positive or negative discretion give way to movement across borders without undue violence and harassment.

Arguing from this perspective doesn't imply that host country officials couldn't exercise appropriate control over their borders, or that they would have to abdicate legitimate powers generally associated with sovereign nations. Ensuring free movement of peoples within and amongst nations will help foster migrants' access to basic human rights, including the right to health care, social services and employment. One model for this vision does exist for states that are members of the European Union (EU). The EU is not a perfect system, since it too creates border-states on the edges of its territory as well as various versions of persecution and exclusion. But if its example were to be followed in the Americas, in Asia and in Africa, en route to an eventual open borders policy worldwide, there would be enormous benefit to all parties of the process.

This then is the case I wish to make, and in order to do so I'll refer in detail to the in-depth interviews I've conducted with people who are insiders to the day-to-day workings of the current systems in the United States, primarily, but also Canada and Europe.

I myself am an immigrant, but in regards to those whose professional work involves defending, interpreting for, prosecuting, healing or integrating undocumented migrants, I stand as a privileged outsider who is bound only by a desire and professional obligation to speak the truth on the basis of my research. As such, I speak openly and freely, and with what Marc Angenot describes as a kind of "deviance and subversion that is *tolerated*, using *ostentatious* language expenditures, and even perhaps a form of satire that is protected by the Powers that be" (Angenot 2004, p. 217). I also speak as a researcher specializing in language theories that relate to translation, social discourse theory and legal argumentation, and I bring to this realm the tools that I've previously employed in research into Convention refugee issues, the narratives of homeless people and issues relating to incarcerated persons in Barsky (1994, 1996, 1997, 2001, 2005). Situated therefore both inside and outside, I attempt to contribute to crucial issues of social justice with the license of a kind of interloper, someone who can go beyond what can normally be said. I find great inspiration for this kind of work from the carnivalesque Fool, or the Clown:

> The Fool does not follow any ideology. He rejects all appearances, of law, justice, moral order. He sees brute force, cruelty and lust. He has no illusions and does not seek consolation in the existence of natural or supernatural order, which provides for the punishment of evil and the reward of good. Lear, insisting on his fictitious majesty, seems ridiculous to him. All the more ridiculous because he does not see how ridiculous he is. But the Fool does not desert his ridiculous, degraded king, and accompanies him on his way to madness. The Fool knows that the only true madness is to recognize this world as rational.
>
> (Kott 1974, pp. 166–7)

The Elizabethan-era fool is an interesting example of an advocate for social justice because he had officially sanctioned access to power via the king, who represented absolute authority, but also granted license to fools or clowns to challenge it. In the modern world, some fiction writers have used the same model, employing the prestige amassed during literary careers to speak out on issues of the day. My inspiration for this work comes from writers like Charles Dickens, George Orwell, John Steinbeck and Émile Zola. Zola is an especially interesting example because his fame as the leading novelist of his day provided him with privileged access to the newspaper *L'Aurore,* where he loudly proclaimed, to quote Hamlet, that "there are more things on Heaven and Earth" or, to recall Gershwin's *Porgy and Bess,* "it ain't necessarily so...". Zola spoke out in the name of justice, and from a standpoint that gave him a voice amidst a cacophony of lies and misrepresentations promulgated by the government and the army. In so doing he put himself at considerable risk, and was murdered for his efforts.

There are some teachers including Noam Chomsky, Bertrand Russell, Edward Said and Howard Zinn who have followed similar paths, shunning the kinds of niceties, intrigues and professional engagements offered to obedient intellectuals in favor of speaking unabashed truth (and derived different but very considerable appreciation for their efforts). Edward Said, whose work on behalf of Palestinians brought wrath upon him from certain quarters, suggested that it's worth making a great deal of one's rare opportunities to work beyond the ivory tower:

> catching the audience's attention, being better at wit and debate than one's opponents. For there is something fundamentally unsettling about intellectuals who have neither offices to protect nor territory to consolidate and guard; self-irony is therefore more effective than pomposity, directness more than hemming and hawing.
>
> (Said 1996, p. xviii)

It's true that:

> no one can speak up all the time on all the issues. But, I believe, there is a special duty to address the constituted and authorized powers of one's own society, which are accountable to its citizenry, particularly when those powers are exercised in a manifestly disproportionate and immoral war, or in a deliberate program of discrimination, repression, and collective cruelty.
>
> (Said 1993, p. 98)

The system of immigrant incarceration is an example of this cruelty, which I now take it as a responsibility to denounce because, as Jean-Paul Sartre wrote:

> The writer is *situated* in his time; every word he utters has reverberations. As does his silence. I hold Flaubert and the Goncourts' responsible for the repression that followed the Commune because they didn't write a line to

> prevent it. Some will object that this wasn't their business. But was the Calas trial Voltaire's business? Was Dreyfus's sentence Zola's business? Was the administration of the Congo Gide's business? Each of those authors, at a particular time in his life, took stock of his responsibility as a writer, and I wish to do so of mine.
>
> (Sartre 1988, p. 252)

Some commentators might challenge the decision to speak out on behalf of irregular migrants in the Americas, in Europe and beyond because this is a group of people who are in defiance of domestic laws, in most cases consciously. Furthermore, the pervasiveness of undocumented people is to be expected in light of the existing marketplace and the state system, and in many cases these people have found ways of surviving despite their irregular status. In other words, they have chosen to run this risk, and then when their presence is deemed a detriment to the interests of a political party, or a voting bloc, or some local situation, they *can be* subjected to arrest, incarceration and deportation on the basis of their being in violation of domestic law. They are considered "illegal", but they are also tolerated, and in many cases even deemed desirable or essential to the smooth functioning of particular societies. This perspective ignores that all people have rights, that these rights include (according to international Conventions and Declarations) the right to free movement, that the punishments doled out to these people are totally out of proportion with their actions, and that tolerating or supporting the status quo is to ensconce the idea that every society is entitled to an underclass of human beings who can be treated as inferiors.

One of the standard lines used against undocumented people is that they steal jobs by queue jumping, and threaten the economies of the host country. In fact, there is actually a significant cadre of experts who support dramatic changes to how we consider and treat border policies as means of *improving* local economies. Moses (2009) has pointed out that respected economists from major institutions have argued for open borders, and to consider his examples and sources suggests that the idea shouldn't be so easily dismissed within the social discourse about border crossing. He reviews recent work by three commentators who hearken from three of the most conservative business organizations, one American, one British and one international: Philippe Legrain, former journalist for *The Economist* magazine (cf. Legrain 2006); World Bank economist Lant Pritchett's (cf. Pritchett 2006) and *Wall Street Journal*'s editorial board member Jason Riley (cf. Riley 2008). The arguments they present are various, but include ideas that this study supports, including: the free movement of people is just as beneficial as the free movement of goods and capital; societies from developed countries need to devise better mechanisms for supporting, integrating and assimilating immigrants from the developing world; and open borders are consistent with some basic values and traditions that underwrite countries such as the United States:

> In choosing these three examples, I do not mean to suggest that all economists believe that the benefits of greater immigration outweigh the costs. Economists, after all, are known for their inability to agree about anything. But even the most skeptical economists realize that the economic costs of immigration—if they do, in fact, exist—are remarkably small and vary by level of aggregation. The costs associated with undocumented immigrants is probably even smaller, as these workers pay local and payroll taxes, but shy away from using many of the public services that these taxes support (indeed, their demographic profile makes them less likely to rely on public support, as they tend to be young male workers, without children and family). Even if we accept a small economic cost to immigration, there is no reason to dwell on these as the political, moral and social gains from immigration are almost overwhelming positive.
>
> (Moses 2009, p. 12)

Few people would imagine that commentators associated with the *Wall Street Journal*, the World Bank or *The Economist* would agree on such a policy, but if we examine the current system of abuse and punishment more closely, it's surprising that more people aren't of their ideological ilk. It's important to spread the word because people all over the world are accustomed to seeing undocumented people doing fundamental tasks, and yet they don't speak out when these same people, especially workers, are subjected to "crackdowns", arrest and deportation (Bloch 2013; Bloch, Kumarappan and McKay 2014; Bloch and McKay 2014). In other words, it's commonplace to think that for whatever reason, when we don't need undocumented workers anymore, when they've finished building our stadium, painting our home, weeding our garden, picking our crops or when they turn out to be human, and make the mistakes that the rest of us make when we slip behind the steering wheel of our car en route to an inebriated ride upon the suddenly blurry interstates that provide us with convenient pathways to our malls and our suburban retreats, then we can unceremoniously make them disappear, forever. A lawyer interviewed for this project said:

> Most immigrants are known for good labor. They show up on time for work, they do their work, and they need the money. And so, the employers seem to look the other way [in regards to their immigration status]. But then when the heat comes down, they give them up. So these are very mixed messages, and employers are very opportunistic. I hear horror stories, and in fact I could have sworn that I've even heard that Wal-Mart, or some other employer, was employing people and making them live in trailers and paying them nothing. It's the new slavery. You make people think you are going to report the person to the authorities if he complains or asks for more money, so in essence, to me, this is the new slavery.

From this perspective, undocumented people would have to be good workers, given the competition for their jobs and, as a scholar-activist noted, they have to be resilient just to make the journey to the host country:

> The boundary enforcement apparatus produces the perfect worker because what it does is it weeds people out. Because it is so difficult to cross now [from Mexico to the United States], the voyage weeds out the relatively weak, because it's just too difficult a trek.

An alternative to throwing up our arms and simply accepting this system, with all of its contradictions, arbitrariness and brutality would be to embrace the population as a whole, and provide the same advantages to all people on a national soil. This sounds utopian but is, from the perspective of one lawyer, simply pragmatic:

> I guess people think if you are too welcoming then you are encouraging people to get here illegally, and then benefit from things such as schooling, medical care, and driver's licenses. I think it is so ridiculous to think that if we don't provide this, they will not come. They are going to come. Why would you not want them to take a driver's test and get insurance and learn the rules of the road? Immigrants are going to be here, and they are going to work, and they are going to do a good job while they are building your house, so why would you not want them? It is for you and me that they are getting their driver's licenses, and their children are getting an education. It is like everybody wants to be blissfully ignorant of reality. The reality is these people are here, building your schools, cleaning your schools, and building your community. Why not embrace them into your community and help the next generation really integrate?

These kinds of questions, which are frank, clear and straightforwardly enlightening in their very audacity, are what made this project enjoyable, despite the real horror that I experience in the face of the draconian, punitive and abusive system it describes. For this reason, I've dedicated this book to the heroes on the front lines, those public defenders, investigators, translators and attorneys who work on the side of the oppressed and the marginalized. I have singled out the public defenders because they consciously and conscientiously choose to work for a very modest salary with a group of people whose cases seem like lost causes from the very outset. What the public defenders taught me is that irregular migrants aren't actually condemned to the worst case scenario when people fight on their behalf, and in an era when public service is under attack, we need to valorize the work of those people who have chosen this vocation as a means of publicly expressing their care for the oppressed.

Note

1 This book contains citations from interviews undertaken with different parties to the undocumented immigrant issue, including lawyers, public defenders, advocates, law enforcement officials, incarceration officials, interpreters and academics. In accordance with the Institutional Review Board (IRB) guidelines that relate to this project, these interviews have been stripped of all identifying features. As such, interviewees are only identified by their profession. These interviews were recorded by the author from 2005 to 2014 in Canada, Europe and the United States, and most of them were transcribed by professional transcribers. In certain cases the citations have been edited to eliminate redundancies, unrelated digressions, pauses, verbal ticks ("like", "you know"), grammatical or spelling mistakes and inaudible or partially inaudible statements.

Bibliography

Angenot, Marc (2004) "What Can Literature Do? From Literary Sociocriticism to a Critique of Social Discourse", in Barsky (2004), pp. 217–33.

Barsky, Robert F. (1994) *Constructing a Productive Other: Discourse Theory and the Convention Refugee Hearing*. Amsterdam and Philadelphia, PA: John Benjamins.

Barsky, Robert F. (1996) "The Function of the Intercultural Interpreter", *The Translator: Studies in Intercultural Communication* 2.1, pp. 45–63.

Barsky, Robert F. (1997) "Outsider Law in Literature: Construction and Representation in Death of the Maiden", *SubStance: A Review of Theory and Criticism* 84, pp. 66–89.

Barsky, Robert F. (2001) *Arguing and Justifying: Assessing the Convention Refugee Choice of Moment, Motive and Host Country*. Aldershot, Burlington, VT, Sydney and Singapore: Ashgate.

Barsky, Robert F. (2005) "Stories from the Court of Appeal", *Dis/Locations*, eds. Mike Baynham and Anna de Fina, Manchester, UK and Northampton, MA: St. Jerome's Press, pp. 217–38.

Barsky, Robert F. (ed.) (2004), "Marc Angenot and the Scandal of History", *Yale Journal of Criticism* 17.2, pp. 163–313.

Barsky, Robert F. and Denise Helly (1996) "Women Through the Eyes of Writers Who Immigrated to Québec in the 1980s", *Ethnic Writing*, ed. Alan L. McLeod. New Delhi: Sterling Publishers Private, pp. 168–80.

Bloch, Alice (2013) "The Labour Market: Experiences and Strategies of Young Undocumented Migrants", *Work, Employment and Society* 27.2, pp. 272–87.

Bloch, Alice, Leena Kumarappan and Sonia McKay (2014) "Women Migrants Today: New Directions, No Papers, Old Barriers", *Working USA: The Journal of Labor and Society* 17, pp. 339–55.

Bloch, Alice and Sonia McKay (2014) "Hidden Dishes—How Food Gets on to Our Plates: Undocumented Migrants and the Restaurant Sector", *Journal of Workplace Rights* 17, pp. 69–91.

Kott, Jan (1974) *Shakespeare, Our Contemporary*. New York: Norton.

Legrain, Philippe (2006) *Immigrants: Your Country Needs Them*. London: Little Brown.

Moses, Jonathon W. (2009) "The Politics of Immigration: Introduction to a Special Issue on US Immigration", *European Journal of American Studies* 4.3. Available at: http://ejas.revues.org/7715. [Accessed: 15 January 2015]

Pritchett, Lant (2006) *Let Their People Come*. Washington, DC: Center for Global Development.

Riley, Jason L. (2008) *Let Them In: The Case for Open Borders*. New York: Gotham Books.

Said, Edward (22 July 1993) "The Reith Lectures: Speaking Truth to Power", *Independent*. Available at: http://www.independent.co.uk/life-style/the-reith-lectures-speaking-truth-to-power-in-his-penultimate-reith-lecture-edward-said-considers-the-basic-question-for-the-intellectual-how-does-one-speak-the-truth-this-is-an-edited-text-of-last-nights-radio-4-broadcast-1486359.html#. [Accessed: 15 January 2015]

Said, Edward (1996) *Representations of the Intellectual: The 1993 Reith Lectures*. New York: Vintage.

Sartre, Jean-Paul (1988) *What is Literature?* Introduction by Steven Ungar. Cambridge, MA and London: Harvard University Press.

Introduction: advocating for those who suffer

> There's a lot of misinformation going on about the law; but I also think that this is to be expected because there's what the law is, and there's how it is being implemented, and those don't necessarily overlap.
>
> (A lawyer interviewed for the project)

This book offers an attempt to understand the experiences of undocumented migrants all around the world, from the moment they consider leaving their country of origin until the time they are deported back to it. I argue that many of the actions that are taken against these people are often arbitrary, and implemented by an array of officials who can exercise considerable discretion, particularly on what I call the "front lines", where migrants encounter host country officials. I also suggest that every stop along the migrant's pathway into and inside of the host country is strewn with language issues, including intercultural communication, interpretation, gossip, hearsay, and *idées reçues.* These language issues are almost always impediments to anodyne or productive interactions with host country officials because undocumented people are always acting "illegally", and their very presence on the territory of a host country makes them susceptible to punishment for immigration violations that can include overstaying visas, illegal entry, illegal employment or illegally re-entering the country subsequent to deportation. This susceptibility renders people vulnerable, irrespective of whether they have been in the host country for a few minutes, a few decades or as long as they can remember. In some cases, these people may have grown up, married, had children and worked in a host country. They may run their own business, pay taxes, employ citizens of the host country and contribute to the community. In any of the 30 countries in the world that recognize birthright,[1] they might also have children who, by virtue of their having been born in the host country, will never live in the betwixt-and-between world that their undocumented parents inhabit, which is of course one of the many "pull factors" that bring people to take the risk of living illegally.

Or, and this is in many cases the arbitrary or, these same people can be pulled over by the police for a burnt-out taillight, be singled out by their skin color, their accent, their inability to speak the language of the host country or by their license or ID (or lack thereof),[2] and be arrested for being "illegal". They may then be unable to meet bail fast enough to avoid a zealous paper-pusher who might make a late night phone call to immigration officials to check on the status of inmates. If they are found to be undocumented, they can be sent to a holding institution (detention center, jail, prison) to await trial, followed by incarceration and deportation and then, a few days or months or even years later, find themselves "back" in a country that some of them have not seen for years. Even Barack Obama, considered "liberal" on the spectrum of those involved in immigration policy, has been an avid participant in the deportation of undocumented immigrants (Khimm 2012), leading to the widely reported statistic that by the end of 2012, deportations under Mr. Obama reached 2 million, "or nearly the same number of deportations in the United States from 1892 to 1997" (Shear 2013, p. A12). If deported immigrants return to the United States subsequent to deportation in order to, say, continue their lives with their families and are singled out (for whatever reason) for denunciation to immigration authorities, they can be subjected to prison terms of 4–6 years (Reasoner 2011); and if they happen to have any kind of felony charge in their past, including domestic abuse, a drug or gun conviction or DUI (drinking under the influence), they can be sent away for long prison sentences under the terms of an "aggravated felony" conviction (Immigration Policy Center 2012).

This particular scenario is the American version of gargantuan efforts underway all around the world to apprehend, incarcerate and deport unwanted undocumented people, in part to punish them for their actions, but also to send a message to others that they shouldn't make a similar attempt either to live "illegally", or even to make a Convention refugee claim under the auspices of the 1951 Geneva Convention, a phenomenon that has been observed amongst numerous groups including Afghans in Europe (Schuster 2011), boat people in Canada (Lieu 2011–12), Vietnamese refugees in Bangkok (Palmgren 2014), Iraqi refugees in Indonesia (Hoffman 2011) and of course Latin Americans in the United States. The growing number of immigrants in prisons for having violated immigration regulations is a result of profiling, surveillance and sweeps[3] which, over a four-year period, have cost the US government alone over 73 billion dollars in immigration enforcement (Simanski and Sapp 2012). These types of efforts, replicated in many countries throughout the world, instil fear and uncertainty, and generate a counterproductive lack of trust in law enforcement amongst immigrants.

In some cities, states and countries there have been efforts on the part of immigration agents and prosecutors to focus on those foreigners who have committed serious crimes, or are deemed national security threats; but this practice is inconsistent, and likely contributes to the unpredictable nature of actions in this realm. It's this unpredictability, this uneven application, and the variation of how the laws are understood, interpreted and applied that were of special interest to me in researching and writing this book. For many people, including those who vote to sustain the current system, the arbitrary and arbitrarily enforced laws described herein are just hearsay, gossip or fear mongering that is no less real than the fairy tales that are told about the American Dream. But there are laws against irregular migration, and when they are applied they bring in their wake prolonged suffering for all those involved, including the society that works against its own best interests, and in contravention of the system of international human rights, when it acts in unnecessarily draconian ways against non-violent offenders.

Many of these examples hearken from the United States, or Western contexts; but in order to reinforce the sense of vulnerability imposed upon illegal people, we can look to a very different context and find similar and similarly dangerous repercussions to keeping people in the limbo of being "illegal" over long periods of time. Ramachandran (2002) reports that up until 1992 large numbers of undocumented Bangladeshis were living in different areas of India, and were being treated like *de facto* citizens. In mid-1992, nationalist organizations of the Hindu right, collectively known as Sangh Parivar, "made the manifold dangers of the unsanctioned immigration by growing numbers of poverty-stricken Bangladeshi Muslim peasants their rallying cry". As a consequence, the "lenient attitude of the Indian state towards these immigrants [had] hardened with astonishing rapidity". This is an old story, whereby a group that had lived undocumented with relative impunity suddenly found itself trapped in a political struggle that created new impetus for a "crack-down":

> Unsettled by this sweeping tide of Hindu chauvinism, a hurriedly enforced "Action Plan" to locate and identify these undocumented immigrants was followed by brisk efforts under "Operation Pushback" to deport them from New Delhi – India's capital city and locus of bureaucratic, political and financial power. Haphazard and sporadic in implementation, Operation Pushback, while unmasking partisan dispositions coursing through the Indian bureaucracy, also exemplified Congress' belated attempts at redeeming its enervated standing. It is also worth noting that the highly circumscribed material realities of the Bangladeshi immigrants residing in Delhi's numerous slums made them easy targets of these perverse politics, and that subsequent opposition, internally and from neighbouring Bangladesh, to the gratuitous brutality displayed towards the first groups of deportees contributed to the Operation's abrupt truncation.
>
> (Ramachandran 2002, pp. 311–12)

This is connected to another area of concern in an era of arbitrary law, which is that laws that are "on the books" but not enforced can be drummed up when it's politically expedient to do so, as for example those draconian 1996 anti-terrorism laws passed by Clinton[4] that were recalled and, moreover, enforced, after 9/11. Many overly optimistic voters thought that Obama would overturn these and other measures in the Patriot Act, but instead they have become further enshrined in American law. From this perspective, laws exist on a kind of continuum, from their being proposed to their being enforced, and the range of possible variations inside that continuum makes certain actions seem arbitrary, or decided on the basis of undue discretion.

This book supplements examples from the American context with examples from around the world, and some of the practices described can make American policies seem somewhat reasonable. But the inclusion of a broad range of practices in different contexts is for purposes of providing an international overview, and is not meant to exonerate the United States (or Australia, Canada, the UK or anywhere else), or to take our attention away from so-called First World practices – on the contrary. Intellectuals concerned with social justice need to take a very careful look at the issues from a host of angles, including, and perhaps in particular, the actions of officials in their own country. Noam Chomsky (1967) writes that Western intellectuals ought to speak out about such issues in their own countries because:

> they are a privileged minority, for whom Western democracy provides the leisure, the facilities, and the training to seek the truth lying hidden behind the veil of distortion and misrepresentation, ideology and class interest, through which the events of current history are presented to us.
> (p. 7)

This seems especially applicable in a country where the government sometimes voices overt disdain for undocumented people through both rhetoric and proposed legislation. One example is a provision to a recent act that would have made the first entry into the United States not just a crime, but a felony. Had this provision passed the Senate and been signed by the President, it would have opened up the possibility of prison sentences for first "offenders" akin to what we now offer to those who actually commit crimes:

> One of the most controversial provisions of H.R. 4437, the "Border Protection, Antiterrorism, and Illegal Immigration Control Act of 2005," or "Sensenbrenner Bill," would have made simply being undocumented in the United States a felony. Although passed by the House of Representatives, the bill was rejected by the Senate after massive street demonstrations around the nation and sharp criticism of the provision criminalizing undocumented presence. Senator Harry Reid (D-Nev.) attacked the bill as "mak[ing] criminals out of and demoniz[ing] a lot of hard-working people who are just trying to provide for their families."
> (ACLU 2010, p. 5)

Resistance to this provision of HR 4437 was the consequence of people getting organized and speaking out against those in power in the House. Those who publicly denounced this law used an approach advocated by Edward Said in which the aim is to:

> use humanistic critique to open up the fields of struggle, to introduce a longer sequence of thought and analysis to replace the short bursts of polemical, thought-stopping fury that so imprison us in labels and antagonistic debate whose goal is a belligerent collective identity rather than understanding and intellectual exchange.
>
> (Said 2003, p. i)

If we are willing to make this effort, which motivates this book, then we cease to be the detached observers who, in William Butler Yeats's perfect phrase, "deliberately sip at the honeypots of our minds".

Overview and organization of the material

The originality of this study flows from the multifarious approach taken to the material, the integration of humanistic and social science insights to the realm of law that relates to undocumented people and, moreover, my insistence that there is a strong language or linguistic dimension to this area of work. Undocumented people enter into a society in which people discuss foreigners, immigrants and illegality in particular ways, and if they are apprehended, they have to try to convince officials to let them be. To do so, as a Methodist minister who advocates on behalf of migrants notes:

> They have to learn the language of this system to push for the rights that they've actually got because they will not be given to them. That's the empowerment piece, it's to give people tools so that when they engage this system, new options open up.

This idea that people have to learn the "language of the system" is crucial, and it's akin to the idea that using the rhetoric of persuasion is like peddling linguistic wares in a kind of marketplace of social discourse. Over and above the linguistic and cultural barriers, this is a complex negotiation that generally favors the well informed and the linguistically astute, which usually means those from upper classes in which such characteristics are favored and taught. A community organizer summed it up well when he suggested that:

> there are more poor people in prisons because they don't know how to manipulate the system and because at the initial level, at the starting point which is with the police officer, the police officer reacts in a

> different way to somebody in the upper middle class or the upper class than he/she will with somebody who is poor.

People tend to construct arguments in regards what they know, or think they know, and this knowledge can be derived from many sources, including public debates, hearsay, gossip, the media, government offices and any number of intermediaries. When viewed from this perspective, we gain considerable insight into how the system actually functions by bringing linguistic and language research to bear upon every aspect of the process, as I will demonstrate throughout this book.

In order to lay the groundwork for understanding the linguistic dimensions of this realm, I will offer an ongoing description of the broad "social discourse" that encompasses everything that is said and also everything that is sayable in a particular society and at a particular time, in regards to undocumented immigrants. This subset can be described as "what people in a given society at a given time say about undocumented people", which in turn relates to how different groups of people talk about issues of borders, migration, foreigners and lawful behavior. The broader category of social discourse is also comprised of gossip, misinformation, propaganda, purposeful efforts aimed at misleading people or convincing them of something, and this collection of discourses can be perceived by undocumented people who then act upon what is said in regards to their plight. From this perspective, undocumented immigrants aren't just a group of people who are uncertain about which laws apply to their particular situations, and therefore seeking information on how to act; they are also people who are constantly trying to figure out what decisions they should make in a particular time and place in a setting in which the relationship between the law and its consequences is always unclear because of the arbitrariness, discretion and non-enforcement described in Chapter 1.

Sometimes, there are efforts made to shift a particular discourse, as for example when an official or an agency publicly announces a "crackdown" on illegals. When an undocumented person hears about this, he/she may react to it on the basis of the contradictory messages he/she has received along the way. On the one hand, the social discourse surrounding migration can be positive, suggesting that there are good paying jobs for hard-working people who are willing to take a few risks for the benefit of themselves or their families (Longazel and Fleury-Steiner 2011). The same discursive realm can also contain negative messages, about how undocumented people are "illegal", criminal, unwanted. In a recent commentary, Bauder (2014) suggests that legal and refugee scholars and practitioners should use the term "illegalized" in order to draw attention to the process by which people are deemed to become "illegal". This is an interesting example of scholars actively trying to shift the social discourse to a particular end, in this case providing the Associated Press (AP) with a term to replace "illegal immigrant", which AP no longer sanctions. AP has proposed: "Person entering a country illegally" or "without legal permission". Bauder, like some other legal scholars and social scientists, prefers instead the terms "illegalized" refugee or immigrant in order to emphasize the processes by which some people come to be classified as "illegal":

> To these writers, the term "illegalized" accurately describes the societal phenomenon that renders some refugees and immigrants "illegal". This commentary builds on this existing scholarship to suggest that the word "illegalized" should be adopted beyond this small scientific community and should be widely used by legal and refugee scholars and practitioners. This suggestion is part of a wider effort to also establish the term among politicians, journalists, educators, and the general public.
>
> (Bauder 2014, p. 328)

Referencing Fairclough (1992), van Dijk (1997) and Wodak and Menz (1990), Bauder (2014) insists upon a crucial insight that runs through this book, the language we employ in specific domains *matters*:

> Language matters in legal debate, public discourse, and everyday exchange. Terminology can imply causality, generate emotional responses, and transmit symbolic meanings. The term "illegal immigrant", for example, implies that an immigrant has committed a crime, that she does not belong, and that someone else (often the speaker) has been wronged. These implied meanings and the emotional responses they elicit can have real consequences, affecting the judgement and behaviour of decision makers and voters, which can in turn influence legal decisions, policies, and legislation. They can also shape the way civic society, employers, and communities engage refugees and immigrants in everyday life.
>
> (p. 328)

If terms carry implied meanings within a social discourse, then it's appropriate to try to shift them or, as we've seen in realms such as feminism or studies of race, we can try to change the terms altogether:

> The suggestion to change terminology follows other similar changes that have recently been adopted. For example, in academic and increasingly in public discourse, the terms "race" and "racial minority" are gradually being replaced by the phrases "racialized groups" or "racialized minorities", which convey that racial categorization is a social and political process rather than a natural condition. In a similar way, the term "illegalized" refugee or immigrant shifts the emphasis away from the individual and towards a societal process that situates people in positions of precariousness and illegality. The illegalization of refugees and immigrants is a widespread international issue that is common practice in

> Europe, North America, and elsewhere. Although there are national and regional differences in the particular ways in which people are illegalized, the term "illegalized" refugee or immigrant has potential for widespread international use.
>
> (p. 328)

As we'll see in Chapter 2, there are sophisticated language theories that bolster this claim and provide some theoretical apparatuses to describe how such changes in terminology can occur inside of a given social discourse. For the moment, though, it's worth noting that social discourses not only contain an array of implications, innuendos and implied meanings, often contradictory, but in addition these messages can shift across time and space, and migrate from realm to realm. For example, technical legal debates in the courts can sometimes offer glimmers of hope, and while it's unlikely that the undocumented people themselves would have access to or even be interested in specific cases, they can nonetheless hear reports in the media about recent deliberations concerning, say, the Human Rights Commission's interpretation of article 12(4) and its potential application to the situation in the United States.[5] Liss (2014) notes that:

> *Prima facie*, it seems that the basic principle underpinning the protection of sociological belonging – the recognition of the greater claim to membership possessed by those whose social conditions and circumstances link them to the common good of the community – is equally compelling in the context of undocumented immigrants.... [T]his seems particularly true in countries, such as the United States, where the presence of formally undocumented immigrants occurs en masse and where there has been a degree of tacit consent to their presence by both private and public actors.
>
> (p. 1181)

These kinds of debates, in popular, political or judicial milieus, can affect undocumented people who, in response to what they've heard, might flee particular spaces in search of more sympathetic discourses; and reports on these debates can also influence voters, who might be called upon to support or reject proposals that relate to undocumented people.

In different times or spaces, particular voters might be inspired to support legislation aimed at regularizing an existing workforce, or, on the contrary, they might back efforts aimed at identifying and cracking down on undocumented immigrants. This book aims to contribute to that "social discourse" by stimulating conversations that might help shift people's views on, for example, the relationship between providing status to undocumented immigrants, and ensuring their active and productive participation in the host society. Investigations into current practices reveal an underbelly as despicable as modern-day indentured labor, with the constant threat of incarceration and deportation. The ways that this process unfolds, and the push-pull effects it has upon people who are considering migrating, are processes I will also describe in Chapter 2.

The most marked characteristic of this domain is the fickle and unpredictable ways in which the broad array of regulations and laws relating to undocumented immigrants can be applied to particular cases; this shouldn't come as a great surprise, though, given the numbers[6] and, moreover, the vast spectrum of possible interactions that undocumented people can have with authorities. Overall, it is nonetheless clear that the most common contact between citizens or authorities from the host country and undocumented people is benign, that is, people just go about their business and leisure without questioning, or without caring about, the legal status of immigrants they encounter. On the other hand, undocumented people *can* at any moment find themselves questioned, arrested and set up for deportation because they live in a state of constant "illegality". Any contact might be their last, the most innocuous traffic violation can cost them their freedom; and if they have been previously deported, they can be set up for long prison sentences prior to their eventual, and usually certain, deportation.[7] This study distinguishes between those who are prosecuted for criminal behavior, and those who violate immigration laws, but I also look at how the two combine because people who have committed criminal offences can face very different outcomes if they are also found to be in violation of immigration regulations, and vice versa. Whether or not people are "looked-up" in the system depends on decisions that law enforcement officers make on *the front lines*, which means that a law enforcement officer can, at his/her own discretion, decide whether or not he/she wants to act like an immigration officer. This whole process, from "looking-up" to booking, begins with the crucial *first encounter* on the side of a highway, or in a government office, or on the street, or at the very border between two countries or regions. The (il)logic of this interaction is described in depth, and with special emphasis upon the array of possibly horrendous consequences of miscommunication, willful or linguistic, in Chapter 3.

Once an officer on the front lines decides to arrest an undocumented person for immigration violations, the stakes, constraints and logic of the entire process shifts. From this point onwards, in most if not all countries, the system is far more codified, and the obstacles faced by the claimant change. In Chapter 3 I emphasize the value of linguistic translators and cultural mediators for the front lines because in those spaces there's considerable risk of misunderstandings and cross-cultural mishaps that can lead undocumented immigrants to acting inappropriately for the circumstance (signing away rights, offering bribes, trying to flee). From the moment he/she is arrested to the time of sentencing, I argue that the time for significant negotiation is probably over, and the claimant needs to have formal representation, including full access to a certified interpreter, rather than a culturally aware translator, who can render his/her intentions in a favorable light to the host country officer. At this stage of the process the claimant is generally offered a trained intermediary to adequately present the case to the officials, but there's still considerable room for arbitrary decision-making, as we will see in Chapter 4.

Once the undocumented immigrant has passed through the system and been found guilty, he/she faces incarceration, and almost certain deportation. There's a high degree of variation even at this stage, however, because the conditions of the incarceration and the rights that are exercised, or not, subsequent to release, depend upon happenstance, chance and the degree of leniency of judges and jailers. At present, the growing numbers of undocumented persons who are interned prior to deportation also represent a new market for industries involved with incarceration. Private prison companies have a strong foothold in the United States, where the lobbying they undertake to secure contracts for the incarceration of undocumented people assures high costs, long prison terms and a perpetual industry of lobbying for being "tough on crime". Recent developments also include efforts by such companies as Corrections Corporation of America joining the Geo Group and two British companies, G4S and Serco, which currently work on developing private incarceration facilities in 11 countries in North America, South America, Europe, Africa and Oceania. I document in this book a wide range of negative perspectives on privatizing incarceration, but I've also included valuable information from specialists involved in the industry who claim that privatization could be vastly improved if governments would practice appropriate and ongoing oversight. Public and private prisons, and life therein for people who are serving time for immigration violations, are described in detail in Chapter 5.

This work mines the efforts undertaken over the years by individuals, organizations and corporations that have advocated for lifting hurdles that hinder the movement of workers across borders, and impede their integration once they do so. The time-consuming and wasteful border procedures in place to protect sovereignty and restrict the flow of goods and people are bad for human rights and bad for business, and in some cases it may be valuable to link these interests to advance the interests of undocumented persons. Transnational corporations are on the front lines when it comes to the waste and pollution created by the long and unnecessary bottlenecks of idling trucks filled with goods that are caught in the quagmire of customs line-ups; and drivers, paid by the hour or the load, waste time and energy better devoted to the transportation task at hand (Sandel 2012). When the social discourse emphasizes the details of elaborate border control and massive deportation, the possible benefits of freer flows of people across borders is lost, and with it discussions about the relative advantages of mobile workforces, or the merits of countries becoming fluent in (say) the languages of their border countries. With a smooth flow of people across the North American Free Trade Agreement (NAFTA) borders, for example, Americans could be further encouraged to learn Spanish or French, while Latin Americans could develop valuable skills in English or French as they all enjoy broad rights to work within and beyond their countries of origin. All of these areas will be the central focus of the Conclusion, Chapter 6.

Notes

1 Antigua and Barbuda, Argentina, Barbados, Belize, Bolivia, Brazil, Canada, Chile, Colombia, Dominica, Ecuador, El Salvador, Fiji, Grenada, Guatemala, Guyana, Honduras, Jamaica, Mexico, Nicaragua, Panama, Paraguay, Peru, Saint Kitts and Nevis, Saint Lucia, Saint Vincent and the Grenadines, Trinidad and Tobago, United States, Uruguay, Venezuela.

2 Specific forms of ID exist for undocumented people, including driving licenses and official municipal identification cards. New York, for example, has recently passed an amendment to make these available to undocumented people to provide them with access to public institutions, which inspired Danielle Simonnet, a far-left candidate who ran in the Paris mayoral in March 2015, to make a similar pledge. This is one of the many ways in which the American example can be proxy for efforts and actions undertaken in other countries.

3 This phenomenon is widely reported, worldwide. For one of many examples in the American context that includes a discussion of the consequences for local communities, see Ortega (2013).

4 A good summary of this connection is offered by Discover the Networks (s.d.): "The PATRIOT Act was no dramatic departure from existing legislation. Indeed, its key provisions were incorporated from an anti-terrorism measure that had been passed by Congress and signed into law by former President Bill Clinton five years earlier: the 'Anti-Terrorism and Effective Death Penalty Act of 1996', which was a response to Timothy McVeigh's April 1995 bombing of the Federal Building in Oklahoma City that killed 175 innocent people. This 1996 Act contained a number of key provisions to combat terrorism, but the ones that immediately inspired the formation of a leftist coalition against the legislation were three particular provisions that: (a) made it a criminal offence to provide 'material support' or 'expert advice or assistance' to terrorist groups; (b) allowed prosecutors to use secret evidence in terrorism cases; and (c) authorized the US Secretary of State, the Secretary of the Treasury, and the Attorney General to jointly designate organizations as terrorist groups based upon available evidence. The most influential civil-liberties voices in the United States alleged that with the passage of the 1996 bill, the rights and freedoms of all Americans were under assault by a government that was seeking not only empire abroad, but totalitarian control at home." Available at: http://www.discoverthenetworks.org/guidedesc.asp?catid=101&type=issue. [Accessed: 15 January 2015]

5 Ryan Liss's recent overview offers a concrete sense of how this process unfolds: "The two principal measures of this sort are the Development, Relief, and Education for Alien Minors Act (or DREAM Act), which has been considered by Congress in various forms since 2002, and the Deferred Action Initiative instituted by the Obama Administration in the summer of 2012. Both instruments focus on providing a channel through which undocumented immigrants who came to the United States as minors can apply for legal residency status and seek temporary protection

against deportation.... However, the Human Rights Campaign's (HRC's) interpretation of Article 12(4) and the recent developments in the United States differ in two important ways. First, both the DREAM Act and the Deferred Action Initiative focus on the proven good character of the applicant. And, second, the American measures are grounded in government discretion, in contrast to the mandatory nature of Article 12(4) protection. Nevertheless, at the core is the recognition of the interest individuals possess in remaining part of the national community to which they are most connected in fact – and an interest against being deported to a place where 'they may not have lived' or with which their association based on a sociological conception of membership is weaker" (Liss 2014, 1181–2).

6 Although this is difficult data to find, there is some comparative data for 13 countries. Available at: http://immigration.procon.org/view.resource.php?resourceID=005235. [Accessed: 15 January 2015]

7 And of course it's all the worse if the individual in question is part of other marginal groups because of, for example, their sexual orientation (Gehi 2012).

Bibliography

ACLU (American Civil Liberties Union) (February 2010) "Criminalizing Undocumented Immigrants", *ACLU Issue Brief*, pp. 1–6. Available at: https://www.aclu.org/immigrants-rights/issue-brief-criminalizing-undocumented-immigrants. [Accessed: 15 January 2015]

Bauder, Harald (2014) "Why We Should Use the Term 'Illegalized' Refugee or Immigrant: A Commentary", *International Journal of Refugee Law* 26.3, pp. 327–32.

Chomsky, Noam (23 February 1967) "The Responsibility of Intellectuals", *New York Review of Books*, pp. 5–8.

Discover the Networks (s.d.). "Issues-Patriot Act". Available at: http://www.discovernetworks.org/guidedesc.asp?catid=101&type=issue. [Accessed: 15 January 2015]

Fairclough, Norman (1992) *Discourse and Social Change*. London: Polity Press.

Gehi, Pooja (2012) "Gendered (In)Security: Migration and Criminalization in the Security State Symposium", *Harvard Journal of Law & Gender* 35, pp. 357–401.

Hoffman, Sue (2011) "Living in Limbo: Iraqi Refugees in Indonesia", *Refuge* 28.1, pp. 15–24.

Immigration Policy Center (16 March 2012) "Aggravated Felonies: An Overview", American Immigration Council. Available at: http://www.immigrationpolicy.org/just-facts/aggravated-felonies-overview. [Accessed: 15 January 2015]

Khimm, Suzy (27 August 2012) "Obama is Deporting Immigrants Faster than Bush. Republicans don't Think That's Enough", *Wonkblog*. Available at: http://www.washingtonpost.com/blogs/wonkblog/wp/2012/08/27/obama-is-deporting-more-immigrants-than-bush-republicans-dont-think-thats-enough. [Accessed: 15 January 2015]

Lieu, Jamie Chai Yun (2011–12) "Managing the Fear of the Tsunami: Canada's Proposed Policy to Detain Boat People and Lessons Learned from the United States' Detention Policies", *Rutgers Race & Law Review* 13.1, pp. 1–68.

Liss, Ryan (2014) "A Right to Belong: Legal Protection of Sociological Membership in the Application of Article 12(4) of the ICCPR", *New York University Journal of*

International Law and Politics (*JILP*) 46, pp. 1097–191. Available at: http://ssrn.com/abstract=2329181. [Accessed: 15 January 2015]
Longazel, Jamie and Benjamin Fleury-Steiner (2011) "Exploiting Borders: The Political Economy of Local Backlash against Undocumented Immigrants", *Chicana/o-Latina/o Law Review* 30, pp. 43–65.
Ortega, Oliver (15 July 2013) "Local Sweeps Jail Many Undocumented Immigrants with No Criminal Records", *The Columbus Dispatch*. Available at: http://www.dispatch.com/content/stories/local/2013/07/15/sweeps-jail-many-with-no-records.html. [Accessed: 15 January 2015]
Palmgren, Pei A. (2014) "Irregular Networks: Bangkok Refugees in the City and Region", *Journal of Refugee Studies* 27.1, pp. 21–41.
Ramachandran, Sujata (2002) "'Operation Pushback': Sangh Parivar, State, Slums and Surreptitious Bangladeshis in New Delhi", *Singapore Journal of Tropical Geography* 23.2, pp. 311–32.
Reasoner, W. D. [a pseudonym] (2011) "Deportation Basics: How Immigration Enforcement Works (or Doesn't) in Real Life", Center for Immigration Studies. Available at: http://cis.org/deportation-basics. [Accessed: 15 January 2015]
Said, Edward (2003) "Preface", *Orientalism*. Harmondsworth, Middx: Penguin.
Sandel, Michael J. (2012) *What Money Can't Buy: The Moral Limits of Markets*. New York: Macmillan.
Schuster, Liza (2011) "Turning Refugees into 'Illegal Migrants': Afghan Asylum Seekers in Europe", *Ethnic and Racial Studies* 34.8, pp. 1392–407.
Shear, Michael (23 February 2013) "Seeing Citizenship Path Near, Activists Push Obama to Slow Deportations", *New York Times*, p. A12.
Simanski, John and Lesley M. Sapp (September 2012), *Annual Report*. Washington: Office of Immigration Statistics. Available at: http://www.dhs.gov/sites/default/files/publications/immigration-statistics/enforcement_ar_2011.pdf. [Accessed: 15 January 2015]
van Dijk, Teun A. (1997) *Discourse Studies: A Multidisciplinary Introduction*. London: Sage.
Wodak, Ruth and Florian Menz (eds.) (1990) *Sprache in der Politik–Politik in der Sprache*. Klagenfurt, Austria: Drava.

Chapter 1

Arbitrariness, discretion and non-enforcement

> Illegal migrants receive really mixed messages. They stay here and work, and they do the jobs that nobody else wants to do, and they do what their employers tell them to do so that their employee records will make them appear legal. So all of these people are looking the other way, even though their employers know that they are undocumented. This creates a sense amongst illegal migrants that maybe they are sort of legal. So on the one hand, people are afraid all the time because they are illegal, on the other hand, it's hard not to get this mixed message. There is real injustice in the way that the system plays out, because it works in an arbitrary and sometimes really targeted way, and people can sense that injustice.
>
> (A lawyer interviewed for the project)

This book undertakes an investigation into how people experience "illegality", and what the current system looks like from the perspective of those most intimately involved in it, notably lawyers, public defenders, translators, interpreters, police officers, employers and undocumented immigrants themselves. Most of these individuals were interviewed in the United States, and therefore some of the details described by interviewees concerning, say, inquiries, arrests and incarceration make direct reference to the American system. Nonetheless, it is my contention that people experience illegality in similar ways in most countries, and that host country officials encounter similar obstacles when addressing issues emerging from the presence of undocumented people. So if, for example, a police officer in the United States or Australia or France pulls someone over, he might decide to ascertain the driver's immigration status. If he does, then the trajectory of possible outcomes that flow from the officer's decision is roughly as follows:

- if the driver is found to be undocumented, the officer can choose to arrest him/her on those grounds;
- if he/she is arrested, the officer or another official can choose to contact immigration officials;
- if immigration officials are called, they can choose to pursue the case;

- if charges relating to immigration status are laid, the case can be deliberated in a courtroom;
- if the person is found guilty in the courtroom for immigration-related violations, the judge will sentence him/her to serve time in a private, state or federal facility depending upon the nature of the violation;
- if the person is incarcerated for said violations, immigration officials can initiate deportation proceedings that would be acted upon once the sentence is served;
- if the person serves his/her time, he/she will then be deported;
- if the person returns to the host country after having been deported, then the immigration violation can become a criminal felony.

Each of these possible outcomes begins with an "if", and this is the beginning of our deliberations about "arbitrary law" because if, say, this officer chooses to simply issue a warning, or else to ignore the immigration status of the driver altogether, then none of the ensuing possibilities are likely to occur. There are certain "ifs" that are more rigidly defined, on account of (for example) mandatory sentencing in cases of a person returning to the United States after deportation, for felonies including any crime that involves a gun, or for crimes involving moral turpitude. A public defender explains the sentencing guidelines:

> It's a federal crime to re-enter the country, and around here they prosecute people for illegal re-entry after having committed an aggravated felony. A lot of the immigrant clients we have also have these more serious offenses. If you're picked up after being deported, especially if you're deported after having committed a crime in Tennessee, you'll be charged with this federal offense. Until a month ago, when the federal sentencing laws changed, that carried a mandatory minimum of six years. There are details, but it's about right. If you're deported for a drug offense and then you come back, and your sentence was for over a year, which it usually is, then the guidelines say six and a half years in jail. If you plead guilty, which is advisable, they'll bring it down to five years. And at that point the judge has almost no discretion.

And so right up to the final stage in this process there is significant discretion, details of the process can be negotiated (Rakoff 2014), and proceedings against the undocumented person can be abandoned or simply not taken up. Because this is the chronological order within which most of these proceedings occur, I have organized this book to reflect these possible outcomes.

Arbitrary law

The concept of "arbitrariness" in law has been researched, deliberated and adjudicated in a host of settings and in the legal literature, and it seems on these bases to be the best term for what I'm describing. As Sandoz (2008) makes clear, this is a term with a long and complex history that ties early use of arbitrariness to the unbridled exercise of power, which is still true, but there's a stronger sense of unpredictability in contemporary usage. I describe arbitrariness in law as existing on a kind of continuum that begins with discretion, broadens towards arbitrariness and can in some cases become fiction. Many if not most of the examples to which I refer in this book include some kind of discretion,[1] of course, but I would suggest that "arbitrary law" is nonetheless the better term for the broader phenomena described because the outcome of many cases to which I refer hinge on factors that are out of anyone's control, and thus not subjected to the decision that discretion seems to imply. For example, the presence or not of (say) a good federally certified interpreter[2] on the day of a court case is arbitrary because there's no requirement that there be one in all cases, and so claimants' chances of having a qualified interpreter on hand is in many cases left to chance. Similarly, law enforcement officers' decisions in regards to undocumented immigrants are often arbitrary, and can depend upon how busy he/she is with other traffic incidents, or how willing he/she is, for practical or ideological reasons, to play makeshift immigration officer on the side of the road. There is discretion in both of these examples, but there are other factors that can contribute to the degree of arbitrariness at play.

The *Oxford English Dictionary* (*OED*) (1971) has discretion as part of the definition of "arbitrary", suggesting that an arbitrary decision or action is "dependent upon one's will or pleasure, discretionary". In the realm of law, the *OED* finds "arbitrary" "relating to, or dependent on, the discretion of an arbiter, arbitrator, or other legally recognized authority; discretionary, not fixed". "Arbitrary" can also suggest that the decision is derived from preference or opinion, and is thus capricious, uncertain and varying, all crucial notions for this book. The term "arbitrary" also implies a lack of restraint or control, an unregulated authority, as in "Acts of Will and Tyranny, which make up an Arbitrary Government" (p. 107). This definition invokes the arbiter (possibly from the French, *arbitre*), who has and exercises absolute power in an arbitrary government. As Timothy Endicott (2014) notes, however:

> arbitrariness is a lack of reason. Whenever any government agency does anything wrong, it goes against reason. But that is not enough to make for arbitrary government. Arbitrary government is a distinctive form of unreasonable government; it is a departure from the rule of law, in favour of rule by the mere will of the rulers.
>
> (p. 49)

This invocation of the "rule of law" points to a widely shared and discussed concern for a fundamental norm for legal systems that some see as definitive of legality as such. Rule of law is generally understood to include non-arbitrariness in the administration and application of law, at all levels of the process. But when the law gets applied and enforced in certain sectors, such as the immigration process, the qualities of regularity or consistency in administering the law is missing. The rule of law standard is typically used to criticize corrupt legal systems (e.g. China, Russia or failed states), but here is a sector of law in the United States and in Europe, for example, that because of its arbitrariness is failing to meet a standard that, outside of Critical Legal Studies, is often deemed to exist. In order to deepen our understanding of this realm of arbitrary law, it's worth examining Wright (2010), in which he argues that despite how central arbitrariness is – in particular for administrative law – there is no way to actually define it and that it always is or "at least it should be, strongly and variously contextual" (p. 840). The meaning of "arbitrary":

> will change significantly as context and the underlying, perhaps conflicting, purposes, interests, and stakes vary. The significance, degree, and frequency of the changes of meaning of arbitrary lead to the conclusion that it is more misleading than helpful to imagine that arbitrary has a standard, convenient, legal definition, even in particular legal contexts, such as judicial review of administrative actions.
>
> (p. 846)

Wright explores the weight of this variation from case to case suggesting that the significance of arbitrariness varies in gravity depending upon the example, and so "the denial of a vacationer's recreational fishing license and the imposition of the death penalty might, in particular cases, both be arbitrary, but we can see that the gravity or seriousness of the interests at stake in the two cases can vary substantially". These considerations can lead to variance in what might be considered "arbitrary", or "they can lead to the relaxation of such standards, and thereby alter the meaning of arbitrary" (pp. 846–7).

To further muddy the waters, the persons involved may have multiple allegiances, or even conflicting allegiances, so the decision-making process may be the choice, arbitrary or discretionary, between multiple options on the basis of a range of factors unknown to the person being affected by the decision because:

> more than one common interest or purpose will likely be in play, and "a given actor may hold more than one interest" just as "different persons may hold different and perhaps conflicting interests, of different intensity, at different times. Thus, even the judge may have some interests distinct from the litigating parties (including the government) during the trial, and another set of interests during sentencing.
>
> (p. 847)

In decisions involving undocumented immigrants, the question of "interest" may also play a determining role, and in cross-cultural situations the claimant may not even understand the context well enough to determine where his/her interests lie, just as the decision maker may not be fully aware of all the stakes and motivating factors that govern his/her own actions:

> More generally, legal contexts can be identified and described by reference to the purposes and interests deemed to be at stake by any interested person. Whether all parties have fully understood their own interests, or those of other parties, is a possible complication. As a further complication, some persons may have interests that actually refer mainly to the interests of other persons. Thus, in addition to the litigants themselves, other persons similarly situated, the broader public, legislative oversight committees, the government, agency decision-making officials or agency branches, trial and appellate courts and private counsel, journalists, scholars, and sundry critics may also have overlapping and conflicting interests at stake.
>
> (p. 847)

To make matters worse, some of the interests, conflicts or presuppositions may not be obvious to those who are involved in the decision itself, so the line between arbitrary and non-arbitrary is difficult to draw, even if we defer to legal definitions:

> For legal contexts generally, a decision is often thought of as arbitrary when it is "founded on prejudice or preference rather than on reason or fact". One problem for such a definition is that arbitrary decisions can also be based on genuinely unrecognized logical or evidentiary gaps, murky reasoning, or flawed methodology. These can be inconspicuous mistakes, hardly resulting from prejudice or willful preference. Another problem is that narrowly politically-driven outcomes may reflect not only prejudice or preference, but also a substantial component of "reason or fact", despite their arbitrariness. Similarly, if we legally define the related term "capricious" in terms of "unpredictable or impulsive behavior", we may lose track of the possibility of arbitrariness as a rigid, systematic, ideological bias, which may be both predictable and far from capricious or impulsive.
>
> (p. 847)

Important examples of unstated factors involved in arbitrary or seemingly arbitrary decisions in regards to undocumented immigrants can include racism, xenophobia or even views on whether migrants support the economy by taking those jobs nobody else wants, or, on the contrary, destroy the economy by taking jobs from citizens.

For instance, if a law enforcement officer is engaged in a routine traffic stop involving undocumented immigrants, he can check on, and report, the immigration status of the offender. His decision to do so is discretionary, and therefore his decision to contact authorities can be entirely rooted in racism or xenophobia, rather than any conception of law enforcement. Embedded within the arbitrary, therefore, are factors that can be at work without any party to the decision ever becoming aware of them. This is why I think it valuable in this book to view arbitrary as the broad category, and discretion as a subcategory thereof, in what is a complex and shifting term, as Wright makes clear:

> From my basic thesis, this sense of a frequent but occasionally evaporating practical equivalence between arbitrariness and alternative standards of review is not surprising. In my view, there is simply no reasonably fixed definitional meaning for arbitrary and its closest cognates. The meaning of arbitrary is actually a variety of meanings, dependent upon variations in contexts, which reflect differences in purposes and interests, and the gravity thereof – the stakes – according to the various actors directly or indirectly involved. Where the stakes are thought to be high, arbitrariness review may be correspondingly demanding, as rigorous in that context as some more formally demanding standard. But it will also be possible to compare arbitrariness review in a low stakes context with more rigorous review under some other standard. And since no meaning for arbitrary and its closest synonyms can be pinned down, there will always be a sense that "arbitrariness" can be the practical equivalent of other standards, but it cannot be so regarded in an exceptionless way.
>
> (pp. 851–2)

From all of this flows the recognition as well that there can be positive and negative arbitrariness, depending upon one's politics and point of view, just as there can be positive and negative discretion. In all cases, one hopes that decisions will be "fair" (to invoke a crucial category of administrative law; on this point see Loveland 2012), but here too the definition of fairness is murky at best. And so just as we can envision a kind of continuum from discretion to arbitrary to fictional, I would suggest that there's another continuum that flows from reasonable to fair to just.

Arbitrary, discretionary, discriminatory

One way of elaborating the category of arbitrary law is to view it in regards to some of these close definitional cousins, in particular discretion. Lucatuorto (2010) usefully distinguishes between arbitrariness and discretion when he emphasizes the importance of discretional decision making for the realm of administrative law. He notes that in principle, the administration's goal is to exercise:

> discretional power without arbitrariness since administrations achieve their purposes by involving all citizens. Wielding this power, the administration can make a choice between all of the compatible solutions in a range, but can also enjoy freedom of choice bounded by the well-known reasonableness principle.
>
> (p. 633)

This principle is the supposed bridge between the decision and the evaluation of it, on whichever criteria (public good, private good, public safety, for example), and "the aim of discretional power is to set the comparative weights of all of the competing interests, and the administration is bounded by this evaluation" (p. 633).

This type of evaluation can come from a range of sources, including analyses of decisions. Miles and Sunstein (2008) have provided a valuable overview of recent debates in the United States, with reference to federal courts of appeals, and in particular the United States Court of Appeals for the District of Columbia Circuit. The breadth of the proposed doctrine is wide-ranging, and has potential bearing upon agencies and decisions to which I refer in this book:

> [T]he doctrine found its origins in judicial decisions requiring administrative agencies to demonstrate that they had taken a "hard look" at the underlying questions of policy and fact. Hence agencies were required to offer detailed, even encyclopedic, explanations for their conclusions, to respond to counter arguments, to justify departures from past practices, and to give careful consideration to alternatives to the proposed course of action. These were procedural requirements, to be sure, but they had significant effects, often shifting regulatory policy in identifiable directions....
>
> (p. 761)

This "hard look" doctrine limits *discretion* by "ensuring firm check on agency decisions that might be irrational or discriminatory" (p. 762), suggesting that in principle discretionary decision making has to be undertaken in a *reasonable* manner, consistent with the statutory powers of the agency in question (cf. *Ethyl Corp*, 541 F2d at 68). This approach was entrenched in a seminal ruling in the case of *Motor Vehicle Manufacturers Association v State Farm Auto Mutual Insurance Co* (cf. 15 State Farm, 463 US) that has been quoted hundreds of times in federal cases, and which states that a decision would count as arbitrary if:

> the agency has relied on factors which Congress has not intended it to consider, entirely failed to consider an important aspect of the problem, offered an explanation for its decision that runs counter to the evidence

> before the agency, or is so implausible that it could not be ascribed to a difference in view or the product of agency expertise.
>
> (p. 43)

Despite the ubiquity of this ruling, it is nonetheless the case that:

> some people object that the doctrine has unfortunate systemic effects on agency decisions. Others believe that the hard look is simply too hard and that a soft look would be much better. Still others fear that judicial biases play a large role in the operation of the hard look doctrine – that in finding inadequate explanations or unreasonableness on the merits, the policy preferences of judges are playing a substantial role.
>
> (Miles and Sunstein 2008, p. 765)

And so it turns out that this ruling on arbitrariness (and discretion) is itself subjected to questions about arbitrariness and discretion in the application of the ruling on that very subject.

This is not only valuable as legal background, but it also leads to a central issue of this book, the question of how flexible authorities and intermediaries should be in all aspects of dealings with undocumented immigrants. Given the cultural dimension of this subject, we could argue that officials are often called to render decisions even if, for reasons of translation or interpretation, they don't have access to the requisite facts,[3] particularly when they are required to render some kind of decision on the basis of vague legal language (see, for example, Marmor and Soames 2013). The ways in which cultural interactions affect outcomes at every level of the system dictate the importance of assessing how information is transmitted from host to home parties, and for this reason I emphasize the linguistic interactions amongst parties, and the role played therein by cultural arbitrators at all levels, from federally certified interpreters to jailhouse translators.

It is the case that discretion and arbitrariness run all through the system that enforces laws against undocumented immigrants in most countries of the world, and that there is often less flexibility or discretion in places where it is especially needed, such as in American judges' leeway in determining the length of sentences for persons who return to the United States after deportation, or Australian judges' ability to not enforce the mandatory five-year sentences for migrants who attempt to enter Australia as asylum seekers (Flatley 2012; Owens 2011). In these examples as in others, arbitrariness and discretion *can* be extremely valuable, since they open the door to negotiation at each level of the aforementioned steps. By the same token, arbitrariness and discretion can be hurtful if empowered host country officials exercise their right, or their responsibility, to act like draconian immigration officers in all possible interactions with immigrants. And so neither arbitrariness nor discretion are in themselves problematic from this perspective, it's how they are used that matters.

Arbitrariness at the executive level

In the American context, the (arbitrary) enforcement of immigration law extends all the way to the White House, as Delahunty and Yoo (2013) argue in a work that touches on distinctions between discretion, deferred action, presidential duties and prerogatives and *de facto* delegation. The authors question and critique the Obama Administration's decisions in certain cases to employ "prosecutorial discretion" in order to *not* enforce statutes. In what reads at times like a jaundiced political speech aimed at Obama's White House (and to a lesser extent at Congress[4]), the authors at one point ask:

> If a President can refuse to enforce a federal law against a class of 800,000 to 1.76 million individuals, what discernible limits are there to prosecutorial discretion? Can a President decline to enforce federal laws barring that class from voting in federal elections? Can a President decline to enforce the deportation statute against all illegal immigrants because of a belief in an "open borders" policy? [if only!]
>
> (p. 784)

Obama's presumed views on those statutes that his White House chooses to not enforce are reflected in less lofty quarters of the immigration system as well, such as in the offices of police commissioners who encourage their officers to *not* question immigration status in routine traffic stops, or even Immigration Control and Enforcement (ICE) officials' decisions to *not* be present to arrest a deportable person who has just been released from prison after having served time for a criminal offence. The White House practices discretion (or, as Delahunty and Yoo might claim, arbitrariness because of the link to power), but in fact, discretion runs all through the system, sometimes causing parties to the process to act in fickle and often unpredictable ways. Recent articles address this debate, and attempt to fill in the legal gap by assessing grounds for the Obama approach to (non-)enforcement (Andrias 2013; Margulies 2014; Price 2014).

I would add to this discussion that no matter where the reader comes down on (say) Delahunty and Yoo's (2013) claim that "there is no general presidential Nonenforcement power" even if "the law requires discretionary decision making on the part of the enforcers" (p. 784), it is the case that non-enforcement, at all levels, is one root of the confusion that undocumented migrants have in regards to if, or how, the various laws relating to undocumented people will be applied in their particular cases. This applies with reference to every party to the process, from the Oval Office all the way down to the side of the road, as a public defender notes in the case of Nashville traffic stops:

> There's also on record a stated difference as to the police's interest in being involved in checking immigration status. In Davidson County

> [Tennessee] the chief himself has said that if it's not a deportable offense, then they will not report the person's incarceration to the Department of Homeland Security. The flipside of that is that you've got local law individual officers who are trying to check the immigration status of everyone they walk up to on the street, not only people with whom they're involved, but people they find who look brown.

With the advanced security technologies, these checks have become increasingly sophisticated, ensuring that the breadth of the inquiry will be vast, as a public defender described:

> It seems like now because of 9/11, or maybe because of new technology, all of the agencies are talking to each other a little bit more. Now they are checking. If you are charged with something a little bit more serious, usually they check on the computer, and they check on if you have any immigration problem. And they can check, because there are many places where they can check. One is called BLOC, and it can give you all kinds of information.... They have BLOC and then have EPIC. EPIC is El Paso Intelligence Center, and BLOC is Blue Lightning Operations Center, and both are hooked with DEA [Drug Enforcement Agency] and ICE, which used to be the INS [Internal Naturalization Services]. So, very quickly they can find out if that person has been arrested, and if he has been deported. Sometimes they are just profiling, and they stop you in the middle of the road, and if they think you might have drugs, sometimes they do, sometimes they don't, they'll do a check. Then they call those agencies, which can tell them: "No, this guy must be deported". So they can detain you even if you don't have any drugs, just because you have been deported before.

Despite differences in terms of what laws are enforced, or who makes decisions about enforcement and non-enforcement, the issues are similar in vastly different settings, from Europe to Latin America to Asia (see Alba and Castillo 2012; Baldwin-Edwards and Schain 1994).

Another example of undocumented immigrants who can be sheltered from the effects of federal immigration law in the United States relates to congregations that "shelter" undocumented immigrants who are subject to deportation orders. This is possible because the ICE agency classifies houses of worship, schools and hospitals as sensitive locations that are circumvented as unofficial policy. From this exception has grown the Sanctuary Movement, an effort that dates back to the 1980s when Daniel Neyoy Ruiz, from Mexico, sought refuge in the Southside Presbyterian Church in Tucson, Arizona. Officials eventually granted him a one-year reprieve from deportation, and this started a movement aimed at assisting the hundreds of thousands of Guatemalans, Nicaraguans and Salvadorians who had been deemed by the

Reagan Administration to be "economic migrants" (even though they were seeking refuge from US-supported violent turmoil). The more recent movement has a website that states that "we are a growing movement of faith and immigrant communities doing what Congress and the Administration refuse to do: protect and stand with immigrants facing deportation" (http://www.Sanctuary2014.org [Accessed: 15 January 2015]). Non-compliance, the promise of new legislation and sheltering from legal repercussions make up a significant gray area in the treatment of undocumented immigrants in the United States, and contribute to the fickle, arbitrary, inconsistent, unpredictable and ever-shifting ways in which immigration laws are applied. And again, similar kinds of issues, including movements resembling the US Sanctuary Movement, exist in Australia, Belgium, Canada, France, Germany, the Netherlands, Norway and Switzerland. Recent work by Randy Lippert and Sean Rehaag (2012) describes its impact within and beyond asylum seekers.

Setting up the research project

This work is the product of a vast research project that included interviews with parties to the undocumented immigrant process, including prisoners who were incarcerated for immigration violations. In order to undertake the fieldwork, in particular with the prisoners (considered a vulnerable population), I was required to present an elaborate description of the research project to the Institutional Review Board (IRB). The basic claim that underwrote this research was that immigrants and asylum seekers are increasingly spending time in local, state and federal prisons for violation of a host of new or recently enacted, or else newly enforced laws in a context of heightened security. Their incarceration is justified by their having been in violation of a series of memos, proposed laws, laws and programs that are all part of a kind of legal fiction that a predictable, known and enforced set of laws that applies to undocumented people exists.

I was aware from the research I'd done preceding these interviews, primarily relating to refugees, that there is a vast level of arbitrariness that can affect decisions made at almost all levels of the enforcement and judicial process (Barsky 1994, 2001). The huge arrays of people who fall into this net (see Dann 2013) provide a whole new definition of the term "vulnerable population", both by their numbers and by the precariousness within which they live (see Bales 1999; Marquardt et al. 2011). An investigator who helps gather evidence for a lawyer described this precariousness with valuable detail:

> I have been trying to find my client's relatives. I know they are here. He tells me that they are here. And so I ask him: "Where do they live?" "In a hotel", he says: "If you go to Murfreesboro Road, between here and here, there is a hotel. The guy you're looking for has a big truck. You can ask

> around there and they will tell you where he lives". I have found people like that with directions like that. Sometimes, they don't know their own address or their own phone number. "Where do you live?" I ask. And they reply: "By Harding Road". "What's the name of your apartments?" "I don't know". They might know their apartment number, and that's it. They aren't established here, and that presents a problem.

The uneven application of laws is of concern not only to the huge population of migrants, but to those who are charged with administering laws and overseeing their enforcement, partly because officials know so little about this transient population, and partly because undocumented people follow employment possibilities and so they "aren't established" in residences, neighborhoods or even particular cities for long periods of time. For this reason, it's perhaps unsurprising that the Tennessee Department of Corrections (TDOC) supported this research, and in particular those aspects that related to intercultural issues. TDOC had little to go on when it came to understanding the experiences of the immigrants they are charged with incarcerating, and the subjective information that would be useful in this regard is hard to come by. As such, I focused upon the situation in the United States for the (unpublished) TDOC report, in the hope of contributing valuable information to lawmakers in the Southern United States. In writing this book, I changed the focus, employed tools from a range of academic disciplines to situate the findings and then moved the lens outwards beyond the United States, where I uncovered similar broad tendencies. It's clear that many other countries look to the US example in developing their own strategies for addressing the complex issues arising from the presence of undocumented people, just as US officials look to (say) Europe or Canada as part of their efforts to share and gain information.

Methodological objectives and proposed approach

The methodological issues for a project like this one are complex and in some ways unique, and for this reason it's worth considering them as such. The factors that contribute to this complexity include:

- First, communities of incarcerated individuals are justifiably terrified, and therefore reluctant to speak about their plight, even when incarceration authorities allow researchers direct access to them in prisons or incarceration centers. The same goes for those who have been incarcerated or have family members who have been incarcerated because they feel they are more likely to be apprehended or observed.
- Second, very few incarceration officials are likely to offer their expertise, particularly in an era when public dissent and whistle-blowing is so harshly punished (pace the examples of Snowden or Assange). It was

valuable to have TDOC support for this project, since it smoothed relations with the many players to ensure appropriate access for interviews. In the end, the project met with less official resistance than I would have expected; and from what I have been told, I also met with less resistance working in the Southern states than I would have encountered in other parts of the country (especially in terms of access to incarceration facilities).

- Third, interviewees for a project of this sort are hesitant to speak out, and anecdotally I would suggest that this is increasingly the case, because "the word on the street", borne from long experience, is to keep away from officials of all kinds; and even as a university professor, I was often considered or treated like an "official" of the host country.
- Fourth, the problem of potential or summary incarceration and deportation has created heightened tension within immigrant communities who find themselves on the wrong side of new laws, and some community officials actively discourage undocumented people to speak out about their experiences.
- Fifth, undocumented immigrants awaiting hearings or deportation are supposed to be held in detention centers because their sole "crime" was to have entered the country illegally, re-entered illegally or overstayed their visa. This system is now gargantuan, costly and vastly inefficient,[5] and, as a result, undocumented immigrants are increasingly locked up in all kinds of different municipal, county and state jails until sentencing.[6] This trend accelerated with legislation like Operation Streamline, a program put into effect in 2005 that prosecutes immigrants who cross illegally with a criminal rather than civil offense.[7] This, of course, makes it very difficult for researchers who need to get past both the IRB guidelines concerning vulnerable populations (next to children prisoners are considered the most vulnerable interview group, and therefore requests are scrutinized with tremendous vigor) and also the ever-stringent policies regulating prisoners.
- Sixth, like any other vulnerable population, incarcerated immigrants are in desperate need of legal, medical, psychiatric, personal and intercultural care. Many are confused by their plight, and in many instances they are unable to communicate their experiences to the appropriate host country officials, and so they act inappropriately, leading to further disciplinary action. Despite being the interviewer, I was often questioned at length by interviewees, suggesting that their participation in the research project was motivated by their desire to learn something useful about their case from someone "official".
- And finally, researching in this area can be so distressing that it's quite challenging to simply do the interviews in an appropriately methodical and professional manner. When the interviewer learns that someone is facing two decades in prison for a combination of a gram of pot, a scuffle

> in a parking lot and a return to the United States to see his children subsequent to deportation, it's really difficult to remain calm or detached.

In order to provide the reader with a sense of how this project was conducted, it's important to describe all of the steps leading up to the IRB's assessment and eventual approval of the project. I started by consulting available data relating to the different areas of the research, and met with experts in the field, using a "snowball approach", whereby each person contacted was asked for a list of other individuals who would be valuable interviewees. Once I had amassed a bank of valuable hard data, and a sense from the interviews of a solid set of objectives and a methodology, I worked on a proposal that I brought before the IRB. The review process was lengthy, and the proposal was revised several times in consultation with members of the IRB.

Information about the potential interviewees was procured through collaboration with the TDOC, local law enforcement for local jails and federal officials. Incarceration officials were asked to identify possible participants, I assessed the information on those who were willing to participate, and chose representative samples of populations to reflect the diversity of concerns (gender, country of origin, status, language). In accordance with the IRB approved mandate, I was not allowed to contact interviewees directly. The script used to contact inmates was non-coercive, and emphasized that participation in the study was voluntary, and that there were no advantages offered to those who participated (in terms of parole, sentencing considerations and so forth). The text that was handed out to the inmates by prison officials, which was to be translated (if necessary) into the native language of the inmate, read as follows:

> Robert Barsky, a Professor at Vanderbilt University, is directing a research project about inter-cultural relations amongst inmates held for immigration concerns. Inter-cultural relations refer to those elements of interactions between people that are affected by the cultural backgrounds of the individuals in question, notably their race, religion, or country of origin. Inter-cultural relations occur on many levels in interaction, and are manifested through behavior that reflects awareness of the other person's culture as shown by, for example, fear, respect, prejudice, which specifically relates to culture. Since your case has some immigration elements, you may be eligible to be interviewed for the study. There are no advantages to your being involved in the study, and neither your participation nor your answers will in any way affect any aspect of your case, the conditions of your incarceration, or your treatment. Professor Barsky does hope to assess and improve intercultural relations amongst inmates and between inmates and officials, which means that your participation may help with this general objective. If you are willing to be interviewed for this study, for a period of (roughly) two hours, please

> indicate below by signing and returning the form to the incarceration official named below. If you choose to participate in the study, you may refuse to answer any question you wish, you can withdraw at any time without consequence. Your identity will be kept strictly confidential in the report of all findings.

I expected that most qualified inmates would be Hispanic, although I was also prepared to work with translators to translate the text into a host of target languages. To ensure the consistency of the interviews, and the safety of interviewees, I was to be present for all of the interviews, accompanied in some cases by research assistants and translators.

The IRB advised me that the incarceration facility might require the presence of an incarceration official in the vicinity of the interview, and so I stipulated that he/she would not be allowed to listen to the proceedings. In the end, all of the interviews with inmates were observed either from a distance, or from behind glass. The rationale for excluding guards from the immediate vicinity of the interview was the fear despite our request that the interviewees would not stick very closely to answering the questions, and that they might make some kind of accusation about abuse inside of the facility that could lead to complicated relationships with the guards. We also felt it important to prepare for the possibility that an inmate reveal something about their criminal case or conviction that was not previously known to the incarceration officials. Many of the inmates had outstanding issues before the courts, including appeals and pending immigration proceedings, making the interviewing process all the more sensitive.

As Principle Investigator (PI), I was responsible for all aspects of the study, including the selection of interviewees, the interviews, the transcription process and the write-up of the reports. The role of the assistants, of which there were several, was to observe and provide input or support as required. The interviews were held in accordance with the availability of prisoners and prison officials, subject to their time schedules. Interviews were held inside the prison facilities, at times arranged by the TDOC, and the individual facilities. The interview procedure was as follows: parties to the interview process were introduced to one another, consent forms were signed and then the interview proceeded. Interviews lasted for up to two hours, depending upon the nature of the discussion and whether or not simultaneous translation was required. I had prepared for the possibility of follow-up interviews, but in the end decided that they were not necessary.

To protect the participants, none of the information pertaining to their specific identity appears in the published findings or in the report that I submitted to the TDOC. No efforts were made to correlate individuals who were named or mentioned during interviews. If it was possible to identify an individual based upon the interview, that part of the interview was not to be cited in the report or published findings. The questions asked focused upon intercultural and migration issues, and any other information gathered that could be deemed harmful if released was not included in the report or published materials. Inmates' proper names were never used, and the type of information that was gathered during the interview process was assessed as regards the entire pool of data gathered, so specific references to utterances by inmates were restricted to those which pertain to the object of study for the project. All interviews with incarcerated persons followed the same procedures, in terms of time permitted with the interviewee, the space provided for the interview, the types of recording materials permitted and so forth.

In order to address IRB concerns about possible hazards associated with the interview process, we had a series of contingency plans. For example, if accusations of abuse or mistreatment had been described by a specific inmate, then the Safety Monitoring Board (SMB) was to be notified within 24 hours, and convened as soon as possible (and definitely within seven days). The SMB was composed of local experts in areas of law, criminal justice, immigrant work and research and ethics, who would work with the PI as needed, and report to the IRB according to the established IRB policy and procedure. The IRB would be informed of the decision taken by the SMB in the case at hand in relation to the safety/confidentiality of the participant.

Methodological findings from the current project

The nature of the process as described seems straightforward, but the nature of the prison system and the fear experienced by undocumented immigrants held therein led to a high level of variability from case to case. The methodology for a research program appropriate for this kind of work must account for this obstacle, and I would offer a warning to those who would hope to unearth some concrete "findings" about this group, or the elaboration of some rigid approach to this material, based on a few interviews. Specifically, I would suggest that undocumented immigrants are so vulnerable because they are subjected to extraordinary levels of discretion that promotes a general feeling of vulnerability and fear that can be manifest in a host of ways, from silence to behaving inappropriately. As such, it's very difficult to generalize about their situation except in regards to the fear that pervades all of their lives in the host country. Their experience in the host country is most likely represented in the way they behave during the interviews because it's here that the many subjective elements of a project like this are revealed, and it's very difficult to correlate what they reveal to the experience that leads them to reveal it.

Despite all the preparation I undertook and guidance I received, the interview process unfolded quite differently from what I'd expected. Although I met with many undocumented immigrants both inside of incarceration facilities and informally in restaurants and community centers, and although I did find their specific narratives valuable, I have decided not to include citations from them in this book. Most of the inmates I interviewed were very reluctant to be recorded, for obvious reasons, and although the experience of being with them and hearing what they had to say was informative, the actual details of the process were better described for our purposes by intermediaries, especially public defenders, lawyers, interpreters and investigators. And so at the end of the day, the interviews that I undertook with undocumented people in jails and prisons remain in the background, for a range of reasons.

First, because of the long lag time between TDOC approval and IRB approval, it seemed logical to begin interviews with persons familiar with the issue of immigrant incarceration first, and then to continue these interviews with prisoners once they were approved. This approach also provided me with an opportunity to speak with experts who could help me draft a questionnaire appropriate to the task.

Second, it became clear that the many obstacles to obtaining meaningful access to incarcerated migrants and the impossibility of gaining access to federal facilities in which refugees and immigrants are held in "detention" meant that the interviews with public defenders, lawyers and interpreters would constitute the heart of the accumulated data. So although one of the original objectives was to analyze some intercultural communication issues in the prisons, it became apparent that a larger pool of interviewees would be required to make useful assertions, and that the real experts in this realm were the translators and interpreters.

Third, I had hoped that interviews with prisoners would provide a sense of the trajectory that had led them to their present status, how they perceive and describe their current situation, what relationship exists between inmates and their families and what they expected the future had in store for them, either in the United States or back in their country of origin. The interviews with migrants were valuable, but primarily as a means of confirming information learned from experts. There were many impediments to prisoners speaking candidly, and it was my sense that interviewees understandably only said what they thought we wanted to hear. Furthermore, inmates often seemed to be speaking to prison officials when responding to my questions, probably because they were convinced, rightly or wrongly, that their conversations were being overheard or recorded. In the end, it was the unanticipated informal interviews with undocumented people in restaurants, workplaces and law offices that provided the kinds of information that I'd originally hoped to gather in the prisons.

My plan was to focus upon short and medium-term recommendations, and in particular to offer TDOC a host of easy-to-implement methods for improving relations between inmates, and between inmates and officials. I also wanted to gather information for a broader study that would complement my earlier work on Convention refugees (those who are applying for status in the country on the basis of the 1951 Geneva Convention), with the hope of assessing the validity of advocating for loosening or opening up borders between countries. The results of the original projects were indeed a vast array of recommendations that I formally presented to the TDOC, and I have subsequently presented some of the project findings to the local community, interested members of the legal profession, academics and policy makers. Many of the findings of this research project were in line with what other researchers were finding in Europe, Australia, and Southeast Asia, but the approach that I took was original and has led to interesting insights that aren't available in the scholarship.

Researchers in this domain also need to consider that someone who is living illegally in a host country can be subjected to a whole different array of legal procedures, arbitrarily enforced, and that the very fact of their being foreign to the judicial system makes them even more vulnerable to this discretion. For this reason it's necessary to consider "arbitrariness" alongside of "methodology" because it is the arbitrariness of decision making that makes it difficult or impossible to elaborate a formal and predictable methodology. Arbitrary law is no more real than the series of haphazard circumstances that leads to it being invoked, and punishments are often difficult to connect to the actions because the laws are applied in such an uneven fashion, often to set an example to others.

The methodology, as originally described and as modified as per discussions here, has served well as a means of establishing key concerns, although the material in this book extends far beyond the purview of the original research project in terms of international examples and the references to secondary literature. The preliminary conclusions are grim, and, regrettably, with the power of "security" and "law and order" discourse, the situation is likely to deteriorate as lawmakers find ways of "putting people away" without, in fact, considering the effects, long and short term, of these practices. A lot of anger is being born in prisons and internment centers throughout the world, and, if "terror" is indeed spread by the alienated, the disenfranchised and those with nothing more to lose, not much good can come of current practices.

Notes

1 It is of course the case, as Ryan Liss (2014) has recently noted, that "the ability of a state to determine who can enter its territory and who can claim membership in the national community is at the core of the traditional conception of sovereignty", and that "where sovereignty equates to control over territory and people, discretion over who can enter and who belongs would seem to be among the fundamental elements – if not the fundamental element – of a state's status as a sovereign entity". Nevertheless, he notes that "while often maintaining the discourse of state discretion, international law has increasingly intervened to constrain the terms of a state's ability to ascribe (or withhold) nationality and to expel non-nationals, with reference to Article 12(4) of the International Covenant on Civil and Political Rights (ICCPR)" (p. 1098). The effects of these efforts are reflected in, say, the

DREAM Act in the United States, and in an array of challenges in Europe and Australia based upon the idea that migrants have rights if they have spent their entire "conscious lives" in a particular host country (p. 1097).

2 The US Court calls persons engaged in the translation of one language to another "interpreters", as per 28 U.S. Code § 1827 – Interpreters in Courts of the United States. This can cause some confusion, since "to interpret" a text can also mean to fill in missing details or undertake some kind of an analysis of what has been said. Nonetheless, I will use legal nomenclature, and use "interpreter" for the work of translating one text into another without any interpretation, and I'll use "translator" to describe those who provide details beyond what is said in order to convey the intention, as well as the precise words, of the speaker.

3 Adrian Vermeule reviews this gray area (Vermeule 2013) and other important aspects of arbitrariness in a host of international settings are discussed in Timothy Endicott's recent work on the judge's interpretative powers in Indian and Canadian settings (Endicott 2014).

4 In the terms of an earlier period of Anglo-American constitutional history, the Obama Administration seeks a "dispensing" power to waive the law. Congress, however, must shoulder some of the blame for enacting stringent immigration rules and then chronically underfunding their administration, which delegates to the President a sweeping *de facto* discretion over enforcement.

5 On 1 October 2014 the ACLU published a report called "Scholars Evaluate the Cost of Locking Up Immigrants for Months and Years on End. The Results are as Bad as You'd Expect" (Tan 2014); therein, "Tan reports that in 2012, the government put a record-breaking 478,000 people behind bars while seeking to deport them from the United States. Many of them are seeking refuge from persecution; others are long-time lawful permanent residents with U.S. citizen family. And people who eventually win their immigration cases are perversely the ones most likely to languish in prison for months or years on end while their cases drag on through the system".

6 Bosworth and Turnbull (2014) report that "[i]n 2011, Immigration and Citizenship Enforcement (ICE) detained an all-time high of approximately 429,000 foreign nationals. Detainees in the US may be held either in specific immigration detention centres, county jails, federal prisons or ICE-owned 'service processing centres'. The majority (67 per cent) of detainees are held in one of the more than 250 local and state facilities. A further 17 per cent of detainees are kept in contract detention centres, followed by 13 per cent in processing centres, and 3 per cent within Bureau of Prisons facilities" (US Immigration and Customs Enforcement 2011). In 2011, the United States maintained a total of 33,400 detention beds.

7 For recent discussions of this program, the *Huffington Post* keeps a dedicated site at http://www.huffingtonpost.com/news/operation-streamline. [Accessed: 15 January 2015]

Bibliography

Alba, Francisco and Manuel Angel Castillo (2012) *New Approaches to Migration Management in Mexico and Central America*. Washington, DC: Migration Policy Institute.

Andrias, Kate (2013) "The President's Enforcement Power", *New York University Law Review* 88.4, pp. 1031–125.
Baldwin-Edwards, Martin and Martin A. Schain (eds.) (1994) *The Politics of Immigration in Western Europe*. New York and Abingdon, Oxon: Routledge.
Bales, Kevin (1999) *Disposable People: New Slavery in the Global Economy*. Oakland: University of California Press.
Barsky, Robert F. (1994) *Constructing a Productive Other: Discourse Theory and the Convention Refugee Hearing*. Amsterdam and Philadelphia, PA: John Benjamins.
Barsky, Robert F. (2001) *Arguing and Justifying: Assessing the Convention Refugee Choice of Moment, Motive and Host Country*. Aldershot, Sydney and Burlington, VT: Ashgate.
Bosworth, Mary and Sarah Turnbull (2014) "Immigration Detention, Punishment, and the Criminalization of Migration", in Pickering and Hamm (2014), pp. 91–107.
Dann, Carrie (11 April 2013) "By the Numbers: How America Tallies Its 11.1 Million Undocumented Immigrants". New York: NBC News. Available at: http://nbcpolitics.nbcnews.com/_news/2013/04/11/17691515-by-the-numbers-how-america-tallies-its-111-million-undocumented-immigrants?lite. [Accessed: 15 January 2015]
Delahunty, Robert J. and John C. Yoo (2013) "Dream On: The Obama Administration's Nonenforcement of Immigration Laws, the DREAM Act, and the Take Care Clause", *Texas Law Review* 91.78, pp. 781–857.
Endicott, Timothy (2014) "The Coxford Lecture: Arbitrariness", *The Canadian Journal of Law & Jurisprudence* 27.1, pp. 49–72.
Flatley, Christine (11 January 2012) "Judge Slams People Smuggling Sentence Law", *The Sydney Morning Herald*, p. A1.
Lippert, Randy and Sean Rehaag (eds.) (2012) *Sanctuary Practices in International Perspectives: Migration, Citizenship and Social Movements*. Abingdon, Oxon: Routledge.
Liss, Ryan (2014) "A Right to Belong: Legal Protection of Sociological Membership in the Application of Article 12(4) of the ICCPR", *New York University Journal of International Law and Politics (JILP)* 46, pp. 1097–191.
Loveland, Ian (2012) *Constitutional Law, Administrative Law, and Human Rights: A Critical Introduction*. New York and Oxford: Oxford University Press.
Lucatuorto, P. L. M. (2010) "Reasonableness in Administrative Discretion: A Formal Model", *The Journal Jurisprudence* 8.2, pp. 633–45.
Margulies, Peter (2014) "Taking Care of Immigration Law: Presidential Stewardship, Prosecutorial Discretion, and the Separation of Powers", *Boston University Law Review* 94.105, pp. 1–53.
Marmor, Andrei and Scott Soames (2013) *Philosophical Foundations of Language in the Law*. Oxford: Oxford University Press.
Marquardt, Marie Friedmann, Timothy Steigenga, Philip Williams and Manuel Vasquez (2011) *Living "Illegal": The Human Face of Unauthorized Immigration*. New York: The New Press.
Miles, Thomas J. and Cass R. Sunstein (2008) "The Real World of Arbitrariness Review", *The University of Chicago Law Review* 75.2, pp. 761–814.
Oxford English Dictionary (OED) (1971) *The Compact Edition of the Oxford English Dictionary*. Oxford: Oxford University Press.

Owens, J. (31 December 2011) "Harsh Penalties for Boat Crew 'Target Wrong People'", *The Australian*. Available at: http://reasonablegrounds.blogspot.com/2011_12_01_archive.html. [Accessed: 15 January 2015]

Pickering, S. and J. Hamm (2014) *The Routledge Handbook on Crime and International Migration*. Abingdon, Oxon: Routledge.

Price, Zachary S. (2014) "Enforcement Discretion and Executive Duty", *Vanderbilt Law Review* 67.3, pp. 671–769.

Rakoff, Jed S. (20 November 2014) "Why Innocent People Plead Guilty", *New York Review of Books*. Available at: http://www.nybooks.com/articles/archives/2014/nov/20/why-innocent-people-plead-guilty. [Accessed: 15 January 2015]

Sandoz, Ellis (ed.) (2008) *The Roots of Liberty: Magna Carta, Ancient Constitution, and the Anglo-American Tradition of Rule of Law*. Indianapolis, IN: Liberty Fund. Available at: http://oll.libertyfund.org/titles/2180. [Accessed: 15 January 2015]

Tan, Michael (2014) "Scholars Evaluate the Cost of Locking Up Immigrants for Months and Years on End. The Results are as Bad as You'd Expect". Washington: ACLU. Available at: https://www.aclu.org/blog/immigrants-rights/scholars-evaluate-cost-locking-immigrants-months-and-years-end-results-are. [Accessed: 15 January 2015]

US Immigration and Customs Enforcement (2011) "Detention Management Fact Sheet". Available at: http://www.ice.gov/news/library/factsheets/detention-mgmt.htm. [Accessed 15 January 2015]

Vermeule, Adrian (2013) "Rationally Arbitrary Decisions (in Administrative Law)", *Harvard Law School Public Law & Legal Theory Working Paper Series*, Paper No. 13, pp.1–24.

Wright, R. George (2010) "Arbitrariness: Why the Most Important Idea in Administrative Law Can't Be Defined, and What This means for the Law in General", *University of Richmond Law Review* 44.2, pp. 839–65.

Chapter 2

Translating the utterances of undocumented immigrants in a hostile discourse marketplace

> These are folks who to a large extent came here for the sole reason of earning enough money to send to mama. And they are doing that. And then, on Friday night, they are there with a car. They would never have had a car where they're from. $500 gets you a damned good usable car here, and you couldn't touch one for $500 in Mexico. And they can drive it. License? Maybe. Then some clown shows up drunk one night and sells one of the guys a $200 pistol. There's a really big tradition in Latin America, where if something is happening that is good, then you fire your pistol off. This guy is not a threat to the community. We take the pistol away from him, we tell him why we don't do that, and he goes on. The reason they are in jail instead is the same reason why my Caucasian clients are in jail: drinking, drugging and being stupid. Just because you come from Mexico and are here to send money home doesn't alleviate any of those three conditions.... But what eventually happens to them if arrested depends upon who is working in the jail, and whether they are looked up on the computer. There's a little line on the computer that says: "Hold for I.C.E." If that happens, then they are screwed.
>
> (A lawyer interviewed for the project)

Most work on migratory flows focuses upon the "push" factors that drive people away from their homes, and the "pull" factors that attract them to new horizons (European Commission 2000). In this chapter I'll adopt a similar approach, but I will add references to the "social discourse" of undocumented immigrants, which denotes the swirl of information, rumors, ideas and general discourse into which people enter, or from which they flee, when they move from place to place. In so doing, I wish to flesh out this idea that migration can be understood with references to discursive practices that occur amongst interested parties, and that examining the details of linguistic interaction provides a much deeper understanding of the challenges migrants face as they try to negotiate their existence in the host country. It has been shown that, for example, Pakistani men undertake the perilous journey to England in order to work, without authorization, as a kind of rite of passage, and many Mexican farmhands decide to bow to the pressure of their villages in order to "be a man", leave for the United States and send home remittances and hone new skills (Ahmad 2008; Lesesma 1998; Maciel and Herrera-Sobek 1998; Schrover et al. 2008). The pressure that these individuals experience comes from actual and overheard conversations about what it means to seek out employment opportunities abroad, which in turn can be tied to crucial tropes in home societies, including, for example, machismo and masculinity (Ramirez 2011).

When migrants arrive in the host country, they enter a social discourse that is most likely negative in regards to "illegal" immigrants, and, in regards to social pressures, may have very different conceptions of manly activities. So rather than encountering an environment that celebrates the achievements and potential of the migrant, they encounter an antagonistic social discourse that's riddled with xenophobia, false stereotypes, horror stories, but also the occasional uplifting tale based on the experiences of particular people. An interpreter provides one such story in the American context:

> I am thinking of a woman who was never incarcerated. I interpreted for her when she was in physical therapy. She was from Oaxaca, and had lived here several years, but had crossed the border between the US and Mexico eleven times. It was very clear in her mind, and in the minds of others like her, why they are here. They are here to work and make a living. They are not bilking the system. They are paying taxes on their $6.00 an hour job, carried out under miserable conditions, and that is why they are here. I admire them. They are very singularly focused on just doing what they came to do, not bothering anybody, giving their kids a better life, sending money back home for their mothers. I think they are cognizant of the risks they take by being here. They have an amazing singleness of purpose, to live every day, and to do their work.

The broad arrays of things that are said about people like this woman both contribute to, and flow from, a prevailing "social discourse", rendering the act of border-crossing a linguistic fact as well as a physical one. When we consider the narratives of undocumented people, we also come to realize the importance of gossip, rumors, and "life story" narratives, whether or not they are true. Such an approach also drives home the fact that undocumented immigrants hear stories about people like themselves, through the filters of translation and cross-cultural barriers. And so in this chapter I will undertake a subjective assessment of how undocumented people experience their life in the host country, and then suggest that one of the many obstacles that undocumented people face is that they are often negatively perceived, and deleteriously described, within the prevailing social discourse. Having set up the backdrop, I will suggest that amongst the array of ways in which undocumented people are described, the most common is to attribute to them the qualities of dirt and filth, that is, matter out of place. And finally, I'll turn to interpreting on behalf of these individuals, and claim that this task is rendered all the more difficult because of the overwhelmingly negative views that circulate about them within the social discourse.

The blame game

Immigrants are often blamed for crimes committed in the country, and news made by partial groups posing as impartial research centers, like NumbersUSA or the Federation for American Immigration Reform (FAIR), often finds its way into the mainstream news media. Of FAIR, the National Council of La Raza (NCLR) (2010) has recently written:

> Overall, FAIR blames immigrants for crime, poverty, disease, urban sprawl, and increasing racial tensions in America and calls for a drastic cut in the numbers of those allowed to immigrate. In radio and TV ads, it attacked former Senator Spencer Abraham (R–MI), saying Abraham's immigration reform proposal could "make it easier for [Arab] terrorists like Osama bin Laden to export their way of terror to any street in America." Print ads featured a photograph of Senator Abraham—an Arab American—next to a photo of bin Laden. FAIR's ads were condemned across the country and caused former Senator Alan K. Simpson (R–WY) to resign from FAIR's advisory board. Another example of FAIR's racist views is reflected in a comment made by Garrett Hardin, a FAIR board member, who argued that aiding starving Africans is counterproductive and will only "encourage population growth." FAIR has also created two affiliate organizations: Choose Black America (for African Americans) and You Don't Speak for Me (for Hispanic Americans).
>
> (p. 2)

These stories make news, broadly, and they affect the general perception that people have of immigrants, and that immigrants can have, therefore, of themselves. The pervasiveness of these organizations, and the ease with which "war on terror" can be applied to almost any criminal activity, from local vandalism to international drug smuggling, is worrisome indeed. From a more theoretical standpoint, this type of fearmongering and hysteria, replicated in settings all around the world, creates a negative perception of undocumented immigrants, and migrants more generally, in the broader social discourse.

Intrinsic to any discussion of how a negative subsection of the social discourse operates is a theory of the whole compendium of discursive practice in a given society at a given time, in this case relating to discourses about foreignness, immigration and otherness within a particular host country. In order to discuss this idea of social discourse, and to consider it as regards a host of push-pull factors, it's necessary to determine what the social discourse is, and to consider its value in understanding the many obstacles that undocumented immigrants face. To undertake this task, we can look to the work of Marc Angenot who, in a broad array of articles and books, sets out a broad and powerful framework that has great value for this domain of inquiry. Social discourse, according to his approach, is:

> everything that is said or written in a given state of society; everything that is printed or talked about and represented today through electronic media. Everything that narrates or argues, if one contends that narration and argumentation are the two basic kinds of discursiveness.
>
> (Angenot 2004, p. 200)

His eventual goal is not simply to catalogue or to list all prevailing discursive tendencies, but rather to uncover the "extrapolation of those discursive rules and topics that underlie the endless rumor of social discourses without ever being themselves objectified" (ibid.). What is said that relates to immigration, say, is in this respect but one practice amidst a massive discursive output that relates, in complex and often contradictory ways, to particular utterances made about immigration and immigrants:

> A culture, a social discourse is in fact never made out of a set of statically dominant ideas, representations, systems of belief, "ideologies". It is thoroughly made out of regulated antagonisms between conflicting images, concepts, cognitive discrepancies, and incompatibilities that are still relatively stabilized without ever reaching a state of equilibrium. Social discourse is made out of a set of ideologèmes [the basic ideological unit of ideas or themes embedded in a culture's language] in tension with each other, of "sociogrammes" thematizing, on divergent vectors, conflicting social representations. It is through and beyond these tensions, conflicts, and compartmentalizations, beyond the cacophonic rumour of social languages that something like a hegemony will be discovered producing precedences and arbitrations between conflicting discourses, concealing topical axioms and basic principles of social verisimilitude, universal taboos and censorship that mark the boundaries of the "thinkable". One should not dissociate from this hegemony the normative imposition of the legitimate language, a language always saturated with tropes and idioms, phraseologies and bombastic structures of feeling. It should perhaps be added that so-called ideologies never go in isolation even if the historian tends to isolate them (i.e. anticlerical id., anti-Semitic id., protofascism, republicanism and so forth) for the purpose of analysis.
>
> (p. 201)

At the same time, however, Angenot recognizes the autonomy of various discursive genres within this broader compendium, and does not make any attempt to totalize social discourse, and thus ignore its traditions, its discursive genres, its stakes, its constraints, its values within the discursive marketplace and so forth.

This approach is tied to a series of disciplines and texts, including argumentation and rhetorical work dating back to Aristotle, and developed through the elaboration of elements that allow for utterances to be linked. Amossy (2002) describes "the unexpressed premise accounting for the passage from one utterance to the other" as a "topos in the pragmatico-semantic meaning of the word" (p. 386), that is, beliefs commonly held by people in a particular group that give the appearance of representing a kind of consensus. This new perspective has proven to be fruitful in several linguistic fields, and it's valuable for our purposes because it implies that to use specific words is to invoke a broader topoi, suggesting that the meaning of a word is determined more in regards to related clusters of terms than to a particular referent.

This may seem a tad obtuse, but its implications for how we "hear" particular discourses, or how we produce particular utterances for specific speech situations, is a crucial issue, especially for people who are foreign to a particular social discourse. If we stick to the example of the "undocumented immigrant" or, worse still, the "illegal", then we can immediately imagine the array of linked topoi including foreigner, criminal, job-stealer, immigrant, outsider – or even worse, such as terrorist. Furthermore, every word the undocumented immigrant says in a given setting is from this perspective saturated by the context within which it is spoken. Her utterances are also bathing in a very particular time at which she speaks, which calls up not only the conditions of the speaking subject but also every element of the context within which, and to which, the word is spoken. An example might be the statement that "I've come to this country from Yemen because here I am free" pre- versus post-9/11 or the shootings at Charlie Hebdo, let's say. Before 9/11 or Charlie Hebdo, this might have seemed like a comment on the West, its generosity and the "dream" that so many people associate with it. Post-9/11 or Charlie Hebdo, a host country interlocutor might construe this sentence differently, as in "free" to act inappropriately, or else using "free" as a negative rather than positive indicator. The point is, the utterance itself might be identical, but it may be "heard" in very different ways, depending upon the moment when it is uttered.

Immediately after 9/11, I traveled from Montreal to New York City, and at the border was accosted by a hostile border guard who was appalled when I said to him: "I don't have my passport because I have never used it to cross this border, and didn't think it would be any different now." He barked back at me: "But we are at war!" I had traveled hundreds of times across the US border from Canada, and was traveling to New York that time in order to offer my support. I certainly never imagined that I would be considered a possible threat, or an imposter. The situation had changed, and not only had the border-crossing rules changed, but the "rhetoric" of the time had suddenly become militaristic, rendering my own reasoning inappropriate or even disrespectful. This type of example leads Angenot (2004) to a crucial preliminary point in his thinking about "social discourse", which is that it's deeply linked to time, and, as such:

> At any moment and in spite of different ideologies in competition, there exists a *diffuse thematic paradigm* that may undergo innumerable avatars but nevertheless provides the basic features of a dominant world-view. Such a thematic paradigm is not necessarily embodied in a specific philosophy or doctrine of the time; it may be more elusive, existing both everywhere and nowhere. Fashionable ideologies of the moment provide successive versions or variants of [it].
>
> (p. 204)

In other words, we evaluate what we hear on the basis of the context, in the broadest possible sense, including (say) what the person listening to the utterances thinks about his/her interlocutor. Herein enter issues relating to racism and xenophobia, but also other factors such as physical attractiveness, or the degree to what is being said accords with the fashion of that particular time. This idea of discursive "fashions" is described by Bakhtin, who claimed that specific utterances are tied to the "speech genres" to which they relate, and to the "situatedness" of the person speaking. For Bakhtin (1981), language is stratified into different speech genres that gain and lose value depending upon the context (the space and the time) within which they are uttered:

> The internal stratification of any single national language into social dialects, characteristic group behavior, professional jargons, generic languages, languages of generations and age groups, tendentious languages, languages of the authorities, of various circles and of passing fashions, languages that serve the specific sociopolitical purposes of the day, even of the hour (each day has its own slogan, its own vocabulary, its own emphases)—this internal stratification present in every language at any given moment of its historical existence is the indispensable prerequisite.
>
> (pp. 262–3)

Consistent with this idea, Angenot suggests that the study of discourse must be clearly inscribed within a broader project of understanding the entire social discourse at a given time and place. This is very exigent, and demands that the reader or hearer possess a clear understanding of the prevailing norms of emission and reception, in order to accord the discursive commodities the speaker is attempting to peddle in the discursive marketplace. The undocumented immigrant is, as it were, selling his/her utterance, and hoping that the buyer will consider it worth the investment.

By way of concrete example, we can imagine an undocumented farmworker who is pulled over for speeding. In his interaction with the officer, he might invoke the importance of bringing in the current crop of tomatoes before the impending storm. If this officer thinks that this is valuable work, and that indeed the storm will ravage the tomatoes because of their fragility, he might let the undocumented laborer off with a warning, or, at the very least, might not call the immigration authorities. The savvy undocumented immigrant, therefore, might try to "direct" his discourse appropriately, in the hope of achieving his desired end. But this is a complex action, because, as Bakhtin (1981) suggests:

> The word, directed toward its object, enters a dialogically agitated and tension-filled environment of alien words, value judgments and accents, weaves in and out of complex interrelationships, merges with some, recoils from others, intersects with yet a third group: and all this may crucially shape discourse, may leave a trace in all its semantic layers, may complicate its expression and influence its entire stylistic profile.
>
> (p. 276)

If we can agree that discursive exchanges do in fact occur this way, then the speaker of any utterance must be familiar with the local fashions, what is acceptable, or even "stylish", in a particular discourse marketplace. Bakhtin describes utterances as living beings, cast forth into a pre-existing ecosystem, such that:

> The word in living conversation is directly, blatantly, oriented toward a future answer-word. It provokes an answer, anticipates it and structures itself in the answer's direction. Forming itself in an atmosphere of the already spoken, the word is at the same time determined by that which has not yet been said, but which is needed and in fact anticipated by the answering word. Such is the situation in any living dialogue.
>
> (p. 281)

Angenot (2004) supplements this approach by describing the social discourse environment, identifying details of its prevailing hegemonies and norms. Whereas Bakhtin often describes this relationship in organic terms, as though the utterance is animate, Angenot is more material-minded in his social discourse approach, and therefore much more apt to think of the utterance as commodity than as living being:

> This division of discursive labor may also be approached in the logic of market and commodities. Discourses circulate, their value is regulated by supply and demand, they are marketed and exchanged. All discursive topologies are subject to a specific economy with its market engineering, supply and demand, planned obsolescence of ideological goods,

> inventories, and clearance sales. A whole new economy with its fashions, infatuations, inflations, and crashes, conflicts with the preservation principle and the need to control the limits and outskirts of the thinkable. Hence the frequency of that classical compromise: the "foreseeable newness," or the art of making new out of old.
>
> (p. 207)

This idea, key to his work on how utterances circulate in a social discourse, moves Angenot away from Bakhtin and towards Bourdieu (1990). Bourdieu's approach, like Bakhtin's and Angenot's, challenges the idea that we can undertake some kind of a formal analysis of language, that we can just record what was said, as the basis for how it could or should work. This might apply in some cases, but in social situations, like for example the relation between an undocumented immigrant and a policeman, it goes beyond just saying the right thing from a purely technical standpoint. The "right thing" has to be uttered at the right time, in the right way, to the person most likely to be receptive to it; and furthermore, determining what is "right" for a particular situation can be enormously complicated.

For Bourdieu, linguistic exchange isn't "living", in the way that Bakhtin describes it, but rather it's a kind of economic transaction between a "producer, endowed with a certain linguistic capital, and a consumer (or a market),...which is capable of procuring a certain material or symbolic profit" (p. 66). Utterances aren't, as he says, "signs to be understood and deciphered; they are also signs of *wealth*, intended to be evaluated and appreciated, and *signs of authority*, intended to be believed and obeyed," which leads him to the very salubrious observation that:

> Quite apart from the literary (and especially poetic) uses of language, it is rare in everyday life for language to function as a pure instrument of communication. The pursuit of maximum informative efficiency is only exceptionally the exclusive goal of linguistic production and the distinctly instrumental use of language which it implies generally clashes with the often unconscious pursuit of symbolic profit.
>
> (p. 67)

This use of "profit" suggests that the examples to which Bourdieu is referring relate more to (say) selling something, or deriving personal benefit from the interaction. In the case of undocumented immigrants, it's not so much profit as it is survival. Like a claimant in a courtroom, the undocumented immigrant is trying to undo labels that have been placed upon him/her, such as "criminal" or "illegal", and trying to substitute instead "hard worker" or "contributor to the host society". He/she may also be trying to disassociate him/herself from a group to which he/she is deemed tied, because of the negative connotations of that association. A legal investigator describes this process:

> Sometimes it's just pride in whatever their country of origin is. Some of them think they are a little bit better than others, and so they don't want to be confused with people from other countries. I've heard statements like: "I don't want to be confused with one of those Mexicans".... Obviously, not every Latin American here comes from Mexico, and each culture, and each country, has their different ways of interacting, even in regards to sense of humor. The common thing is that we all speak Spanish, but then you have your different cultural aspects, and they are very different from one country to another.... But I think it is also very typical of Americans to group people, like all the Hispanics. So here it's assumed that I am Mexican.

Bourdieu's work goes a long way in explaining why a Latin American legal investigator might not wish to be labeled as a Mexican, and certainly why Mexicans don't want to be labeled "illegal". The links here are not just linguistic ones, tying the sign to the signified, because by the association between labels in a particular topoi, the Mexican can be viewed in the first instance as a criminal. Describing someone instead as "undocumented", or *sans papiers*, is somewhat better because it doesn't relate so much to their person, as it does to their possessing, or not, some kind of documents. It's still negative, but much less so than "illegal", because if this person enters into the discourse marketplace as an "illegal", it's as though the words that he/she is offering are being sold by some kind of a criminal.

And so in order to survive or derive profit from a foray into a discourse marketplace, the speaker counts on, and attempts to establish, some basis for the communication of his/her value, credibility or viability. But the process is highly complicated because, according to Angenot (2004), the underlying rules of the social discourse:

> comprise a thematic repertory, an implicit cognitive system (or perhaps several cognitive systems in competition), and a regulated topology, a division of labor in the discursive realm. These are the basic components of what engenders the sayable, the writable, and the discursive acceptability at a given historical moment in a given society.
>
> (p. 200)

Herein are echoes of Bakhtin's idea that any narrative consists of complex interrelationships, consonances and dissonances, such that "understanding" is active and interactive. All this helps to explain why it's difficult for someone foreign to a speech context to discern the right way to direct a narrative because, to use Bakhtin's (1981) formulation, a speaker's:

> ... orientation toward the listener is an orientation toward a specific conceptual horizon, toward the specific world of the listener; it introduces

> totally new elements into his discourse; it is in this way, after all, that various different points of view, conceptual horizons, systems for providing expressive accents, various social "languages" come to interact with one another.
>
> (p. 282)

This means that the utterances aren't unified, and they aren't untainted by the exterior world, because:

> All words have the "taste" of a profession, a genre, a tendency, a party, a particular work, a particular person, a generation, an age group, the day and hour. Each word tastes of the context and contexts in which it has lived its socially charged life; all words and forms are populated by intentions. Contextual overtones (generic, tendentious, individualistic) are inevitable in the word.
>
> (p. 293)

These contexts evolve constantly, so the relationship between the speaker and the language he/she produces "is always found in a state of movement and oscillation that is more or less alive" (p. 293). Angenot (2004) suggests that this complex and unfolding relationship is nevertheless regulated by rules which, even if fluid and variable across genres, are nevertheless discoverable. The problem is:

> ...to try to connect the literary, scientific, philosophical, political fields, and so forth, and without neglecting stakes, constraints and traditions of these individual fields to extrapolate trans-discursive rules, discover vectors of exchange, and set up a global topology of the prevailing *sayable*, accounting therefore for using "Social Discourse" in the singular, and not social discourse*s* as a simple coexistence and juxtaposition of genres, disciplines, and local cognitive strategies.
>
> (p. 200)

The difference between Bakhtin, Bourdieu and Angenot, then, resides where each of them chooses to place the emphasis. For Bourdieu, the "sayable" is linked to the circulation of discursive goods in the marketplace, while for Angenot it is tied to the conditions under which the speaking subject produces his/her utterance, and for Bakhtin (1981), whose work subtends both, that same word, however constrained, is nevertheless the product of living, speaking individuals who are situated in very specific ways, in space and in time. Utterances are therefore living entities that interact with the environment, even as they act upon it:

> The living utterance, having taken meaning and shape at a particular historical moment in a socially specific environment, cannot fail to brush up

> against thousands of living dialogic threads woven by socio-ideological consciousness around the given object of an utterance, it cannot fail to become an active participant in social dialogue. After all, the utterance arises out of this dialogue as a continuation of it and as a rejoinder to it—it does not approach the object from the sidelines.
>
> (p. 274)

The idea that dialogue itself is somehow organic, and tied to a living space where dialogue occurs is crucial, for Bakhtin, because:

> ...in any actual dialogue the rejoinder also leads such a double life: it is structured and conceptualized in the context of the dialogue as a whole, which consists of its own utterances...and of alien utterances (those of the partner). One cannot excise the rejoinder from this combined context made up of one's own words and the words of another without losing its sense and tone. It is an organic part of a heteroglot unity.
>
> (p. 284)

This latter approach is a sign of Bakhtin's time (1895–1975 with the brunt of his work undertaken in the early part of the 20th Century), tied to the contemporary interest in vitalism (cf. Burwick and Douglass 1992), and linked to his earlier work on the carnival. Nonetheless, it's the crucial linchpin in the work of both Angenot and Bourdieu, who see discourse as produced within a context, in an ongoing way, directed towards particular ends. When brought to bear upon the act of translation, this becomes all the more fascinating because in a situation in which the added component of traversing linguistic and/or cultural bounds is added into the equation, the utterance faces multiple hemispheres of ideology, situatedness and context; and since home languages translated into host situations tend to be fraught with politics, the idea of each utterance bathing in ideology becomes all the more significant.

Against the backdrop of social discourse, the discourse marketplace and Bakhtin's vitalistic approach to discourse, we can assess the challenges facing undocumented immigrants. Since they are necessarily outsiders to the host country, they experience a sense of indeterminate outsiderness that feeds into feelings of unease and tension, described by a lawyer:

> I think that on one level, people who are undocumented are aware that they are susceptible to being detained or deported at any moment. People I talk to as witnesses for violations by undocumented persons are aware of that and they live in the fear of that all the time. On the other hand, it's impossible to live with that all the time, so you sort of try not to think about it. I think that people assume that there is a more fair system than there is, that if you're reasonably discovered that you would be quickly detained and deported.

This lawyer identifies the central issue that ties together the "awareness" that undocumented people have of the risks they are running, the "fear" that they will get caught and the effort to "not think about it" so that they aren't incapacitated. This is a complex mental game made much worse by the swirling array of laws, proposed laws and programs that they can be subjected to. A brief description of some such laws and programs can help us appreciate the challenges these people face.

Awareness, fear and the backdrop of punitive actions

The social discourse surrounding undocumented immigration issues has undergone important changes in the last decade, particularly in the United States. As we've seen, many new and draconian measures flow from the adoption of new (but at that time mostly unenforced) laws in 1996. After 9/11, many of the new laws were enforced either for the first time, or more stringently. So much new legislation has been debated, proposed or passed in their wake that any research project in this era has to look critically upon data or frameworks developed pre-9/11. A community organizer summed up the situation as dramatic:

> I think what 9/11 did was legitimize prejudice. We had this Know-Nothing Party [a political party that flourished in the 1850s in the United States that was an outgrowth of the strong anti-immigrant and especially anti-Roman Catholic sentiment that started to manifest itself during the 1840s], and we have this history of anti-immigration, and I think what 9/11 did was justify the kind of prejudices that were already out there.... I think that it's because of 9/11, which legitimized people doing nasty things to foreigners.

Social discourse can shift dramatically after an event like 9/11, a natural disaster, the sinking of a vessel containing undocumented people, the murder of journalists or cartoonists or reports of abuse directed against migrants. In regards to the cultural aspects of the social discourse, it's also worth keeping in mind that the more distant one is from the host culture, the more difficult it will be to successfully work (within) the system. For this reason, people who are refugees, homeless, foreign or for whatever reason marginal can be subjected to a complex array of discriminatory actions that are taken in regards to the dominant and hegemonic social group.[1] But the situation of undocumented people is growing in size and dimension, and it has become so egregious, and abuses are now so widespread, that it now defies both logic and consistency. This is even affecting law enforcement officials who find themselves charged with assessing complex immigration data and convoluted immigration regulations; and it's a growing concern for officials involved in the process of incarcerating foreigners on grounds which can be murky to officials, and often incomprehensible to those who find themselves in the system.

Reports and rumors about new legislation concerning irregular migrants

The last decade has been witness to a plethora of recently enacted or newly proposed legislation affecting foreigners, emanating from different federal, state and local offices. These changes are in themselves a source of great anxiety amongst immigrant and asylum communities, and amongst those charged with enforcing new laws. It's noteworthy that each of these programs has been discussed in the media, but not all have been adopted; and even when adopted, they are not consistently enforced from one state, or even one county, to the next. Furthermore, new proposals are constantly being put before state and local legislatures, but a lot of them look like posturing on the part of legislative members trying to prove their "toughness" to constituents. In fact, there has been such an array of proposals aimed at curbing illegal migration that an exhaustive list would be a chapter-length work, particularly if it included local, state and federal initiatives. It's worth mentioning a few of them, though, because they provide a concrete sense of where a social discourse comes from.

For instance, when I first started interviewing people for this project, there was significant discussion of the 2005 "Operation Streamline" that enforces criminal prosecutions against virtually every person caught illegally crossing stretches of the US-Mexico border. The Operation was described in Congress, and was of course widely reported in the media, which created an atmosphere of fear and uncertainty amongst the population targeted. A lawyer I interviewed noted that:

> There's an overarching anti-immigrant sentiment that has developed since September the 11th that has made people much less sympathetic, if they were ever sympathetic to undocumented people in this country. There's this sense that people are surprised that people get any basic rights as undocumented people. It seems like it's getting worse, and that may be a function of the media.

There is significant debate about this Operation, and many reports that describe activists protesting against it; whether it is eventually dismantled or not, its impact will continue to be felt as undocumented people hear stories about the law, its effects, and its uncertain future.

Even more to the point, though, is the incredible amount of legislation that is put forward, debated, modified or changed in city, state and federal districts every month. Each of these new initiatives, and challenges, comes in addition to the vast array of legislation that exists in local, municipal, county, province, state and national settings. Immigrants hear about these proposals, first or second hand, and are susceptible to acting on the basis of what they hear. This is destabilizing, but also justifiable, since there can be significant variation from one state to another in terms of openness to migrants, as a public defender indicated with reference to the United States:

> I think our government right now is very immigrant unfriendly, and it makes me angry to consider how immigrants are treated.... There's also a huge contrast between [different states] in terms of embracing and celebrating different cultures. It would be hard to be an immigrant right now.

Amidst this variation, there's also a consistent anti-immigrant theme that emerges at various levels of vociferousness depending upon the political climate, and all of it has an effect, because the lag-time between propositions, implementation and knowledge is so long that people may still believe that they are still in force even if they no longer exist.

In light of all the contradictory things that people hear, they are likely unsure of how to act, what to say and, pace Bourdieu (1990), what will "work" to get them safely back to their homes or to their jobs. Typically, the undocumented immigrant won't know what is "correct", appropriate or, to use the terminology from Bourdieu or Angenot, they don't know what they should offer up to the marketplace of discursive practice, and they risk saying something that cannot be "heard" or, worse, they might employ a discursive or practical tactic that works in Mexico, but not here (offering to pay the fine in cash, invoking friends in the hope that the officer knows them, and so forth). These linguistic and cultural obstacles could be better overcome in the presence of a translator or interpreter, so I'd like to begin by thinking about what kind of training such a person should have, and what the "field" of translation studies should look like. To do so, it's important to recognize that interpreting on behalf of undocumented people is akin to arguing on behalf of the unwanted, the undesirable or, worse, people who are deemed dangerous because they are quite literally "out of place", an idea best understood as regards censorship.

Social discourse, censorship and translation

Translation is one of the disciplines at the intersection between culture and knowledge transfer, and as such it deals with the selection, transformation and dissemination of information against the backdrop of the prevailing social discourse described above. At this intersection, however, stands an array of tasks that are so different in nature that they aren't even captured in the oft-mentioned distinction between translation and interpretation. This distinction is nonetheless an appropriate place to begin, and so I use the accepted terminology of "interpretation" to refer to the work involved in linguistic translation *tout court*, and "translation" to mean linguistic interpretation that is supplemented, or even supplanted, by information that helps describe what the speaker is trying to say, or means to say. This of course far exceeds what we normally think of as the task of translation, or translation studies; indeed, even if we defer to the many definitions provided in the monumental Doorslaer and Gambier (2013), we're generally led to the quest for efficacious and accurate renderings of one language into another, without (in my opinion) sufficient reference to concrete impediments in the social discourse.

And so informed by work by Angenot, Bakhtin and Bourdieu, and from a somewhat outsider perspective relating to what literature and law can teach us about the situation of the undocumented immigrant, I'd argue that we need to think carefully about what translation means in the context of marginalized peoples, and what kinds of things should be taught in the realm of translation studies, which leads me to wonder what should be involved in that kind of work. Of course the definition game for emerging or underrepresented fields like translation studies can be tricky because it demands that practitioners undertake an exercise deemed unnecessary in established fields, such as, say, anthropology or sociology (even though they too suffer from constant and justifiable identity crises). In order to contribute to our understanding of the translation process, I would like to think about what translation studies *do* from a somewhat uncharacteristic perspective that focuses not only upon the transformation of linguistic material from one national language to another, but also on the resistance to this process. This is best understood with reference to materials deemed inadmissible, that is, material that is not necessarily just untranslatable, but rather undesirable in translation, and therefore untranslatable. By invoking censorship, I hope to contribute to our understanding of translation in the context of the undocumented immigrant discursive paradigm, and then to efforts at solidifying translation work inside institutions of higher learning.

To begin, I want to take us back in time to the case of a famous couple of translators and publishers, Henry and Ernest Vizetelly, and their involvement in the translation and dissemination of works by Émile Zola that were deemed obscene in France, and prosecuted as such in England. With the insights of that example, and discussions about what obscenity charges teach us about translation studies, I'll then turn to more contemporary concerns regarding illegal immigrants, drawing attention to the overlap between what was said against Henry Vizetelly at his trial,[2] and what is said about illegal immigrants, in terms of their involving the representation of "filth" and "dirt", that is, the treatment of matter that is deemed in its filthiness to be "out of place". These two examples point to challenges faced by translators and translation studies, both in terms of its acceptance as a discipline and course of study, and its formulation as an adequate description of those tasks translators should learn to undertake in order to meet these challenges. Thinking in academic ways about what a translator should be allowed to do in a situation of intercultural translation, assessing the multiple competing definitions of translation studies and debating technical matters about what kind of translating methods should be taught to students, it's easy to forget the real object of translating for marginal groups like undocumented immigrants. No matter how accurate the translation, or how sophisticated the methodology, or how wonderful the certification process, the real obstacles to translation are often elsewhere, in, for example, preconceived notions about the nature of the material being translated, or the person speaking the foreign language.

I'll also underline the fact that when translators work on behalf of these undesired or so-called undesirable elements, they themselves can come under fire as being the vessels through which unwanted individuals are given passage into the unwitting and innocent host society rather than as useful vehicles, mediums or intermediaries in a complex transformational linguistic process. This means that translation studies should indeed undertake the broad tasks usually associated with this realm, including, for example: applied interpreting and translation, the analysis of contextual meaning, "extra-linguistic" aspects of communication, cross-cultural sensitivity, sociolinguistics, dialectology, localization and terminology management. But this already broad training could nonetheless benefit from a deep understanding of what kinds of contextual impediments can prevent the admission of the discourse, on the grounds that its very presence threatens the sanctity of the host or home society (a point driven home by such events as the shooting at Charlie Hebdo). As such, translation studies needs to be conceived of within a much larger humanistic enterprise that is bolstered through study of history, philosophy, literature and politics; and to see why, it's instructive to look into the realm of obscenity.

Obscenity and translation

In 1857 two seminal texts came before French tribunals, and their authors, Gustave Flaubert and Charles Baudelaire, were both charged with obscenity. Despite the differences in genres, and in the approach taken by the defense, the rhetoric of both trials can be seen as a precursor to arguments that would be made against Henry Vizetelly in 1888. *Les Fleurs du mal* was denounced as being disgusting to the point of causing a kind of infection, and its author was portrayed as a purveyor of garbage (Guyaux 2007), and similar accusations were made against Vizetelly for his translations of Zola's novels. In spite of the many differences between Zola via Vizetelly, Baudelaire and Flaubert, the critical vocabulary deployed against them all seems to make one thing clear: in the eyes of many of their contemporaries, and certainly in the courtrooms of justice, the works that were being scrutinized were all portrayed as a kind of dirt that was imposed upon an unsuspecting reading public that risked, in its exposure to it, an irreversible infection. This idea of utterances acting like infections in a social discourse is a common theme throughout obscenity trials, as de Grazia (1993) chronicles with rigorous detail across a plethora of examples. My claim is that the translation of unwanted texts or utterances – no matter how felicitous, how professional, how rigorous – will be impeded if the reader or hearer is averse to their contents. And this applies to "obscene texts" or any other unwanted discourse, or discourse uttered by unwanted people.

The reference to "dirt" tells us a lot about the cultural understanding of unwanted texts (or undesirable people), particularly through the lens of William James's definition of dirt as "matter out of place" (James 2008, p. 104). From this perspective dirt is the exception that proves the rule, the anomaly that reinforces the norm, the ambiguity against which distinctions come into definition. Dirt occupies another space, or it invades a space, and so it is unwelcome and yet, like the sacred, it is also from another realm, and in that respect separate and prohibited, exalted and defiled. Dirt, recalling R. Sieburth's (1984) work on poetry and obscenity, "exists outside of system, it escapes classification, it represents a disorder which must be excluded, bounded, interdicted, so that order may be instituted and maintained" (p. 345). From this standpoint, we can see the risks and perils of trying to introduce the "foreign", be it obscene or other in different ways, because in so doing we are asking for the integration of something that stands outside not only linguistically, but also in terms of accepted norms and codes of representation. Foreign texts resemble the dirt to which they are compared because they are not discerning, and their effects are multifarious and uncontrollable.

Inappropriate utterances or themes can attack the institutional *purlieu* of poetry, in the case of Baudelaire, unsuspecting women in that of Flaubert and the vulnerable uneducated classes in that of Zola via Vizetelly. Sieburth recalls the work of anthropologist Mary Douglas, who observed that "fears of pollution tend to focus on the danger of margins, that is, on any borderline object or event which threatens the coherence or integrity of the physical or social body" (p. 352). From this perspective, James is indeed correct, dirt is "matter out of place" because, as Sieburth notes, "its location is always somehow liminal, interstitial, in between; its lack of clear differentiation is precisely what renders it so potentially defiling" (p. 352). These examples suggest that when the body's flesh is opened up, it creates spaces of ambiguity and marginalization that challenge identity and allow the reader or viewer to entertain indeterminacy. The open flesh also allows for the entrance of dirt, pollution, foreignness, which suggests that Baudelaire is obscene because the dirt that his poems represent is unknowable and mysterious, betwixt-and-between and neither here nor there. By these descriptions Baudelaire's poems are deemed marginal, illicit, illegal and unwanted, just as utterances made by undocumented immigrants are, which has the effect of rendering the book of poetry, and the body of the immigrant, undesirable, illegal and untranslatable into any acceptable language.

As we further reconsider the task of the literary translator as regards the case of Vizetelly the translator, and, moreover, the case of Vizetelly the translator of the defiled work of Zola, we find oft-overlooked issues beyond the formal task of translation, even when attempts are made to account for the relevant context within which this task is undertaken. We can begin by looking at the language employed against Henry Vizetelly in the face of a "Pernicious Literature Debate" described in the House of Commons. The proceedings were assembled as a pamphlet called *Pernicious Literature* by the National Vigilance Association (1889), alongside of a report from the Old Bailey and newspaper comments concerning the trial and conviction of Henry Vizetelly. Therein, we find the reproduction of an article in the London *Star* that suggests that while Rabelais is obscene, Chaucer is coarse and Boccaccio's ladies and gentlemen are all too frank, "Zola's novel 'La Terre' has none of the charm the humour, the style, which redeemed the works of the authors named; it is simply unrelieved and morbid filth," and it is therefore "impossible to excuse its reproduction into English" (p. 22). The editor of *The Methodist Times* notes:

> Zolaism is a disease. It is a study of the putrid.... No one can read Zola without oral contamination, and the only plea that can be made is that the disgust inspired destroys the fascination of the evil. It is time that the legislative action was taken against other authors besides Zola, who are contributing to the literature of the Sewer.... Broadcast translations are an offence which demands the utmost severity of punishment and repression.
>
> (p. 24)

The editor of *The Western Morning News* agrees:

> Whatever may be said in favor of the state shutting its eyes to the circulation of Zolaesque literature, there can be no question that Zola is filthy in the extreme, and obscene to the point of bestiality. He is more unclean, and realistically so, than any other writer,...We could prove our point in a moment if in the very proof we were not likely to do the evil which we deprecate.
>
> (p. 25)

So from this perspective translation is linked directly to border-crossing undertaken by those who are deemed undesirable in both the home and host countries: "A class of vile scoundrels came over to England simply because the freedom of our laws enabled them to carry on their nefarious trade which their own country probably would not allow" (p. 8). One witness suggested that law enforcement officials need to do more to limit the incursion of unwanted texts: "We ought not to have stood by while this terrible pestilence was spreading throughout the country. In other countries, the State undertook this duty" and that "on the whole, it was a much better and a more thorough way of dealing with this evil". He then suggested that one role that the state should play is to "create a sounder public opinion" and the House of Commons "could do that" (p. 10). All of this is an interesting take on the role of the state which suggests that its representatives should actively intervene in the social discourse; as though the state, through some kind of education or propaganda, could modify this great compendium of discourse practices. Interestingly, the Secretary of State replied that:

> the public judgment was a safer guide than that of any official, and if the general moral sense of the community did not compel individuals to prosecute, no good would be done by trying to create an artificial moral sense by the actions of the prosecutor.
>
> (p. 12)

At the same time, though, in this example the literary translator is not valorized for his/her knowledge or skill, he/she is demonized because he/she actually threatens the health of the body politic by bringing the foreign to bear upon the healthy native population. In these same hearings, a Mr. De Lisle, of Leicestershire, suggested that the state intervene as a kind of gatekeeper for unwanted discourse because:

> The evil affected the class of persons who were least able to resist it. Those who were rich and had comfortable homes might keep the evil from their doors; but the poor, who had little scope for the higher enjoyments of life, naturally picked up the literature which was nearest at hand. It was a terrible evil that this filth should be thrown in the faces of the people day after day; and therefore he hoped that the House, if it did express an opinion on the matter, would speak most emphatically, and be prepared, if necessary, to limit that liberty of publication of which in most respects we were so justly proud. The highest duty of Conservatives was the safeguard of the morals of the people; indeed he was convinced that if they allowed the corruption of moral sentiment, which had been going on for years, to continue, there was no system of government which could be erected which would long stave off the threatened clouds of revolution.
>
> (p. 11)

The Secretary of State of the Home Department interjected, suggesting that:

> So far...as he could influence the Public Prosecutor,...he would certainly urge prosecutions in any cases in which it did not appear that more harm than good would be done by dragging them into the light of day.
>
> (p. 13)

Another witness, Mr. Mundella, from Sheffield, noted that there was an antidote in the form of a kind of vaccine, notably "the supply of healthy literature, and an intellectual training to preserve the young from the pernicious effects of the poisonous stuff to be met with" (p. 14).

So what is emerging here is an image of a moral duty, to be carried out by presumably enlightened officials, to control the borders by choosing appropriate imports as part of a broader censorship of public morals. And interestingly, this control is to be effected on behalf of the poor, the downtrodden, those who cannot protect themselves from the plague by closing the gates of their communities, or by those who have intellectual or cultural prophylactics that can act to vaccinate the people against nefarious threats from the other, in text or in body. And the person who is quarantined, interdicted or held responsible for this plague is exactly the one who is trying to explain its meaning: the translator. What kind of a task does the translator face when the issue is undocumented immigrants rather than obscene literature? It's more or less the same thing.

There is an enormous corpus of work that ties undocumented, or dare I say "illegal" immigrants to crime, and its profusion accounts for the link in many people's minds between "illegal" people and "illegal" activities:

> Paramilitary groups trading fire with U.S. agents. Kidnappings and murders of U.S. citizens. Members of al-Qaida, Hezbollah and other terrorist organizations infiltrating the border on a routine basis. We are not talking about Iraq – but Texas. One of the clearest indicators the United States has lost control of its southwest border is the ease with which thousands of tons of drugs and millions of illegal aliens are crossing the U.S. border on an annual basis. This open borders policy has opened the door to more than just cheap labor. The presence of millions of undocumented persons in our country has provided a perfect cover for various forms of criminal activity, ranging from drug trafficking to prostitution to identity theft.
>
> (Civitas Institute 2007)

Challenging or dismounting the misinformation of this connection has been a task undertaken by many scholars, journalists and politicians (Hagan and Palloni 1999; Sampson 2008), but the task is daunting because the connection between criminality and the illegal is so easy to make, and because "tough on crime" is often a surefire platform. It's also a political landmine, as is made clear by Governor Christie of New Jersey:

> During his most recent campaign for reelection, New Jersey Governor Chris Christie claimed he would vote in favor of passing the Tuition Equality Act, New Jersey's version of the Dream Act that recently passed through the State Senate. Under the new reforms, undocumented students that have attended a public high school for at least three years would

> qualify for in-state tuition rates at any New Jersey public college. Despite his earlier pledge of support, Christie announced on November 25th that while he is still in favor of extending in-state tuition rates for the children of immigrants, he would not sign the Senate's version of the bill, claiming that the bill approved by the Senate was "overreaching" by asking for more funds than the federal version of the bill. In response to his announcement, New Jersey Senate President Steve Sweeney accused Christie of "once again turning his back on those who need us most.... When he was running for governor he supported it, now that he is running for President he does not." MSNBC columnist Steve Benen noted how Christie appears to be cross-pressured in trying to appeal to Latino and moderate voters within his state, while still keeping favor with the national Conservative base, which have become increasingly polarized on immigration issues.
>
> (Political Research Associates 2013)

This reportage contributes to the confusing social discourse that swirls around the issue of undocumented immigrants. The Governor seems on-board, and then not, he pledges support, it sounds like a sure thing, and then it evaporates. It's difficult enough as an American citizen to keep up with the various sides, and who is on them, but the flip-flopping aggravates the situation considerably. Not only are there physical borders and boundaries, there are also borders between issues that are crossed and re-crossed, as undocumented immigrants, led to believe one news story only to have it shot down by another, feel double-crossed.

From censoring ideas to patrolling national borders

We learn a lot about our borders when considered in this light, and it justifies Petrilli and Ponzio's (2006) suggestion that we distinguish in translation between "listening" and "hearing", whereby "listening is connected with hospitality", and "wanting to hear aims to distinguish, classify, reduce to identity, define, judge", a more narrow definition imposed when interlocutors are intending "to defend one's own rights to the disadvantage of the rights and viewpoints of others" (p. 192). This approach insists that it's the translator's role to challenge the imposition of inappropriate labels, like filth and bestiality, broadening the task of the translator and adding to his/her responsibility to translate the text or the utterance, a responsibility as well to its author or speaker. Therefore, the translator is called upon to mediate in the encounter between languages, signs and cultures, and this task demands that he/she participate in processes of migration and globalization from the perspective of linguistic, ideological and physical borders.

What we saw in the Vizetelly case is the idea that controlling borders has to include censoring ideas that undermine prevailing systems of public morality by impeding the passage of unwanted filth akin, from Petrilli and Ponzio's perspective, to "absolute alterity". Absolute alterity, they claim, requests hospitality and therefore questions identity, and for them:

> This request cannot be registered, it cannot be acknowledged, it resounds like an accusation, even if this is not the intention. In fact, the request for hospitality evidences a bad conscience in the good conscience of identity, it evidences those characteristics of the capitalist system that are preferably ignored: underdevelopment, oppression, segregation, poverty, famine, illness, death, war—all being irreducible excesses of this same system.
>
> (p. 207)

Crucially, this "request for hospitality made by migration comes from an alterity that cannot be assimilated by the community" (p. 206).

In the case of obscene literature, as in the case of "illegals", the request for entrance is inassimilable because it's being made by absolute alterity. The host, deemed to be somehow pure, homogenous and sanctified, is threatened by this infection. Censorship is deemed legitimate, therefore, because it protects its population, and trials against imposters are appropriate because they flush out the unwanted filth. To combat such a monologic perspective on identity rights, Petrilli and Ponzio call "for translation understood in terms of hospitality; his/her existence calls for listening, for understanding of his/her irreducibility to the system, consequently for transformation of this very same system" (p. 207).

In light of these observations, it seems that a broad definition of translation and interpretation studies is crucial in order to account for such phenomena as intralingual translation, intercultural translation and the reception of translations and interpretations. As we've seen, certain utterances, or certain migrations, come to be deemed filthy, and this categorization then resists or closes down any kind of translation, including inter- or intralingual translation into the host society. In truly accounting for the complexity of these processes, we come to realize that even the work of the lawyer is a kind of translation, since he/she helps translate the experience of the undocumented in terms that will be understood by the judicial system. This is indeed why undocumented people come to rely upon lawyers, or should do so, if they are actually arrested or booked. Before then, as I argue in the next chapter, they need translators on the front lines, people who try to ensure that the dreaded arrest never happens.

The multiple disciplines of translation

With a sense of the social discourse and the discourse marketplace, we can return to the multiple tasks of translation, and think differently about how to translate on behalf of the "illegal" who, like the dirt to which he/she is implicitly compared, must be resisted rather than understood. In my own interviews with interpreters from this realm, I've found competing views on how this should be accomplished. For example, federally certified interpreters insist upon the need for high-level, disinterested, certified and recognizable training, while those who work on more front-line cases, traveling for example with police officers patrolling immigrant neighborhoods, argue for methods that are closer to the aforementioned distinction between being listened to and hearing. The latter doesn't have as a prerequisite the need for a technically accurate link between the immigrant discourse and the translation thereof, except in ensuring that the perspective of the other be understood with ethically grounded empathy.

Rather than choosing one or the other, I'll return to the literary examples again briefly to recall that the problem with Zola's novels in England is the way in which they infect by virtue of their being out of place, foreign and corrupting to the local public mores. Exactly the same kind of discourse is employed against so-called "illegals". What they are doing is not necessarily undesirable, but their very presence is pernicious because of their otherness. And so even though Latin Americans tend to share basic family, economic and religious values with the host population, they are guilty before opening their mouths because they speak from a liminal space. The profiling that singles them out does so using the categories of visible dirt, as though law enforcement officers, who patrol highways and systematically target visible minorities for random stops, are cleaning up the highways to rid them of unclean elements. The enemy of this flow is the idea of a homogenous American culture or, in linguistic terms, a monologic entity that will be threatened by the infection of outside influences. This image moves from the theoretical to the actual with the horrendous details of the detention of a nine-month pregnant undocumented woman in Tennessee, who was pulled over in 2008, and found to be illegal. The officer, following an Immigration and Customs Enforcement program that authorizes local law enforcement officers to enforce federal immigration laws, took her to a correctional center where she was incarcerated. The details of what followed are repulsive:

> On July 5, 2008, after being held at the detention center for two days, Villegas' water broke. She began to go into labor. According to court documents, sheriff's deputies did not release her, nor did they allow her to call her husband. They handcuffed her, shackled her ankles together with leg irons, placed her on a stretcher and drove her to Metro General Hospital. In details taken from the court record, two male deputies came into Villegas' private room and monitored her as she undressed and put on a hospital gown. When medical staff asked the deputies to uncuff her for her obstetrical examination, they refused. A physician wrote a "no-restraint" order, which the deputies disregarded. Villegas' right arm and

> left leg were shackled to the hospital bed throughout the exam and active labor, until a sympathetic deputy broke department protocol and freed her from the restraints. He kept them off during the actual birth and for a few hours afterward, but replaced them when his shift ended.
>
> (Wood 2014, p. 2)

The persecution of Villegas persisted after the birth, leading her to develop complications from being denied access to a breast pump (deemed by the officers as not legitimate medical equipment), and being separated from her baby and her son. The only way to understand such barbarity is to consider that the parties to this persecution, and the legal system itself, refused to view this young Mexican woman or her child as human beings like themselves, but saw them instead according to all the categories thus described: filth, dirt, infection, foreign, matter out of place.

The remedy for such horrific events can be found in changes to both law enforcement and the justice system, which are to be distinguished in this case, because law enforcement is ostensibly whatever the highway patrol wants to do with the "illegal", which ranges from nothing at all to deportation, whereas justice is doled out by judges on the basis of codified legal argumentation, adequate representation and judicial norms that ensure the attainment of what is fair, moral, right, merited and in accordance with the law. Translation in those two settings is so different in each case as to exceed any single definition and surpass any specific set of technical competencies. One translator who works in legal cases with immigrants in Tennessee recounted the story of a hospital that reluctantly admitted an illegal immigrant in a small rural town because she was about to have a baby. After the birthing process, specialists in the removal of hazardous materials, wearing special suits of the type we saw during the crises in the Japanese nuclear plants, were called in to disinfect the operating room where she had her baby. Exposure to this woman, like the exposure to Vizetelly's translations of *La Terre*, risked contaminating the integrally pure and monologic realm of the United States.

Conclusion: translation studies and the quest for deep time

One of Vizetelly's strategies for defending himself was to note that Zola's work was available in France and England already, and that his translation was expurgated of those passages that might be offensive to the English sensibility. This defense failed because by their very nature Zola's books were as pernicious as the bodily secretions of the undocumented immigrant giving birth, and their presence in the territory was only proof that actions needed to be taken to clean things up. Undocumented people are in these examples akin to diseases, filth or undesirable pests who should be treated as such, and so the translator, caught between two languages but also between opposing worldviews, needs to be trained to recognize obstacles beyond linguistics that stand in the way of him/her doing his/her job. At the same time, we should advocate for translation studies, since it could help sensitize people to the need for this kind of work, and in turn train people to act as the advocates and intermediaries I've described thus far.

Translation studies are hardly prominent in the university system, except in some of the more cosmopolitan cities in which translation is of daily importance (Amsterdam, Geneva, London, Montreal, New York) or in areas where a core group of scholars has assembled to build through great efforts and solid scholarship a strong program, in Manchester, United Kingdom (UK). Furthermore, translation studies, like the rest of humanistic and social science training, is under siege from the dearth of funding, the result of this prolonged recession and ever-more forceful insistence by administrators that they can do away with core humanities training in favor of science and technology or some kind of distance learning. In such a climate, one way to protect and promote translation studies is by calling attention to its more technical side, insisting on the importance of training people for federal certification. Every interpreter I've interviewed or worked with for research projects on homelessness, undocumented migrants and refugee determination has mentioned the dearth of certified translators, and yet very few universities are equipped or funded for this crucial task.

But beyond this more narrow objective, translation studies needs to be firmly entrenched into the curriculum of Liberal Arts, an enclave that is generally deemed essential for all undergraduates, no matter what their eventual professional objectives. Interpreters could argue a role for themselves in Anthropology departments, in particular, but also in Sociology, Medicine and Law, where they can assist by explaining not just the dictionary meanings of specific utterances, but also offer critical cross-cultural interpretation to help overcome misunderstandings and deleterious stereotypes. A successful example of this is the burgeoning area of Narrative Medicine, which has convincingly argued that the transmission of information concerning symptoms, from patient to medical practitioner, is as much an intercultural linguistic issue as a medical concern. In an era of global multiculturalism, it is inconceivable that intercultural interpretation would not be a value added to medical training and practice.

The same applies to legal hearings involving immigrant or refugee communities or the huge undocumented or *sans papiers* populations around the world. These two programs, translation and interpretation studies, account in different ways for globalization, interdisciplinarity and geopolitical developments, and they would have to work from humanistic and technical perspectives. Dividing the field clearly on these grounds, and arguing for them individually, reflects the reality that different kinds of translation and interpretation would help us deal with the complexity of multicultural societies in an era of high-profile xenophobia that renders the foreign filthy. The result of such a multipronged approach to integrating translation studies into the university would be to show that translation is a humanistic enterprise, requiring as much cultural understanding as technical savvy; because filth, in whatever language, won't be deemed desirable to a host population fearful of any infection that a couple of squirts of Purell can't ward off.

If we want to argue against the kinds of nefarious treatment of undocumented people that we've seen here, it would also be valuable to focus upon the second generation. In most public discourses in America, Australia, Europe and even in parts of Asia, there already is the idea that we are all immigrants. But this is not a discourse sufficiently convincing in light of the more "expensive" terms, the terms that trump all other terms, such as "security" or "terrorism". So from a language or propaganda perspective, we need to find ways to overcome these terms with value-laden ones, particularly in the face of an opposition that usually finds little in ideas of compassion, civility or forgiveness. One way to overcome this *différend* is to make reference to the second generation, the children of the incarcerated people who will grow up in our country without the guidance of the fathers and mothers who help make them whole. A public defender notes that:

> Family members disappear, and this is not simply in terms of Latinos. It happens with Latinos also, but also in terms of anybody who goes to prison, initially the family visits for the first little bit, and little-by-little the prisoner is forgotten. Within the Latin population, it becomes a double whammy because the person in prison can no longer provide, and since somebody has got to provide for the wife and children, there is another guy who comes in.

When consequences of such dynamics are traced through time, things begin to look a little different. Immigration is not, therefore, a present-day phenomenon, it is, a multilayered and complex process of *longue durée*, connected to the past. It's also a process that looks to the future, and the future of our societies depends upon how we deal with generations to come. If this is the orientation we take, "family values" over "security", children of immigrants over illegal immigrant parents, there may be sway. An activist scholar noted that:

> We need to appeal to these sort of family values, and the actual effect of the destruction of families and the weakening of families that inevitably takes place as a result of the various types of exclusions associated with immigration boundary control.... It's not something Americans have to ... think about. It's not something that they see.

Translators, interpreters and publicly funded efforts to bring the conversation out of the dark margins and into the bright light of justice and human rights could go a long way to advancing this work, and challenging the distinction between the clean inside and the dirt outside.

Notes

1 This is also why Pierre Bourdieu's work on "language and symbolic power" (Bourdieu 1990) is always valuable for this kind of research, because he explains the (ill)logic of the discourse marketplace, which buys most discourses from "foreigners", particularly poor foreigners, at a discount.

2 In 1888 Henry Vizetelly was prosecuted for "obscene libel" on account of his having translated Émile Zola's novel *La Terre* into English. For the offense, he was fined £100; and when he continued translating, albeit abridged versions of Zola's works, he was again prosecuted, fined £200 and imprisoned for three months.

Bibliography

Ahmad, Ali Nobil (2008) "The Romantic Appeal of Illegal Migration: Gender, Masculinity and Human Smuggling from Pakistan", in Schrover et al. (2008), pp. 127–50.

Amossy, Ruth (2002) "Doxa and Discourse: How Common Knowledge Works", *Poetics Today* 23.3, pp. 369–94.

Angenot, Marc (2004) "Social Discourse Analysis: Outlines of a Research Project", in Barsky (2004), pp. 199–216.

Bakhtin, Mikhaïl (1981) "Discourse in the Novel", in *The Dialogic Imagination: Four Essays by M.M. Bakhtin*, ed. Michael Holquist, trans. Caryl Emerson and Michael Holquist. Austin: University of Texas Press.

Bakhtin, Mikhaïl (1986) *Speech Genres and Other Late Essays*, eds. Carly Emerson and Michael Holquist, trans. Vern W. McGeed. Austin: University of Texas Press.

Barsky, Robert F. (ed.) (2004) "Marc Angenot and the Scandal of History", *Yale Journal of Criticism* 17.2, pp. 163–311.

Baudelaire, Charles (1857) *Les Fleurs du mal*. Paris: Poulet-Malassis.

Bourdieu, Pierre (1990) *Language and Symbolic Power*. Intro by John Thompson. Cambridge, MA and London: Harvard University Press.

Burwick, Frederick and Paul Douglass (1992) *The Crisis in Modernism: Bergson and the Vitalist Controversy*. New York: Cambridge University Press.

Civitas Institute (2007) "Illegal Immigration: Drugs, Gangs and Crime". Available at: http://www.nccivitas.org/2007/illegal-immigration-drugs-gangs-and-crime. [Accessed: 15 January 2015]

De Grazia, Edward (1993) *Girls Lean Back Everywhere: The Law of Obscenity and the Assault on Genius*. New York: Vintage.

Doorslaer, Luc van and Yves Gambier (eds.) (2013) *Handbook of Translation Studies*, 4 volumes. Amsterdam and Philadelphia, PA: John Benjamins.

European Commission (2000) *Push and Pull Factors of International Migration: A Comparative Report*. Luxembourg: Statistical Office of the European Communities.

Guyaux, André (2007) *Baudelaire: un demi-siècle de lecture des "Fleurs du mal", 1855–1905*. Paris: Presses de l'Université Paris-Sorbonne.

Hagan, John and Alberto Palloni (1999) "Sociological Criminology and the Mythology of Hispanic Immigration and Crime", *Social Problems* 46.4, pp. 617–32.

James, William (2008) *The Varieties of Religious Experience—A Study in Human Nature.* London: Arc Manor.

Lesesma, Alberto (1998) "Undocumented Crossings: Narratives of Mexican Immigration to the United States", in Maciel and Herrera-Sobek (1998), pp.67–98.

Maciel, David and Mar'a Herrera-Sobek (1998) *Culture across Borders: Mexican Immigration and Popular Culture*. Tucson: University of Arizona Press.

National Vigilance Association (1889) *Pernicious Literature: Debate in the House of Commons. Trial and Conviction for Sale of Zola's Novels. With Opinions of the Press*. London: National Vigilance Association.

NCLR (National Council of La Raza) (2010) *Know Who You are Dealing With: Key Hate Groups and Their Representatives in 2010*. Washington. NCLR Factsheet. Available at: http://www.nclr.org/images/uploads/publications/62243_file_KnowWhoYouAreDealingWith_factsheet_1.pdf. [Accessed: 15 January 2015]

Parkes, Matthew (13 December 2013) "Issue Brief: This Month in Racial and Immigrant Justice". Political Research Associates. Available at: http://www.politicalresearch.org/tag/justice/#. [Accessed: 15 January 2015]

Petrilli, Susan and Augusto Ponzio (2006) "Translation as Listening and Encounter with the Other in Migration and Globalization Processes Today", *TTR: Traduction, Terminologie, Rédaction* 19.2, pp. 191–223.

Political Research Associates (2013) Available at: http://www.politicalresearch.org/2013/12/13/issue-brief-this-month-in-racial-and-immigrant-justice-2/#. [Accessed: 15 January 2015]

Ramirez, Hernan (2011) "Masculinity in the Workplace: The Case of Mexican Immigrant Gardeners", *Men and Masculinities* 14, pp. 97–116.

Sampson, Robert J. (2008) "Rethinking Crime and Immigration", *Contexts* 7.1, pp. 28–36.

Schrover, M., J. Van der Leun, L. Lucassen and C. Quispel (eds.) (2008) *Illegal Migration and Gender in a Global and Historical Perspective*. Amsterdam: Amsterdam University Press.

Sieburth, R. (1984) "Poetry and Obscenity: Baudelaire and Swinburne", *Comparative Literature* 36.4, pp. 343–53.

Wood, Heather (30 October 2014) "Juana Villegas Now has Legal Standing to Live in the U.S. Other New Mothers may not be so Lucky", *Nashville Scene*, pp. 1–4.

Chapter 3

"First encounters" with host country officials

> Since 911, you see more bullshit with immigrants. You also see what I call stacking of charges. The cops will bring them in and they will charge them with all kinds of stupid stuff. You know, like, if they bring an undocumented immigrant in for a DUI. Say he says, or is perceived to have said: "Screw you!" to the cop. Well, they will charge him with disorderly conduct. If he moves his hands, then they will charge him with resisting arrest too. If he did not pull over quickly enough, then they are going to charge him with evading by motor vehicle. I think that this is a kind of harassment.
>
> (A public defender interviewed for the project)

Everyday interactions between citizens and undocumented people are fraught with the kinds of symbolic power relations that can be as lethal as material attacks. These relations between unequal participants to an encounter are frequently represented in literature, such as Tom Robinson's story in Harper Lee's (1960) *To Kill a Mockingbird*, a particularly apt reference when we consider an earlier American population who has suffered from this othering process. These everyday interactions can be as fickle as Mayella Ewell's accusation, a concrete manifestation in language of barely concealed xenophobia, racism, classism and resentment that simmers beneath the veneer of America's melting pot. The flames of xenophobia are fanned by violent political commentary that helps feed the draconian language of codes, decrees, proposals and laws that are handed down by municipalities, counties, states and federal instances charged with securing the homeland in the face of vague and constant threats.

Even though the challenges that face undocumented immigrants in frontline confrontations are as tangible as they are daunting, in the first instance they are perhaps better understood with regards to an array of language and communication issues that relate to the production and reception of discourse across discursive and cultural lines. In order to understand the first encounters from a discourse standpoint, it's valuable to first consider the prevailing "social discourses" described in the previous chapter, as well as the "linguistic marketplace" that is constituted in their wake. Therein lies an array of "shared opinions" concerning illegal migration that is captured in a term that is employed in rhetoric and argumentation theory:

> Inherited from ancient Greece, the notion of *doxa* as common knowledge and shared opinions haunts all contemporary disciplines that put communication and social interaction at the center of their concerns. To be sure, the specific term is not always used: *doxa* appears under various guises, such as public opinion, verisimilitude, commonsense knowledge, commonplace, idée reçue, stereotype, cliché. Broadly speaking, however, all that is considered true, or at least probable, by a majority of people endowed with reason, or by a specific social group, can be called doxic.
>
> (Amossy 2002)

The particularities of a *doxa* can be captured by some of the fashionable discourses within the prevailing discourse marketplace, worldwide, which in regards to undocumented immigrants can at any given time include such catchphrases as "tough on crime", "illegal immigrant" and "stealing our jobs". This *doxa* can vacillate in time and in space, however, particularly when it comes up against other perspectives, because they too can generate their own *doxas*. So, for example, while in many if not most societies "illegal" immigration is scorned, the idea of respecting families or workers, no matter what their origin or nationality, is not; and so there can be contradictory *doxas* that come into play when undocumented immigrants encounter individuals from the home country, particularly if there is some kind of personal connection between the parties to the encounter (shared workplace, for example). Despite the force and prevalence of xenophobia, or racism, however, encounters between undocumented immigrants and the home population is frequent, necessarily, and generally non-confrontational. The same could be said even in regards to officials who (with varying degrees of discretion) can choose to *not* act in the face of an undocumented person, which arguably occurs in many if not most cases. This inaction can also be tied to the idea of the *doxa* because if an official chooses to *not* take action against an undocumented immigrant, he/she might do so on account of his/her "sympathy for the other", or his/her "respect for difference", which are both in accord with other *doxas* that make up the social discourse.

I am not suggesting here that these discursive *doxas*, or the realms of discursive exchange within which actions are taken, exist outside of memoranda, laws, orders and responsibilities that define various officials' roles. What I am saying is that actions are taken against the backdrop of specific *doxas*, and in regards to the broad array of social discourses, sometimes contradictory, that pertain to the subject at hand. For this reason, we can view the specific actions taken by law enforcement officers in regards to *doxas*, and against a backdrop of the prevailing discourse marketplace and its dominant ideology. Concretely, then, when law enforcement officers act, they do so against a multifarious background of what is said within the social discourse about their roles as, say, representatives of the state who have been charged with acting in the face of an action deemed criminal. This pertains to border enforcement, of course, but can also play a role in the relationship between lawyers and their eventual clients, as a lawyer suggested:

> When I was a DA [District Attorney] I worked with a gentleman who is a lawyer, but he was a good ol' boy. I do not think he understood that there were Hispanic people who are professionals, who paid a mortgage, and who were just like everybody else. He and I worked on a case when we actually ended up going to Mexico, and he kept saying, and I was so embarrassed when he did so: "They are just like us". I guess people may not realize it but I think it does affect them. They do picture everybody running across the border, and crowding into cars and trying to be smuggled in. They do not realize that they are people just like us.

By the same token, prevailing social discourses, and the *doxas* that swirl inside of them, play a role in determining the types of laws or measures that are put into effect, and even the decision on the part of front-line actors to act upon these measures in particular cases can in turn have an effect upon the social discourses. From this perspective, social discourses can be said to establish the continuum of discretionary possibilities, and may play some role in legitimizing particular decisions taken by officials on the front lines. Discretion diminishes as we move further and further away from the front lines, into police stations and courtrooms, and so it's important to cordon off this area, and consider the complex realms of front-line contact between host and home country.

Confrontations on the front lines

In this chapter I will move the camera further in, to address what is happening on the front lines where law enforcement officers or immigration officials endeavor to fulfill their professional obligations while recognizing, and acting in accordance with, the broad margin of maneuver that discretion and arbitrary law offer. My goals here are descriptive in the first instance, but I will also be prescriptive, and offer suggestions aimed at addressing situations that can degenerate unnecessarily into profound and dangerous conflict. My overriding claim is that when officials meet vulnerable undocumented people in an era of discretion and arbitrary law, the subsequent interactions don't need to be aggressively confrontational, first, and second, in many cases these potentially lethal confrontations can be defused if there is some real communication between the two parties. This suggests that the host country authority might need to understand the particular situation of the migrant, and, moreover, that the migrant certainly needs to understand the constraints within which the officer is operating. This is not to say that clear communication won't lead to an arrest, or even eventual deportation; but it is most certainly the case that many complications arise solely on the basis of misunderstandings, many related to communicative breakdowns, which occur on (say) the shoulders of interstate highways.

The chain of events that leads to undocumented people being arrested, and eventually charged, incarcerated and deported, can begin right at the border between home and host countries. There is very little that can be done in such cases, particularly if the migrants are captured as part of some kind of crackdown, such as the Greek Operation Xenios Zeus (Cossé 2013), the Malaysian "Ops Bersepadu 6P" (LBJ 2014) or the American "Operation Streamline".[1] Despite the different contexts, the stories emerging from such operations tend to be very similar, and the resulting hardship for all parties involved is usually vast. In the Greek case, for instance, Eva Cossé, a Greece specialist at Human Rights Watch (HRW), suggests that "It's cruelly ironic that the authorities named the sweeps Xenios Zeus, after the ancient Greek god of hospitality." The HRW report that she authored shows that "in fact, Operation Xenios Zeus is anything but hospitable to migrants and asylum seekers, who are regularly stopped, searched, and detained just because of the way they look". In the Malaysian example, the Ops Bersepadu 6P aims to round up 400,000 undocumented immigrants from a broad array of countries who will be held in 10 areas that have been gazetted as "detention centers" (Bernama 2013).

In the American context, Santos (2014) described Magistrate Judge Bernardo P. Velasco of Federal District Court boasting that he makes decisions on cases of migrants caught sneaking into the country with great efficiency, and, to quote him, "my record is 30 minutes" to address the entire case of an undocumented immigrant. According to this time frame, the accused migrant has roughly 25 seconds to hear the charges, enter a plea and receive a sentence:

> This is a part of the battle against illegal immigration that many Americans have never heard of. Known as Operation Streamline, it is the core of a federal program that operates in three border-states, using prosecution and imprisonment as a front-line deterrent to people who try to cross the border illegally. It is part of a broader strategy of increasing the consequences for people who break immigration laws. Unlike the civil immigration courts spread throughout the country, where deportation cases are handled as violations of the nation's administrative code, the courts used for Operation Streamline treat unauthorized immigrants as criminals and the act of illegally crossing the border as a federal crime.
>
> (p. A12)

Although not fictional or discretionary, this Operation does smack of injustice and arbitrariness, even as described in this ostensibly expository article. This arbitrariness begins with the varying ways that the same act can be punished (illegal entry is a misdemeanor and illegal re-entry is a felony, but claimants can avoid the latter in some cases by just pleading guilty), the different ways the sentences are served (in prisons, jails or detention centers) and the varying ways in which the sentencing can occur (plea versus ruling from the bench). But from Judge Velasco's perspective, "as ugly as some people think it is, it's a bargain for the defendants. What we do is constitutional, it satisfies due process. It may not look good, but it does everything the law requires." This cynical reasoning on the judge's part is, to cite Fernanda Santas, "assembly-line justice", a big part of the gigantic deportation machine run by the Obama Administration that led, in the month of December of 2013 alone, to the arrest, incarceration and deportation of 1.9 million people:

> Sentences range from 30 days to six months and are served in federal prisons, county jails and private detention centers that operate under contract with the government. Keeping the migrants from their families and the possibility of jobs to sustain them is one part penalty, one part incentive for them not to try to come back. (An illegal re-entry conviction carries a maximum of two years in prison, but it can be up to 20 years if the migrant has been deported before and has an aggravated-felony conviction.)
>
> (p. A12)

In this realm, no matter how punitive the consequences and different cases are from one another, the outcomes are determined in a matter of minutes.

A recent phenomenon in the neoliberal state is the use of non-state actors on front lines, most notably international carriers who are increasingly shouldering both the burden and the responsibility for verifying the status of migrants. Rodenhäuser (2014) sets forth the legal implications of these efforts, adding another brick to the arbitrary law discussion in what he calls "first instance immigration control":

> Under carrier sanction legislation, carrier personnel are obliged to control migrants' documentation at the point of embarkation, and to deny boarding to undocumented migrants. In this respect, private carrier personnel become a first instance immigration control, having to deal not only with migrants, but also with asylum seekers who may be in need of international protection. In border control situations, the *refoulement* of refugees by state agents would violate the state's *non-refoulement* obligation. Carrier sanctions pose two particular difficulties for the establishment of state responsibility: first, the potential rejection of asylum seekers at the point of embarkation is executed by non-state actors, whose conduct is only

> under certain circumstances attributable to the state. Second, while states' obligations to protect human rights apply to persons under their jurisdiction, embarkation control takes place on the territory of another state and, therefore, is arguably outside the controlling state's jurisdiction.
> (p. 223)

The best description of a multifarious system, of state and private actors that render people vulnerable throughout the duration of their stay, comes from the realm of fiction, especially Kafka or Orwell. A public defender indicated as much:

> The present system is taken straight from Orwell's *1984*. If you look at *1984*, what you had was the inner party that had privileges and was not terrorized at all, and that's what we have with the rich and the wealthy. You had a small middle class, the outer party that was controlled by terror, and you had the [rest] who were neglected. And if they became inconvenient you bumped one off. The difference between *1984* and our society right now is that the middle is not being kept by terror, but rather by a combination of carrot and stick. There will be a little carrot for you if you do the right thing. If you don't do the right thing, we don't have to kill you, but you are out, and you are going to fall into that mass of people and your kids won't go to university, etc. In other words, we do not have to use the Ministry of Law and the rats and the cage.

Some undocumented people do manage to live their entire lives by remaining invisible to Big Brother (although this varies widely from country to country), but it's probably fair to say that most undocumented people have difficulties at some point, especially if they break the law or find themselves in need of social services. But even without direct contact with the authorities, there is a broad array of screening that operates on an ethereal front line, where computers signal unusual financial transactions or even unhabitual travel arrangements. In some ways this exceeds what Orwell imagined because the tools available to officials are so ubiquitous. Hintjens (2013) notes in a special issue of *Surveillance & Society* that authorities in the UK are able to:

> cross-check their databases for "indicators" of a person's intent to cross borders illegally, through systems similar to those used to screen "terror suspects". Erratic use of credit cards and last-minute travel arrangements, for example, can be viewed as indicators of risk, but so too can skin colour and religious appearance. There is increasing police surveillance of pro-migrant organisations, and raids on businesses known to hire undocumented workers have increased in recent years. Stop and search policing has intensified, with spot-checks on cars and in public transport in many countries being intended also to detect "illegals". Detention and deportation can result for

> those unable to present their legal papers. At Christmas time in the UK, police routinely stop cars to check for drunken drivers.
>
> (pp. 89–90)

Despite the employment of these high-tech tools, most problems still arise when the migrant is forced into actual contact with host country officials, through traffic stops, crackdowns or when migrants seek out authorities for issues relating to health, welfare or the procurement of other state services.

There is no doubt that these stops are motivated, in many cases, and that specific types of individuals are targeted. Hintjens notes that even though official border guards aren't supposed to employ "underhand methods to exclude people", they nonetheless defer to "profiling" to decide which people to question and take aside. Our interviewees, including a lawyer, offer a plethora of evidence to confirm this trend:

> They get stopped under some pretext that our system says is legal as long as you can cite a moving violation. The police have a list of their favorite moving violations to target anyone who looks like they might be Mexican, or anything that does not involve Caucasian or White skin. Out-of-state license plates can create a pretext to pull someone over. Usually it is things like following a tractor-trailer too close.

One interpreter who was originally from Latin America describes the difficulties experienced by her own son who, although born in the United States, was nonetheless targeted on a regular basis because of his physical appearance:

> My son was stopped all the time. I do not remember if he was ever searched, but he was ticketed for all kinds of things, like going 37 in a 35 MPH zone, the kinds of things most people would not be stopped for. You know, I hated to be right on that point, but he did later say that he did not actually want to hear that but he finally learned. Now when he gets stopped, he takes his sunglasses off and speaks deferentially. He tries to wear his hair back rather than letting it run wild.

This is an interesting observation because it shows both sides of the profiling; the police are profiling on the basis of certain physical attributes, and at the same time if those likely to be profiled know how to avoid detection, they can downplay some of the physical characteristics that attract attention in the first place, like the wildly unkempt hair of this example.

Some of these tactics, in particular those resembling racial profiling, are illegal, and so various organizations undertake front-line interventions like one from the National Coalition of Anti-Deportation Campaigns (NCADC) in the UK. They endeavor to warn irregular migrants to stay out of cars because the Border and Immigration Agency is especially active during the holiday season. If someone is caught up in this effort, the "NCADC will as ever be providing emergency cover throughout the period to 'Signpost' friends of persons detained what actions if any can be taken" (NCADC 2007). This is a fascinating example of front-line efforts aimed at preventing immigration-related traffic stops and intervening when they do occur because, Hintjens (2013) notes, these can lead to the kinds of interventions that forever deprive undocumented immigrants "of any possibility of regularisation of their status" (p. 90).

The NCADC "stay out of cars/stay out of detention" motto is important, but it presupposes that people have access to alternative forms of transportation. In the UK and indeed most of Europe, these kinds of alternatives usually exist, while in other settings, including the United States, there may be no alternatives available because the country lacks the kind of extensive public transportation network for those who work outside of urban settings, most notably in agriculture, food processing, construction and domestic settings. In these underserved regions, highways can be transformed into a kind of sieve through which people are compelled to pass; and since immigration officials often patrol the highways, or are within easy reach of traffic stops, highways become critical front-line spaces where much of the home and host country interactions occur.

One problem faced by undocumented immigrants during traffic stops is the amount of time that they can be compelled to spend with law enforcement officers, which can be quite substantial. The stops themselves can be arbitrary, and the discretion of the officers during the stop is very high; so if an officer chooses to extend the time spent with the driver, in order to lure him/her into some kind of misstep or misstatement, there's very little that can be done. The stop can be justified by the age or condition of the car, the way in which the person is driving or else by a concerted effort to target immigrants. Articles like Elizabeth Ricci's (2011) "DWU: Driving While Undocumented", published by the American Immigration Lawyers Association magazine *Voice*, helps to set out basic traffic stop concerns:

> St. Louis immigration and criminal defense attorney Raymond R. Bolourtchi has witnessed a dramatic increase in arrests of Hispanics by local and state police. "In some instances, the clients have not even been cited for any offense until after they are verbally 'warned' and questioned about their immigration status," Bolourtchi said. "We have noticed a dramatic increase in our removal cases with suspicious factual grounds leading to initial arrest and now find ourselves with over a hundred motions to suppress and terminate being filed over the past two months." Bolourtchi went on to say that he has "failed to find any ordinance, or...statute making it illegal to 'drive while Mexican.' I cannot seem to find any probable cause for the vehicle to be curbed, which in turn resulted in the client being issued 'no license' citations, and arrested subsequently only

> to be delivered to Immigration and Customs Enforcement." Bolourtchi mentioned having several clients that weren't even driving when arrested but walking home. "I can only hope that immigration judges will grant our motions and order police officers to testify in immigration court. If so, this may work toward curbing what I consider to be racial profiling."
> (p. 18)

And so before proposing remedies for the front lines, we need to look beyond laws and statistics, and into front-line reports of how these stops occur, and what their outcome is in different cases. In order to do so, the best source of information is the police officers, public defenders, lawyers and interpreters who address these questions each day.

The particularities of the traffic stop

The array of ways this stop can occur is vast, and depends upon the nature of the host country. In Europe, the kinds of efforts associated with borders have now moved onto state territories, so that people can be asked to present papers in a wide variety of circumstances (Guiraudonn and Lahav 2000; Zolberg 2003). Broeders and Engbersen (2007) describe the ongoing fight against illegal immigration in Europe:

> Illegal aliens are at the top of the policy agenda, and politicians, fuelled by popular fear and uneasiness, have heavily invested in the various manifestations of the European border (including seaports and airports). Strategic borders have been strengthened with guards, watchtowers, fences, and state-of-the-art technology, such as infrared scanning devices, motion detectors, and video surveillance. And yet despite funding and political backing for the "fight against illegal immigration," the presence of irregular migrants remains a fact of life for most EU countries. The realization that borders alone cannot halt irregular migration has already led to a widening of the scope of immigration policy. Border control is "moving away from the border and outside the state" or is becoming "remote control" or is moving "upwards, downwards and outwards". Now other actors, such as supranational actors (the EU), private parties (e.g., airlines and transport companies), local governments, and public institutions, also have a role to play in the fight against irregular migration.
> (pp. 1592–3)

In addition to this kind of profiling, there's also a host of ways in which countries are employing strategies aimed at internal migration control:

> One of the turns that policy on illegal aliens has made is toward internal control. Border controls, though still important, are increasingly being

> supplemented with policies of exclusion and discouragement of those unwanted aliens who passed the border. When it comes to irregular migrants, exclusion is now the stated aim of policy. For those illegal aliens who cannot be discouraged or deterred to come, exclusion is meant to complicate and frustrate living and working conditions to such a degree that they will turn round and try their luck elsewhere. The goal of discouraging irregular migrants has led to a shift toward internal migration control, which comprises a wide array of policy measures such as employer sanctions, exclusion from public services, surveillance by the police, incarceration, and expulsion.
>
> (1592–3)

I would add to this list the fear instilled in those who travel in countries such as France by automobile because the Compagnies Républicaines de Sécurité (CRS) regularly sets up traffic stops at roundabouts. At the same time, though, French law regarding arrest and incarceration of undocumented immigrants has undergone a significant shift in light of a July 2012 French Court of Cassation ruling that held that undocumented immigrants can't be taken into police custody simply for being in the country illegally. This ruling can be traced back to two important rulings on the cases of El Dridi and Achughbabian that were handed down by the Court of Justice of the European Union, which both dealt with the EU Returns Directive. The French ruling was "idiosyncratic" and, according to Beduschi (2014), "is the result of a unique interplay between French criminal law and European Union law" that has resulted in transforming "detention from an extraordinary measure of last resort into an ordinary tool for combating illegal immigration" (p. 334). The way in which this occurred speaks volumes about the fickleness of legal systems that are brought to bear upon a group that is deemed undesirable by the government. What started as a relaxing of policies concerning incarceration has turned into a much more draconian system that stands further outside of the French rule of law. Beduschi's conclusion, invoking a legal dance, is an apt description of a policy upheld by power rather than law:

> The new procedure of detention for the verification of identity and legality of stay provides fewer guarantees of fundamental rights than the procedure of placement in police custody. Hence, by declaring the latter unlawful, the supposed step towards a less criminal treatment of undocumented immigrants in France has, in reality, resulted in a more restrictive and less protective procedure. One step forward by the Court of Cessation has led to two steps sideways by the legislator. The government, wary of promises to stamp out illegal immigration made during the presidential campaign, has tried to keep the balance in the dance by performing impressive legal pirouettes. Although the trio of dancers

> may have avoided tumbling into politically risky territory, their dancing shoes have trampled mercilessly on the rights of one of the weakest social groups in France.
>
> (p. 347)

In the American context, the most frequent approach used by law enforcement to effect these kinds of investigations into migrants' status is to apprehend drivers on highways, especially interstates. Once a person is pulled over or stopped and asked for identification, there is a range of potential scenarios, and what we often see from the very outset is the risk of a communication breakdown. From here, things can degenerate quickly, particularly if the officer is motivated, for whatever reason, to verify the individual's immigration status, or requests to search the person and/or his/her vehicle. There are some interesting examples of municipalities, cities or other regions that encourage their officers to defy policies that require officers of the law to check immigration status, as was the case recently in New Orleans.[2] Such efforts remain the exception, however, and so even in a routine traffic stop there's a strong likelihood that the officer will check the driver's immigration status, and if it's found to be irregular, there will be subsequent conversations that set the stage for disaster. A lawyer notes:

> Officers cite drivers for minor traffic violations as a way of questioning the driver about her status, and this is where it all happens. You get pulled over for speeding, and you have no license. So the officer says: "Oh, well now we have to arrest you, and we have to search your car. Ah look, you have half a joint, so now you have that charge too. And a pack of rolling papers, that's a paraphernalia charge", and they just pile that stuff on.

So it begins with racial profiling (driving while Mexican, or driving while undocumented) that can become the impetus for motivated searches that begin with immigration status checks and then move on to narcotics. A lawyer describes the "motivated" side of the scenario:

> Other than the driving while Mexican, there's another sinister deal. Everywhere there's an interstate highway there is a grant to the local police to monitor that interstate highway for drugs. Easy enough to do that: "Stop everyone who is brown. If we stop 'em all, we're bound to get someone soon!" I get these cases for speeding and no driving license, and on the affidavit, there are 8 police officers listed for a speeding with no driving license. So I know what happened without even talking with him. They pulled him over, they got consent to search his car, the K-9 unit showed up, four other units showed up, and damn! This time they didn't find a thing, so they have to cut the poor bastard loose, for only driving with no license and speeding. I know immediately when I see this

> that when I look at all these cops. All they're doing is cruising around in unmarked cars, and they see [foreigners] and say: "This looks like a hit". They call in the traffic unit, a marked car, and they say: "Follow him until he, say, changes lanes without turning on his turn signals. Bang! We got you"!

Lithwick (2014) comments upon a December 2014 Supreme Court ruling in the United States, providing details that confirm, and in some ways even exceed, what we've seen thus far:

> *Heien v. North Carolina* was the first big criminal case to come down this term, and it involved a question of whether a cop's mistaken understanding of a state traffic law—a misunderstanding that led to a traffic stop for wholly innocent behavior—should be used to throw out a drug conviction that resulted from that stop. On Monday, eight justices ruled that although the police officer stopped a car for having only one working brake light, and having only one working brake light is actually legal in North Carolina, the stop was "reasonable" under the Fourth Amendment. Thus, the baggie of cocaine the officer found in his resulting search of the car was admissible in court.

According to the police officer's testimony, in 2009, Nicholas Heien and Maynor Javier Vasquez were driving down a highway in North Carolina. Vasquez was driving while Heien napped in the back seat, and a police officer noted that the driver seemed "stiff and nervous" and was "gripping the steering wheel at a 10 and 2 position, looking straight ahead". When the officer noted that one of the rear brake lights wasn't working, he pulled Vasquez and Heien over:

> mistakenly believing that state law requires two working tail lights. He gave the driver a citation, got permission to search the car from Heien, and eventually found a baggie of cocaine. Heien was sentenced to two consecutive prison terms of 10 to 12 months for drug trafficking.

The officer had no grounds to make the traffic stop in the first place and, as Dahlia Lithwick argues:

> Heien has argued that since ignorance of the law is never an excuse for citizens accused of crimes, it defies logic to create that double standard for police. This week, that argument lost by a wide margin. As Chief Justice John Roberts wrote for the majority: "To be reasonable is not to be perfect, and so the Fourth Amendment allows for some mistakes on the part of government officials, giving them fair leeway for enforcing the law in the community's protection."

This is an extremely important ruling that has the potential to justify a wide variety of police stops made without proper legal justification:

> Because Vasquez wasn't stopped by the cops for having a broken tail light. He was trailed by an officer because he was driving while looking "stiff and nervous" and for "gripping the steering wheel at a 10 and 2 position, looking straight ahead." In other words, he was a Hispanic man driving a beat-up car in North Carolina, and the officer followed him for doing what the rest of us do every single day: driving while holding on to a steering wheel and looking forward.

An interpreter who works with undocumented immigrants adds the linguistic component to a scenario like this one, which exacerbates the problem because of the likelihood that the driver will quickly relinquish his/her rights:

> The big issue that comes up in all of the court proceedings has to do with the Miranda Rights. There are some officers out there who think that they speak Spanish. We hear this a lot: "I had a one week Spanish survival course." So they have this little card, with the Miranda rights on it, in Spanish. Some of them have a few phrases like: "May I have permission to search your car?" We had this in a case recently. The policeman who was on the stand was from Meridian, Mississippi, and they asked him how he would have said in Spanish: "May I search your car?" I was doing the interpreting, and I had to stop. I literally did not know what language he was speaking when he said that. It happened so quickly, and as an interpreter, you are always a few steps behind what is going on. You are listening, and you are speaking what was just spoken, so by the time they got back to English, I was sitting there thinking: "What was that? Oh, that was supposed to be Spanish!" I mean, I had a total blank in my interpretation. I had no idea what he had said. And this guy, on the basis of the fact that he thought he was asking the right question, thought he was speaking Spanish. Then the immigrant sort of smiled. He was nervous, and so he smiled, and [the officer thought]: "Oops, that means yes!" So the officer searched the car, and got the evidence. We are seeing more and more of that. The basic rights that Americans are guaranteed are not being afforded to some of these guys. The lawyers can tell you more about that. I just know, from what I have heard of their Spanish, that this is very, very common. They offer these one-week courses, and the officers think that it's all they need to get permission to search the car.

This type of example demonstrates that intercultural issues can become linked with legal ones, even when people are going about the most innocuous of business. A lawyer who represents farmworkers, who in the Southern

United States are largely illegal immigrants, provides us with a sense of the magnitude of this issue, within and beyond the highways:

> I have heard of a lot of people who have some kind of traffic offense that then gets them run through the computer, which then reveals that they have immigration holds. Those are most of the people that I talk to. Or the people who don't even have a traffic offense but are entered into the computer, and found to have immigration holds. Or people who are entering the courthouse. There's a practice in upper east Tennessee where there's an officer who would schedule hearings on Monday in one county and Tuesday in another county, which corresponded to the days when the Spanish interpreter was there, and he would be in the courthouse looking for whoever looked Hispanic. There's no criminal offense in those cases, an immigration agent has the authority to stop any of us and ask us about our immigration status. And so far as he's concerned, he's not discriminating based on a constitutionally protected category. He's not actually allowed to ask all the Mexicans about their immigration status, but if he asks everyone in the courthouse, then he could do that. People also have the right to not answer his questions, but people are so afraid of what's going on, and because of the meshing of the different law enforcement officers and their roles, the officers are playing on that. So these are people who just happen to be in the courthouse paying a ticket who can get arrested based on that, and then incarcerated on a prior deportation order.

The loci for these encounters are as broad as the host country itself, and even include the jails and prisons that incarcerate loved ones who have been swept up in these arrests. A public defender states that "I have heard stories about people who have a partner who has been incarcerated for some allegedly legitimate reason who goes to bring clothes to that person, and gets picked up at the jail after their name is run through the system when they sign in to bring the materials". Another public defender notes that such checks can even occur, in a systematic way, in schools:

> I have heard stories about school officials questioning kids, because in many communities there are enough settled citizen kids with parents who are still without status, about renegade school officials who question all of the kids about the status of their parents and report parents to the Immigration and Naturalization Service (INS), who then try to detain them.

Some of these initiatives that target immigrants are unlawful, and can be overturned in court. The problem in this domain is that there are so many ways in which this fundamental right can be waived, and it can happen in a range of settings, from the side of the road all the way up to the deportation hearing. A lawyer described the issue as follows:

> Consent has to be knowing, intelligent and voluntary, and for that, language is critically important, as is age and educational background. This is something we can challenge, and the way to do it is get a Spanish speaking expert witness who will watch the tape and say: "This officer said 'do you want eggs with your toast?' or something that was not 'can I search the car?'". We have had some success with this, but a lot of times courts bypass those requirements and find other reasons to justify the search after the fact. When [it turns out that] there are four or five kilos of cocaine found in the car, the courts are inclined to say: "Listen, these cops had a hunch, and they acted on the hunch". There are many more cases where I think that we should have been successful than cases in which we really were successful.

This is an astonishing example of arbitrary law, since it demonstrates that even judges can arbitrarily find ways of justifying illegal searches. Furthermore, no matter how hard we might try to ensure that people are accorded rights that can apply to encounters with figures of authority, they will naturally be scared, and in most cases immediately they will give in to authority. A public defender notes:

> When Spanish-speaking clients are pulled over, even if they don't understand what the officer is saying, there seems to be this desire to appease or consent, and I think that we see that sometimes with our clients, they consent without an understanding. I don't know if it's a reflection of the way that the justice system works in Mexico, or if it's more tied to the culture.

One of the reasons why these traffic stops are so common is in part because officials are offered incentives to entrap, coerce and trick unsuspecting prey, particularly on the front lines. A lawyer explains the process:

> In this county, both the county and the city policemen, almost all of them have video cameras, and with the homeland security crap they are getting digital. They have diddley[-squat] going on, but they can record and then download each evening every stop onto their computer. If you are unlucky enough to be on such a stop, the cops might say: "Here's your warning citation, I'm going to give you a warning citation because I'm a nice guy, when I could have given you a ticket. Here's your citation. Oh, by the way, you don't have any contraband in the car, do you?" "No." "Mind if we take a look?" The blue lights are still flashing, the cop is still wearing a gun, he still has his hat on, and his nightstick, and

> if you say no, and that's on that tape, now you've got some bargaining power.

Most vulnerable people will not say no, of course, because they fear the repercussions. But even if they do decline, law enforcement officials may have some kind of incentive to continue the search, which they can do by bringing in the K-9 (canine) unit. A lawyer states:

> These dogs are full of shit. They are going to circle your car, and how many times have you seen in the last six months a story of a guy who buys a car at a government auction and the fuel tank ain't right, so he has the tank taken out and they find three kilos floating around in there, which are cutting the gas off, and then floating back. The bumper is full of pot. And nobody has ever found it. Now with those damned dogs, they use it as an excuse, and the dog doesn't alert off of the presence of narcotics, it works off of the scent of narcotics. The scent? Yah right. And so it alerts, well that's a pretty damn nebulous term too.

A refreshingly irreverent lawyer like this one can help protect people from the dangers of that initial interaction, but if only if he is present on each stop, which is of course improbable. Furthermore, in this example he provides a clear sense of why the cards are so stacked towards abuse, particularly if the person pulled over doesn't speak English, or doesn't know his/her rights. The point about the dogs, though, is that once a scent is detected, for whatever reason, the stakes and constraints of eventual charges shift because they provide the basis for "probable cause", says a lawyer:

> They'll pull them over, and most of these officers in their police training learn one or two sentences in Spanish, usually garbled, like: "Can I search your car?" They invariably consent, and if drugs are found, the process begins. If they don't consent, the standards are relaxed for cars, so the police will never need a warrant to search a car. But they will need probable cause. And in many cases, they don't have probable cause. They'll try to cobble together probable cause by saying: "He seemed nervous". Or "I talked to the driver, who told me they were coming from one place, and passenger said somewhere else, and that heightened my suspicion". In a lot of cases, now, the Supreme Court has said that very little is required for a drug dog to do a sniff search. And many of these patrols will have the dogs with them, and will look for some pretext, and then bring the dog out immediately. If the dog alerts, and we don't even know what that means, then it will become the basis for probable cause. Then consent is no longer an issue. In most cases, the officers will be very friendly, and 9 times out of 10, the stop is video-taped. The officers will have a video camera in the cruiser, and they'll ask a series of questions in English, and

> most Spanish speaking people will understand a word or two, but not much. Then they'll ask in Spanish if they can search, and the vast majority of times there's a nod, and they'll allow a search, even when there are drugs in the car.

When we move from legal rights to language issues that impinge upon access to those rights, the magnitude of the problem is revealed with brutal clarity, bringing us to the value of approaching the home-host country encounter from a linguistic perspective.

Language skills on the front lines

In spite of American laws protecting citizens and non-citizens against arbitrary searches, there is no way to exercise the rights that they accord unless pertinent information is conveyed in a way that is both comprehensible and *hearable* to the undocumented immigrant. But even if those rights are properly conveyed, the desire to appease rather than confront authority will generally prevail. A lawyer sums up the issue with a single question:

> The cop is supposed to have to tell the person that he can refuse to have his car searched. But if you pull some guy over who doesn't speak any English, how the hell do you explain to him that he doesn't have to consent?

The "hearable" side to this equation is convincing the person that he/she does have rights, and can exercise them (cf. Lithwick 2014), while the linguistic side is the transmission of the information in the target language, a challenge in a system construed in this way, according to a lawyer:

> I had a federal case where they got permission to search the house. They brought a jailor out who speaks Spanish. She read him the rights in Spanish, and asked if the people in the house understood. So I said, "Tell me in Spanish what you told them." What she told them was: "You have a right not to use your rights." I said, "Come on judge, that's not an explanation of rights!" It passed muster for that day in court. The evidence wasn't suppressed. This happens all the time.

This version of translation, in which the utterance is supplemented with advice as to how to answer a question, is so rampant that I'm motivated to invent a new term: *interpretadvice*, perhaps? or maybe *comminterpretation*?

> For a long time in general sessions court, we had someone who was incredibly well intentioned, a sweet, dear man. But he absolutely perceived his role in the system to be that of sort of a friend of the court, who just sort

> of explained things to people. I would be standing in back listening to this non Spanish speaking lawyer who would say things like: "Tell the guy that he has a right to go to trial", and the man would say: "You can go to trial but you sure don't want to!" And I am over there saying: "No, no wait! He did not translate what you said!" or: "Can't you tell that he has been talking for 5 minutes and you only translated two sentences?"

Language skills on both ends of this equation exacerbate the problem tremendously, and can lead to an actual shift in the legal categories that apply to the case. Because the linguistic resources are not usually in place at local levels, these already criminalized individuals find themselves committing new crimes with each moment that passes. A lawyer provides the following example:

> We had a girl who was taken into custody. She had gone to drop something off at the jail for someone else, and she left her kids in the car for ten minutes while she went in. They wouldn't wait on her quickly, because she was Hispanic, and because she spoke no English, and so it took her fifteen or twenty minutes. So they cited her for leaving her kids in the car. She was taken into custody, run through the system, and landed up in immigration court. The perception of the community is that either these no-reason cases, or low-level misdemeanor citations are being used as a funnel to incarcerate immigrants.

If translators were available on the front lines then they could act as valuable advocates when these people, who are as terrified as they are ill-informed, are willing to do or say anything at all just to avoid the threat of punishment. The motivation for giving in to authority is obviously very strong on the front lines, even in cases in which the driver is engaged in criminal activities:

> The guy might think: "Maybe if I tell him it's okay to search, he'll think I don't have anything and let me go", even though he knows that there are two kilos in the trunk, which aren't going to be hard to find. Or else he thinks that he can stop the search and limit it to the front seat, which he can. At any point he can say: "Stop, I don't want you to search anymore". But the cops aren't stupid, so as soon as he says yes, they are going to drag his ass to the police car and lock him in the backseat where he cannot say anything to them about anything because they cannot hear him anymore. So he cannot limit the search because he has been removed [from the vehicle].

These kinds of legal details don't apply to all countries, and even in the United States most people are unaware of how to act around law enforcement officials. A lawyer provides some tips:

> If you say no, they cannot arrest you and impound your car. In fact, there's pretty good Tennessee law that applies if there's a delay of 20 or 30 minutes while they get a dog out to your car. Now if they find dope, you have an argument that you were illegally arrested for that 20 or 30-minute period, so anything found after that should be suppressed. It isn't always, but it should be. And so the word is always: "No. No. And you ain't going to pat me down. Is there some reason why you're afraid of me officer? Because you ain't going to pat me down". There has to be some kind of articulable fear, and to search your car, the officer has to have an articulable suspicion. They can also confiscate your car if they find something. And they can search the navigator too. It's a racket.

This is a "racket" because it isn't just racism, or xenophobia, or even law enforcement: it's income for the local police department, and so the stops and searches can in some cases be motivated by money, according to a lawyer:

> They are investigating corruption? They ought to be investigating the cops. And they do multi-million dollar seizures lately around here, and whichever organization was participating in the bust will get a piece of that. And all of that money is controllable by the sheriff himself, not the county commissioner. We have four helicopters here in Knox County. That's more than Davidson, Shelby and Hamilton counties combined. [The police chief] there is spending money like a drunken Japanese sailor.

This is incentive for negative discretion because any goods that have been purchased with funds obtained by illegal means can be confiscated, which means that certain types of police work can provide funds to offset the costs of enforcement. This is a crucial area of concern, particularly in dealing with commodities such as drugs. An article from the Australian context by Fisse and Frasier (1992) describes this as forfeiture that is put into play as a deterrent:

> [A] fundamental aim of asset forfeiture as a means of controlling crime is economic pressure. Those who would circumvent the level playing field of a properly regulated market are punished by forfeiture and are thereby deterred from future illicit economic activity. The cost of doing illegal business is dramatically increased as both capital and income are forfeited and, if the regulation is effective, illicit activity is made unprofitable.
>
> (p. 738)

Whatever the motivation of asset forfeiture, it can easily lead to profiling on the basis of preconceptions, as a lawyer indicated:

> Are some immigrants more targeted than others? I don't know, I think that the drug task forces want to get as many drugs as possible. They certainly do want to get drug mules, like anyone else. But they work on preconceptions. They think that people of color are more likely to have drugs, but I don't think it matters where they're from, in particular.

In certain instances, law enforcement officials are subjected to policies that oblige them to act in ways that they themselves consider inappropriate or counterproductive. We saw the example of the New Orleans official bucking federal immigration policy in order to maintain strong ties to immigrant communities; but there are also times when police officers are punished for *not* carrying out deleterious duties or enforcing ineffectual laws. A recent American example came in light of challenges to the "stop and frisk" policies in New York City (NYC), where policemen were being demoted for not meeting quotas (Goldstein 2013). Currently New York residents are experiencing the inverse, since police officers are protesting the NYC mayor by cutting back on citations, another excellent example of both discretion and arbitrary applications of law (Goodman and Baker 2015).

In all of these front-line cases, the presence of a sympathetic cultural interpreter, or a police officer rendered sympathetic by incentive to act lawfully instead of trying to extort resources, could go a long way towards reducing abuse and suffering. A lawyer describes how draconian the current system can be with reference to the case of a man involved in selling contraband:

> He came into the States years ago, and he did some kind of drug or drug trafficking thing. He got convicted, and then he was sent back to Mexico. Then he came back, led an exemplary life, got married, had kids, and this life went on for 10 years. One day he is walking down the street and because a car had been stolen nearby that day, the police pick him up and they notice by his driver's license that he is illegal. He didn't do a damn thing wrong, but now he is in jail, in federal jail, because he illegally re-entered after an aggravated felony conviction. He stands to go away for upwards of 8 or more years . . . and all the attorney would have to prove is that he is here illegally.

In other words, no matter how competent the interpreter, how solid the lawyer, how sensitive the judge, the defendant in this case will serve hard time because further up the procedural ladder there is little or no discretion or room to negotiate if the case involves a felony such as returning to the United States after deportation. So what is to be done?

Remedies for the front lines

Betts (2010) has argued that in spite of "the existence of international human rights norms that should, in theory, protect such people, there remains a fundamental normative and institutional gap in the international system" that can be addressed by: "First, the consolidation and application of existing international human rights norm into sets of guiding principles for different groups of vulnerable irregular migrants; and second, improved mechanisms for interagency collaboration to ensure implementation of these norms and principles" (p. 533). In other words, he is looking to existing human rights legislation and norms to establish what can be applied to cases involving undocumented immigrants:

> In a world in which irregular migrants are often perceived by states as an undesirable security threat, it is often forgotten that irregular migrants have human rights qua human beings under international human rights law. This means that people who cross borders are entitled to be treated in a certain way and according to certain sets of norms prior to being returned to their country of origin. Where they have particular vulnerabilities, either as a result of the situation in the country of origin or as a result of circumstances during movement, these may create additional sets of entitlements and obligations under human rights law, which a host state would need to meet prior to the migrants' return. Furthermore, as has been increasingly recognized under international human rights law's notion of "complementary protection", there are also a range of circumstances in which irregular migrants—even if they are not refugees—may have an entitlement not to be forcibly returned to their country of origin but to receive temporary or permanent sanctuary.
>
> (pp. 534–5)

This approach would necessitate the instruction of lawyers, public defenders, advocates and the migrants themselves in regards to these oft-neglected or little-known areas of law. As Betts points out:

> The problem, however, is that although these human rights standards exist, and states have signed up to them, they are rarely fully implemented in states' responses to irregular migration. Neither the rights that all irregular migrants are entitled to—nor the additional entitlements and obligations that arise from specific vulnerabilities—are clearly understood and recognised by states. Nor is there any clearly defined international institutional responsibility for ensuring the implementation of these rights and obligations.
>
> (p. 535)

This approach would be of great value, particularly if there was some kind of international oversight to identify and ensure that application of pertinent legislation. But the problem with this approach, and one that Betts himself identifies, is that most of the human rights legislation to which he refers applies to migrants who suffer particular types of vulnerabilities, such as conditions in the country of origin or shifts in their situations on account of their having fled the country of origin. Except in certain cases, these kinds of claims don't apply, or would be difficult to argue, for people coming from (say) Mexico unless there was some obvious persecution on account of interactions with drug cartels, sexual orientation or other documented form of persecution. One category that Betts invokes is that of the "stranded" migrant, defined by Dowd (2008) as:

> [T]hose who leave their own country for reasons unrelated to refugee status, but who become destitute and/or vulnerable to human rights abuses in the course of their journey. With some possible exceptions, they are unable or unwilling to return to their country of origin, are unable to regularize their status in the country where they are to be found, and do not have access to legal migration opportunities that would enable them to move on to another state.
>
> (p. 4)

If this category of persons were to be recognized, and if their rights were to be ensconced firmly, then a significant number of persons currently in limbo could find relief. Currently, however, those who are (say) trapped in a host country because they fear re-crossing the border are unlikely to find much sympathy from host country law enforcement.

For these reasons, I would suggest that positive discretion and sympathetic translation on these crucial front lines could offer some relief as we await viable permanent solutions, including "soft-law" frameworks and proper international oversight.

Positive discretion and sympathetic interpretation

As we've seen, undocumented people on the front lines need advocates who can help render pertinent information that is "hearable" to host country officials, before the situation gets any worse. In cases of undocumented persons who are unfamiliar with host country norms, linguistic and otherwise, this process might involve many layers of translation and explanation. In one particularly evocative example that sums up what I mean by this term "translation", an interpreter describes the kind of effort that can be required in certain cases:

> Imagine this: You've got this mountain guy, a young guy who has been in the mountains since way back. And he is part of one of these communities that are really isolated. I might give my son a CD for Christmas, and it would be all wrapped-up, with a bow on it, and all that sort of stuff. If

> I were to give this same CD to one of those mountain people, he might take it and think: "That's it! This is a beautiful object! It's wrapped in paper, decorated with a bow, and everything!" And I would actually have to take off the ribbon, and take off the wrapping paper, and then when he sees that shiny plastic case inside, he thinks: "That's it!" Maybe it's something he could use as a decoration, with its hard, shiny case. He understands that no, it's the silvery thing inside [the case]. That's it. So I show him that he can open the case, and there's this object that is silvery and beautiful inside. And maybe he thinks "That's it!" because he can hang it up on a tree, and it would swirl around, and give off life, and maybe scare birds away. But that's not it either. There is actually information or music on that CD, and for that, he will need a machine [to play it]. So these are layers, and layers, and layers of incomprehension.

And so the "translators" that I'm promoting need to be advocates who are able to interpret into the target language, of course; but in line with this analogy, they also need to be able to unwrap the linguistic utterance, remove its bow and wrapping paper, unearth the text on the CD and then translate it, as part of this effort aimed at expressing the intentions of the migrant, and the responsibilities and efforts of the law enforcement officer.

Sometimes these "layers" are far less complex; an interpreter who was born in Latin America provides an oft-cited example of the culturally specific impediments to this process:

> There is no doubt in my mind that for Latino males, there is obviously a problem with drunk driving. In Latin America, we don't enforce laws against driving while intoxicated as we do here. It is a different culture there, and it is more common than it is here. With the backing of the law, cops are able to stop people when they even suspect that they have been drinking while driving, and then prosecute them, and go from there. A lot of Latino males are targeted for that.

In other words, Latino males can also be "targeted" for acting in ways that are deemed acceptable or even normal in their country of origin, which makes them sitting ducks for those who wish to see them excluded from American society. Another cultural difference that can lead to disaster is the propensity, also more accepted in Latin American culture, of dating or having sexual relations with people who are considered minors in the host country, as a lawyer indicated:

> There have been more problems with statutory rape simply because this is a cultural problem. There are gentlemen who do not realize that you cannot have relations with girls who are 14–15 years old, whereas probably in their own country it was okay. A lot of the Hispanic males who are

> a little bit slower or a little less competent are going after these girls who are 15 or 16 years old, and are a little bit smarter. These girls are using these guys for money and rides and stuff like that.

The same goes for corporeal punishment of children; in some contexts this is a normal part of parenting, while in others it's equated with child abuse. A community organizer recalls such a case:

> I know the child got hurt, but I don't know if that child's getting hurt was child abuse, I really don't know. The mother did whack the kid with shoes, which is pretty unacceptable in the United States, but I guess not in Mexico. And the mother doesn't have much of an education. She probably grew up in a one-room or two-room house. And sexuality issues are not the same thing either. It's just not the same world.

This is a two-way street, of course, and there are endless examples of similar phenomena from the opposite standpoint, when, for example, Americans act inappropriately in foreign contexts. Recent high-profile cases include Obama being cited in the Chinese press for chewing gum (Macleod 2014), or when Michelle Obama was skewered in the British press for throwing her arms around the Queen of England, provoking humorous responses in the United States (Walker 2011). These kinds of incidents are particularly notable because we can assume that both the President of the United States and the First Lady would have been briefed on appropriate behavior in the host country; if they nonetheless managed to act inappropriately, we can only imagine how easy it is for undocumented immigrants to do so.

Examples like these suggest that *linguistic* accuracy needs to be complemented with *cultural* accuracy; but translation also has a *legal* component, the transmission of useful legal knowledge that can help prevent undocumented immigrants from unnecessarily compromising themselves through indecorous actions, and then invalidating whatever chance they might have for restitution by waiving their basic legal rights. On one side of the discursive equation, intermediaries might help to prevent what a high-level prison official described as "the potential for corruption": "If you pull this guy over and you are a crooked cop, you may pray that this guy is illegal, so you can say, maybe for $50.00 I'll let you go and that's the end of it." On the other side, an undocumented immigrant might think that the official expects some kind of bribe, and then learns the hard way that it can become the factor that leads to the arrest and the deportation. This is more arbitrariness, because from the undocumented immigrant's point of view, it's pretty much impossible to predict which of the two pathways is most appropriate and, given cultural differences with his/her country of origin, he/she's probably ill-equipped to read the signs displayed by the law enforcement official, signs with which a trained intermediary could help out.

Translation, interpretation and the time of the interaction

In light of these observations I'm suggesting that in the interest of actual and productive communication of useful information, we should make a firm distinction between linguistic accuracy (interpretation) and cultural/legal accuracy (translation), and that we should advocate for the latter on the front lines of interaction between home and host country. Approaching a discussion about the relative merits of interpretation versus translation once again calls attention to the role of the *time* when the conversation occurs. Translation is crucial during the initial encounter because it is during this period of negotiation that a sensitive and qualified translator can keep a claimant from incriminating him/herself, or mis-communicating the situation to authority. Linguistic accuracy is paramount later on, when (say) the claimant is in the presence of counsel, who can ensure that the claimant receives appropriate advice on what to say, and how to say it. And so with this distinction in mind, I would propose three principles that we need to consider when dealing with at-risk populations, especially foreigners who speak little or no English and, moreover, foreigners who don't have status in the host country:

- First, most important moments for vulnerable persons occur in the initial interactions with authority, which tend to take the form of conversations with employers, civil servants, border guards or enforcers of traffic laws.
- Second, it is in these initial verbal interactions that the so-called laws that govern relations with such categories of individuals as undocumented persons, Convention refugees, asylum seekers or immigrants can be shown to be almost entirely arbitrary in conception and application, particularly if the dialogue occurs between a native and a non-native speaker of the national language. Therefore, this is a moment when negotiation can occur between the two parties.
- And third, the first two statements mean that vulnerable populations experience the world as a constant violent conflict between themselves and the host population, effectively rendering their existence so stridently conflictual that they should be considered as victims of an ongoing war that is sustained by the host country, often for financial gain. To help protect them, we need to distinguish between moments when interpretation or translation is most suitable, and provide assistance accordingly.

These statements apply to virtually all vulnerable people, including those who live under the duress of poverty, homelessness, statelessness or even personal uncertainty brought on by strained domestic relations. But for the "foreigners" in these groups the obstacles to justice, and the concomitant strain brought upon them as a consequence, is unfathomable and needs to be considered if we are to offer some kind of sustainable assistance for the long term. As it stands now, our advocacy, our legal work and our desire for adequate translation and interpretation on behalf of migrants will only impact a tiny proportion of the vulnerable population unless we consider ways of intervening at the most intimate levels of interactions between home and foreign populations.

If an undocumented immigrant is arrested following a front-line interaction, the information he/she has conveyed will contribute to the dossier used at the eventual hearing. Signed statements, video recordings and statements made by terrified "illegal" people can be unduly incriminating, and for those who have been misled at those front lines, there is only the good faith of officials that can prevent draconian decision making.[3] Bad faith in any setting can contribute significantly to the harm, and so if we are going to nominate translators to advocate on behalf of people on the front line, the selection process has to include some measure of both how competent they are to act as linguistic and cultural intermediaries *and* how sympathetic they are to the vulnerable population. In regards to the former, there is a useful distinction between translation and interpretation that can help in our selection of these intermediaries:

> Whoever is somewhat familiar with the professional practice of translating from one language into another, one being his native and the other a foreign language, knows this simple, yet helpful truth: it is always preferable to *translate* from foreign into native, while *interpretation* work is simpler when done the other way around. This rule is based on the strict necessity to thoroughly comprehend the original (source) message. When you hear an oral utterance in the foreign language, you have neither dictionaries at hand, nor time to consult them about a word or phrase which might be unknown; all this becomes possible and is easily done when translating. At the same time, an utterance in your mother tongue is at any rate almost always sure to be clearly understood.
>
> (Nikolayev 2001)

So the translator can help to negotiate by conveying information that will either prevent the individual from entering the system (as in, for example, a case involving a potential arrest), or from making crucial mistakes in articulating the claim (as in filling out initial forms at the airport, required for a Convention refugee claim). I might add that an incompetent translation of initial events, if done in the spirit of negotiation and discussion, is probably less detrimental to an eventual case than an incompetent interpretation because the latter is more formal and therefore probably less open for debate in the formal court setting than an effort at cross-cultural translation might be. An approach that emphasizes the first encounter as the appropriate space for translation may help clarify where limited resources can be best allocated in cases of extreme conflict – as in, for example, the conflictual relations that can arise between host populations and "illegals", and the competition that has been set up for the possession of goods by virtue of the aforementioned right accorded to some officials to seize the assets derived from criminal activities.

The logic of providing legal remedies to those who have been incorrectly charged with crimes is that wrongs can be righted in the second instance by authorities who have been provided with pertinent facts of the case, communicated via highly trained interpreters to competent lawyers and sensitive judges. Such an apparently obvious assertion, also rooted in time, is in fact erected upon fallacious assumptions because much of what happens in the eventual hearings depends upon information provided during the initial encounter; and in the case of undocumented migrants this information is often incomplete, inaccurate or misrepresented because a sympathetic translator was not there to adequately convey the claimants' utterances on the front lines. And so I would suggest that in addition to advocating for translators for these front lines, we need to also find a way to downplay or even discount information gleaned during the initial interactions. First encounters almost always occur under duress, and without satisfactory linguistic or legal representation, and they should therefore be at least reinterpreted by the court or tribunal in a way that accounts for the inadequacies of the communicative setting that led up to the later hearings. This idea, that decision makers could discount information obtained during the initial encounter, would challenge the way that law enforcement works, so it's very unlikely. Furthermore, immigration proceedings fall under the jurisdiction of administrative law, and in that realm "reinterpretation" or successful appeal usually occurs only in those rare cases in which the court corrects egregious errors of procedure. For instance, a qualified interpreter can review the tapes of the initial interview and find that the official misunderstood crucial answers provided by the interviewee, and acted on the basis of this misunderstanding. But in most cases, as a lawyer explained, excuses are regularly made for missteps in the course of (say) a search ("he didn't have consent to search the car, but he was acting on a hunch based on his experience, so it should be allowed"), or else there is no clearly ensconced legal right to refuse a search because searches are effected on the basis of pure power relations.

There are very few rights that are accorded to undocumented people (Tapinos 2000; Van der Leun 2003), although in some cases the nature of the immigration violation has some bearing upon how they will be treated by authorities. Broeders and Engbersen (2007) offer valuable distinctions, and consider as well the social, political and legal issues that arise out of irregular migration:

> The nation-state is an exclusive club in which rights and privileges are awarded to citizens and semi-citizens (denizens) only. However, decades of immigration research has shown that access to the clubhouse, the territorial state, does not necessarily depend on membership status or even advance approval. Irregular migration comes in many shapes and sizes.

> Many of those we call irregular migrants started their journey perfectly legally, for example, by traveling on a tourist visa, and became "illegal" or "irregular" when they stayed on after its validity expired. Most typologies of irregular migration are therefore set up around three main criteria. There is legal and illegal entry, legal and illegal residence, and legal and illegal employment. These criteria can combine in many ways and produce many forms and degrees of irregularity. Irregular entry and residence are clearly in defiance of the state's claims to control its population and territory. The prominent place that the fight against illegal immigration now occupies on the policy agenda in most western European states is because of both a political and a social shift in attitudes toward this group. Politically, irregular migration adds to the accusation that states have lost control on immigration; a group of immigrants who are by legal definition excluded should not appear to be growing. Socially, popular resistance against this category has, after years of indifference, been steadily mounting. Irregular migrants are generally feared and perceived as a problem.
>
> (p. 1594)

This mounting fear can be drastically exacerbated when people make a link between the "illegal" presence of a foreigner and the dangers of terrorism, and it's this connection between undocumented people and state security that has made it such that the very worst prosecutor is federal, particularly in the United States; and indeed the higher one moves up the line from the traffic stop to the federal appeals court, the worse it gets. A lawyer describes this surprising progression as follows:

> If a guy is here illegally and he is charged in federal court for drugs or guns, then he's screwed: he is going to get a sentence, he is going to serve the sentence, and then he is going to get deported. If on the rare occasion you have someone with a green card, or resident alien, or some legal status, then yes, there may be ways to work out a case that doesn't affect his immigration status, but in the federal system they don't tend to do that. In the state system, I can do that all the time, I say: "Look, this is a crime of moral turpitude". So in immigration court, if they find him six months from now because of a driver's license issue and they find his conviction, then he gets deported. So we make a deal where the state gets what they want, and he gets what he wants. You get that kind of thing in the state system, but the federal system is out for blood, and they ain't interested in working things down.

For those of us who have worked in the refugee determination domain, this is an anomaly because there, you are usually better off dealing with federally certified interpreters and codified legal apparatuses that exist beyond the fields and freeways. This is a crucial distinction between the treatment of undocumented people and Convention refugees because for the latter they can only hope to be treated as they are in highly codified federal systems like that of Canada, while in the former, most deals can only be made informally, before people enter the system, usually with the help of good translators.

Translators preventing arrest and deportation

The consequence of the arbitrary, inconsistent and draconian systems that have been set up worldwide to confront issues of irregular migration is that undocumented people learn to become fearful, resistant and resentful. These feelings contribute to behaviors that are often described as cagey, inconsistent and conflictual, and they tend through their interactions to provide grounds for the failure that they generally endure at later stages in the process. A lawyer commented that illegals tend to be nervous, and they act in ways that put front-line officials on their guard:

> A lot of them are hiding things. They are very careful about what they are saying and they frequently change their stories. Some of them have speech impediments, some of them are missing teeth, and some of them are so shy and nervous that they just will not speak up. More generally, there is a cultural barrier, for instance with Guatemalans, who tend to be very deferential, so they do not want to answer any question directly. Many of their answers begin with: "Thank God that...", and then just continue along beginning at a point that is 2 years before anything happened. For a translator it's very difficult, because they want to just go all over the place, and the answer has nothing to do with the question.

That the answer is unrelated to the question may or may not be an issue in terms of information conveyed, but in a situation involving illegal immigrants it's clear that an interpreter bound by professional ethics would be of little value. Their instinct is to either just get away from the situation as expeditiously as possible, or to try to convince the authority figure that they are in fact linguistically competent, and therefore worthy of a place in America. One lawyer noted:

> I have represented Spanish-speaking men, and they will tell me that they understand English. They might understand it on a very basic level, enough to get through a day, but certainly not enough to convey the details of their case. I do not know if this is due to shame, or if they just are sitting there and say do you understand and they say: "Yes". I think that they might be too embarrassed to say that they do not understand what you are saying. It is kind of, an: "I can take care of myself thing. I do not need an interpreter. I understand. I speak English".

This kind of attitude is particularly dangerous on the front lines, which are rife with officials who can offer clemency or release in exchange for signed affidavits, which in turn become legal grounds for stripping individuals of rights before they are deported. So what began as a minor infraction grows with each passing moment, leading to a disaster.

If translators are most suited for initial encounters, then they are likely to be helpful for preventative measures as well. Many incidents that involve law enforcement can be easily prevented, especially if the message is spread within the foreign-born community that certain actions are likely to lead to arrest and deportation. For example, the largest community of foreign-born people in the Southern United States hearkens from rural Mexico, where guns are shot off at parties, people often drive drunk in cars that are old and poorly maintained, and law enforcement officers are open to accepting bribes. Each of these examples can be grounds for a felony conviction in the United States, so translators could help out by reaching out to the community before trouble starts. One lawyer noted that "there is a much greater percentage of the illegals who are here who never have contact with the legal system than amongst the domestic population", which implies not only lower criminality but an active avoidance of officials. Nevertheless, he said, "you can take any population and there'll be a certain number of them who drink too much, who use drugs, and who will be stupid, no matter what you do". And when immigrants "act stupid", the risks are very high that they will get caught because of profiling. Similar tendencies can be seen in any country with a significant population of undocumented immigrants, such as India,[4] Australia (Wright 2014) or the European Union (EU) (Hintjens 2013).

Prevention also implies communication between the home and the host country, which is crucial because the population of undocumented people often considers itself to be living through a constant violent conflict, an invisible but nevertheless pernicious war. The stakes in this conflict are high, and include the proverbial midnight knock on the door, the arbitrary arrest, the unprovoked attack, the sanctified arrest, the stripping of rights, the confiscation of property and, in more unofficial combat, sexual abuse, rape as an instrument of punishment or coercion and the possibility of other unchecked and un-reportable violence. Not even the most accurate or sensitive of interpreters can help in most of those cases; but reaching out to the community can because it can provide useful information that can help people negotiate on the front lines, rather than simply react to what they feel is an attack against them. A scholar activist suggested that in the current juncture:

> we've moved from sort of the welfare state to the warfare state. So much of what the state does now is provide biophysical security, whether or not it is in the disgustingly huge prison industrial complex in the United States to the gloating military budgets to the war on immigrants that is taking place on the U.S./Mexico boundary.

If the emphasis were to be placed on prevention, then undocumented people might feel a kind of "buy-in" to their adopted culture, which would help them contribute to the host country, rather than resist it.

Remedies for the battlefield

In addition to their being sympathetic to the plight of undocumented people, and active in the work of preventing discordant interactions between people from the host and home countries, translators on the front lines also need to have verbal and linguistic skills that ensure more effective communication between an abusive system and its designated victims. These kinds of intermediaries require special skills, described by an interpreter as:

> a good grasp of, I don't know how to say this, like an intuitive grasp of meaning, beyond just the words, but without going too far, as well as stamina, sufficient stamina, which implies knowledge of your own limitations and a willingness to be open about those.

This "intuitive grasp of meaning, beyond just the words" is often related to cultural sensitivity, as described by another interpreter who suggested that:

> if a Latino or Latin American person does not make eye contact but looks down, it is probably more a sign of respect than it is of guilt, whereas we would assume that not making eye contact creates suspicions. Cultural differences can have an ill-effect on the situation of the immigrant in terms of their relationship with law enforcement or even with court personnel.

Another lawyer-advocate suggested that interpreters have to be qualified and in tune with local dialects and with the aforementioned category called speech genres described here in terms of slang:

> We have serious problems with the interpreters, who oftentimes have no experience with the vocabulary that our clients use. For instance, agricultural slang is not something that they test on the interpreters. So we try generally to use only federally certified interpreters, which is the highest level of training that one can have, but in the state of Arkansas there is only one, and in Tennessee I'm sure there are less than ten.

There really is no substitute for good interpreters because, as the lawyer-advocate said, "poor interpreting is sometimes worse than not interpreting at all".

The huge numbers of migrants in most countries means that there is a broad pool of qualified people from which to draw in order to recruit the kinds of cultural mediators I've described. For any given setting, it would be valuable to set up a web-based information center to help connect lawyers to trained cultural brokers, investigators, interpreters and translators. This way when a particular case comes up, there would be someone to contact, as a lawyer indicated:

> Even at a national level the listserve for immigration attorneys is almost ad hoc. And if you are trying to find qualified cultural experts around the country in different cultures, it's even harder. So there needs to be some kind of national listserve set up, a web-based system where anybody who goes on, types in your country, and boom, you get the expert in that area. You could either call or email, that would be fantastic. Unfortunately, in some cases the nearest expert might be in Georgia or New York City, so there also needs to be an effort to train people in all the major cities to do these certain kinds of work. The hard part for the immigration practitioners is: How do you find people? How do you know where to look? And how much time do you have to look for this?

The state could perhaps fund these investigators to assist public defenders and lawyers with their cases, and also to go into the community to meet with migrants and representatives of cultural groups, as one investigator suggested:

> When I worked for the Metro Public Defender, I would go into the community and bring a book, and I'd tell them: "This is how it works, this is what you do if you get arrested. If you don't have any money, you go to the Metro Public Defender, and you apply for a lawyer". Or: "This is what you do if you get stopped by a police officer". I just gave them information on what to do if they get a citation: "Here is what you need to do, and these are the places where you can get help for this or for that" ... Doing that [kind of work], I had to make all kinds of connections in the community.

As this investigator suggests, some of this community outreach work is going on now, but aside from the occasional do-gooder, fellow immigrants generally perform it, which has its own set of associated drawbacks regarding inconsistency and the diffusion of inaccurate facts. One lawyer who actively counsels community members said:

> We need to try to educate people with the facts, something that could be done in churches or community institutions. The religious communities in the Southern US wield tremendous power, and interpreters could go into Churches and community groups to offer advice and assistance.

Much of this education could focus upon how immigrants should carry on basic activities in the host country, such as commuting:

> You need to try to educate people with the facts. You need to say, "Look, you can buy that $200 car. And you can drive it without a license, and you might make it for a couple of weeks until somebody stops you for driving while Mexican". But, I also ask them: "How are you used to driving while in Mexico?" "I didn't drive in Mexico", they say. "And how long have you been driving here?" I'll ask. "Six or eight weeks". I say: "You can have a wreck, and I'm saying that because you don't know how to drive, and it's not just you, nobody with that experience knows how to drive. And you are going to be unlucky enough to hit a BMW".

Sometimes the details are minute, and unlikely to be known even by the domestic population, such as the risk of having a nondescript car, or even only one key on a chain:

> Early in my career, I represented a client who was stopped traveling on I-40 coming through Nashville. He and another young man in a Nissan Sentra, which apparently turns out to be an indicator, according to the 20th judicial task force, that you are drug-running because you are traveling in a sort of nondescript car, such as a Nissan Sentra. They stopped them and saw that they only had 2 keys in the ignition, which is another indication that you are drug running since you do not have, say, your house key. You know, I feel like I could teach a seminar on how to run drugs properly.

At the end of the day, though, it's the very fact of being on an interstate that inspires most traffic stops, a fact as likely to bear upon a white tourist in Rwanda as a Mexican undocumented person in the United States:

> In answer to your question, the interesting part of the story is that my client's family drove to Nashville I think 5 times during the pendency of that case to you know, make court dates, meet with the lawyers and that sort of thing. We are talking about his father, mother, his two younger siblings who were small children, his grandfather came a couple of the times, his wife and his two small children. So you know, this is a large family, loaded into like a Tahoe or something. Every trip they took, they were stopped at least once. Some trips they were stopped multiple times. Every trip, their entire car was searched on the side of the road.

At the end of the day, prevention, networks of sensitive and sympathetic translators connected by a kind of website and greater education for the host country's officials about the vicissitudes of this process would make a huge difference to how brutal these front lines are for those who are brought into combat upon them. But even with the best of intentions and efforts, people will still get arrested. The experiences of those people who have entered into the system, and recommendations about how to improve that process, are the subject of the next chapter.

Notes

1 The numbers in this entire game are gigantic, reports Santos (2014): "The Border Patrol, which releases statistics by fiscal year, apprehended about 818,000 migrants in the Tucson Sector from Oct. 1, 2008 to Sept. 30, 2013" (p. A12).
2 The details of the case (Case 2:11-cv-00225-SS Document 95-3 Filed 08/09/13) are interesting (and available at: http://nowcrj.org/wp-content/uploads/2013/08/OPSO-Policy.pdf [accessed: 15 January 2015]).
3 This, of course, is a huge area of work, and discussions about its meanings can be undertaken with reference such works as Levin and Mather (2012).
4 Ramachandran (1999) "identifies and explores the convoluted ties between the phenomenal growth of the Hindu nationalist forces and clandestine population flows from Bangladesh. The paper argues that while the official sanitized transcript of *hindutva* positions Indian Muslims at the margins of the Hindu nation, undocumented Muslim immigrants from Bangladesh are increasingly viewed as a severe threat to the security and integrity of the Hindu nation. The staggering signal of an 'invisible invasion' of India by Bangladeshi 'infiltrators' has been expressed through an overt discourse circulated through the media and '*hindutva* press'".

Bibliography

Amossy, Ruth (2002) "Introduction to the Study of Doxa", *Poetics Today* 23.2, pp. 369–94.
Beduschi, Ana (2014) "Detention of Undocumented Immigrants and the CJEU's Decisions in France", *International Journal of Refugee Law* 26.3, pp. 333–49.
Bernama (9 September 2013) "Areas Gazetted as Detention Centres for Offenders Under 'Ops Cantas' and 'Ops Bersepadu 6P'". *The Mole*. Available at: http://www.mole.my/content/areas-gazetted-detention-centres-offenders-under-ops-cantas-and-ops-bersepadu-6p. [Accessed: 15 January 2015]
Betts, Alexander (2010) "Soft Law and the Protection of Vulnerable Migrants", *Georgetown Immigration Law Journal* 24.3–4, pp. 533–52.
Broeders, D. and G. Engbersen (2007) "The Fight against Illegal Migration: Identification Policies and Immigrants' Counterstrategies", *American Behavioral Scientist* 50.12, pp. 1592–609.
Cossé, Eva (12 June 2013) "Greece: Abusive Crackdown on Migrants: Police Sweeps, Invasive Searches, Arbitrary Detention", Human Rights Watch. Available at http://www.hrw.org/news/2013/06/12/greece-abusive-crackdown-migrants. [Accessed: 15 January 2015]
Dowd, Rebecca (June 2008) *Trapped in Transit: The Plight and Human Rights of Stranded Migrants*. Geneva: United Nations High Commissioner for Refugees, Research Paper No. 156.
Fisse, Brent and David Frasier (1992) "Some Antipodean Skepticisms about Forfeiture,

Confiscation of Proceeds of Crime, and Money Laundering Offenses", *Alabama Law Review* 44, pp. 737–61.
Goldstein, Joseph (20 March 2013) "Stop-and-Frisk Trial Turns to Claim of Arrest Quotas", *New York Times*, p. A23.
Goodman, David and Al Baker (5 January 2015) "For a 2nd Week, Arrests Plunge in New York City", *New York Times*, p. A1.
Guiraudonn, Virginie and Gallya Lahav (2000) "A Reappraisal of the State Sovereignty Debate: The Case of Migration Control", *Comparative Political Studies*, 33.2, pp. 163–95.
Hintjens, Helen M. (2013) "Screening In or Out? Selective Non-Surveillance of Unwanted Humanity in EU Cities", *Surveillance & Society* 11.1/2, pp. 87–105.
Kubal, Agnieszka (2013) "Migrants' Relationship with Law in the Host Country: Exploring the Role of Legal Culture", *Journal of Intercultural Studies* 34.1, pp. 55–72.
LBJ (2 February 2014) "Pinoys among 153 Illegal Immigrants Nabbed in Malaysia Crackdown", *GMA News*. Available at: http://www.gmanetwork.com/news/story/346644/pinoyabroad/news/pinoys-among-153-illegal-immigrants-nabbed-in-malaysia-crackdown. [Accessed: 15 January 2015]
Lee, Harper (1960) *To Kill a Mockingbird*. New York: Harper Collins.
Levin, Leslie C. and Lynn Mather (eds.) (2012) *Lawyers in Practice: Ethical Decision Making in Context*. Chicago: University of Chicago Press.
Lithwick, Dahlia (16 December 2014) "The Supreme Court Ignores the Lessons of Ferguson", *Slate*. Available at: http://www.slate.com/articles/news_and_politics/jurisprudence/2014/12/heien_v_north_carolina_as_the_rest_of_the_country_worries_about_police_overreach.html. [Accessed: 15 January 2015]
Macleod, Calum (11 November 2014) "Gum-Chewing, Limo-Eschewing Obama Riles Some Chinese". *USA TODAY*. Available at: http://www.usatoday.com/story/news/world/2014/11/10/obama-gum-chewing-riles-some-chinese/18801757. [Accessed: 15 January 2015]
NCADC (National Coalition of Anti-Deportation Campaigns) (2007) "This Festive Season", Right to Remain. Available at: http://www.ncadc.org.uk/archives/filed%20newszines/oldnewszines/Old%2051-100/newszine89/festive.html. [Accessed: 15 January 2015]
Nikolayev, Serghei G. (2001) "The Importance of Knowing Your Local Vernacular", *Translation Journal* 5.1. Available at: http://accurapid.com/journal/15interpret.htm. [Accessed: 15 January 2015]
Ramachandran, Sujata (1999) "Undocumented Bangladeshi 'Infiltrators' and the Hegemony of Hindu Nationalism in India", *Interventions: International Journal of Postcolonial Studies* 1.2, pp. 235–53.
Ricci, Elizabeth (2011) "DWU: Driving While Undocumented", *Voice* 2.1, pp. 18–22.
Rodenhäuser, Tilman (2014) "Another Brick in the Wall: Carrier Sanctions and the Privatization of Immigration Control", *International Journal of Refugee Law* 26.2, pp. 223–47.
Santos, Fernanda (12 February 2014) "Detainees Sentenced in Seconds in 'Streamline' Justice on Border", *New York Times*, p. A12.
Tapinos, G. (2000) "Irregular Migration: Economic and Political Issues", in *Combating the Illegal Employment of Foreign Workers*. Paris: OECD, pp. 13–43.

Van der Leun, J. (2003) *Looking for Loopholes: Processes of Incorporation of Illegal Immigrants in the Netherlands*. Amsterdam: Amsterdam University Press.

Walker, Sarah (25 May 2011) "God Save the Queen from Americans", *Huffington Post*. Available at: http://www.huffingtonpost.com/news/michelle-obama-touches-queen. [Accessed: 15 January 2015]

Wright, Chris F. (2014) "How Do States Implement Liberal Immigration Policies? Control Signals and Skilled Immigration Reform in Australia", *Governance* 27.3, pp. 397–421.

Zolberg, A. R. (2003) "The Archaeology of 'Remote Control'", in A. Fahrmeir, O. Faron and P. Weil (eds.), *Migration Control in the North Atlantic World: The Evolution of State Practices in Europe and the United States from the French Revolution to the Inter-War Period*. New York: Berghahn Books.

Chapter 4

Entering the system, from the arrest to formal sentencing

> Some people were deported twenty years ago, and now they're back in the country. They have been working for fifteen years, and they have American kids. These are people who should be able to apply for residency, and instead they're going to spend seven years in prison ... In some cases the person is a drug dealer, and that's who these laws are made for. But they're hurting people who are responsible, and are just here to take care of their kids. There's no compassion. I've had cases where the defendants were very sympathetic, but there's nothing that can be done.
>
> (A public defender interviewed for the project)

If a customs, traffic or other enforcement agency officer on the front lines determines that someone is undocumented, and if he/she furthermore decides to act on this basis, then he/she can arrest the individual and take him/her into custody. At this point, the migrant has entered the "system", formally. In most countries, irregular migrants are breaking a law, and so they can be taken into custody solely on those grounds. Or else, in yet another way in which like cases can have unlike outcomes, an individual can be arrested for committing a crime and then have his/her immigration status checked while he/she is being held in custody. If he/she is found to be an undocumented immigrant, then he/she might face new charges. In either of these cases, it's worth drawing a line between the moment on the front lines before someone is formally arrested, and everything that happens subsequently. Once this line is crossed, the migrant is usually transported to a headquarters, or a center, or a station, where his/her case will be processed according to the varying tenets of the system. This chapter thus marks a break away from the "front lines" and into a realm where the rules, regulations and laws are more systematically applied, and as a consequence, the range of possible outcomes is usually diminished.

I nonetheless wish to emphasize that even at this point in the process, the "legal system" into which migrants enter is still rather fluid, sometimes very fluid, and that categories of arbitrariness, capriciousness, variability and unpredictability remain. The degree of fluidity depends upon the nature of the system, the predicament of the undocumented person, the country in which the arrest has taken place and, as per previous discussions, the prevailing "social discourse" swirling about the process. For the American case, one lawyer sums up the predicament with remarkable eloquence:

> The problem is, you can take fifteen illegal immigrants out in this parking lot, put them in a van, and start calling the police on them, one after another over a twenty-four hour period. Some of them will be taken out, booked, make bond, and they're gone. Others will be taken out, get booked, and be picked up by immigration officials, and it's only because Bubba came out on the midnight shift, and Bubba, who is making $10-an-hour to be a jailer—and the only reason you'd take that job is because you want to fuck with people. Why would you want $10-an-hour in a dungeon? You are indoors, you ain't seeing the sunshine, and you're dealing with unhappy miserable people who don't want to be where they are. Well Bubba don't like the fact that these damned Mexicans are walking around here anyway, so Bubba, if they don't speak good English, is calling Immigration. And there's no rhyme or reason. You get one guy on aggravated assault, and he gets a bond and goes home, you get another for driving with no license and he gets an immigration hold.

Some of the details here have been exaggerated for effect, but he makes a point that is generalizable and central to the conception of arbitrary law described thus far, and that is confirmed by another public defender:

> They pay terribly for guards. You want to make them want to be there. I think it is already such a hard job, and all the more so when you add the immigrant factor to it. The prisoners are in stressful situations, scary situations, and they are not at our best when they are in the Criminal Justice system. And to get people to work as guards under those conditions, they need to be compensated, especially for those who speak a second language, since that is a skill that most people do not have. Why would I want to work for the prison for you know $10 an hour? To get good people, you have to be willing to pay them, but also have decent facilities. And the problem is that once people get to prison the perception in society is that it is not a vacation, so why should they have all these perks? So you are fighting this, on the one hand wanting good people to work there, and you want to pay them well, but on the other hand, as tax payers or voters, they say that there is no way.

Another lawyer describes how during the period between being charged and making bond the claimant becomes a pawn in a nefarious struggle between the criminal system and the immigration system:

> What will happen, and this is a nightmare, is that sometimes immigration authorities will be able to grab them when they are in the midst of the process. I had a client who was charged with auto theft in Rutherford County, and who was in jail in Rutherford County. He made the resources to make bond, but immigration authorities had placed a hold on him. He could not get out on bond. Immigration picked him up, and they took him to some place out in White County, way out in a private facility where he sat for a while, before he ended up down in Louisiana on the Immigration stuff, or the Homeland Security stuff. People can get really screwed that way. That guy ultimately is getting deported. They do not really even care about the car theft thing.

Most countries have laws on the books that allow for this kind of detention and deportation for undocumented immigrants, but they aren't enforced until there's some kind of pressure to do so, as a lawyer describes:

> The ability to make bond has changed, because a lot of people used to look the other way when people were undocumented. Nobody used to call Immigration, because everybody knew they would not get here. Now, more and more people are being caught, and more Immigration holds are being placed on people, so therefore, more and more people cannot make bond. This happened to me a couple of weeks ago, when before my client could make bond, Immigration slapped a hold on him.

The crucial point here is "before my client could make bond", which means that every moment an undocumented person is physically in a jail or in a police headquarters increases the chance that new charges can be laid. When justice comes to be linked to a ticking clock, it is indeed arbitrary.

Even if the undocumented immigrant is singled out, and authorities called, the "legal system" that will be brought to bear may still treat like cases in unlike ways, and may defy the logic of prediction by releasing more serious offenders, while severely punishing those whose who have committed minor violations. One might argue that this level of variation is often – or even always – the case in law, and that depending upon the wealth or connections of the accused, or the color of his/her skin, or his/her age, or even his/her physical attributes, outcomes different from what the system predicts may occur. But in the case of laws that relate to undocumented people, the level of arbitrariness is much greater, if only because it's an area that is so ideologically charged, and so steeped in histories of scapegoating (Barrera and Robinson 2012; Malecki 2014; Sharma 2011). For these reasons, decisions to "crack-down", enforce laws on the books or just to release a person who is in clear violation of immigration law are often politically motivated. The fickle and variable treatment of people in such a broad array of possible institutions can hardly be considered a "system" because there's very little that is systematic about this process. In fact, the system can often seem more of a fiction that is invented when needed, and otherwise ignored, often on grounds that seem arbitrary.

Gender, status and the migrants' perceptions of their legal counsel

If an undocumented immigrant is arrested and brought into custody in the United States, and if Immigration officials are called, then the initial stages of the incarceration unfold as follows, as per a public defender's description:

> [Undocumented immigrants] are generally arrested by the Bureau of Immigration and Customs Enforcement. They are then brought into the federal courthouse, and either through an indictment or a complaint, the public defender's office is notified. Almost 100 percent of the time they qualify for assistance from our office. They are given a statement of their rights, a four or five page document that details the initial proceedings in court, and their basic rights under the Constitution. They then appear before a magistrate judge. If there has been an indictment, they will be arraigned, which is where a plea of not guilty is entered. There are no circumstances where they'd plead guilty at that stage. They are then taken to a facility either in Nashville, or somewhere else in Tennessee or Kentucky, and then they are processed in the same manner as English-speaking clients. If they don't speak English, they're just out of luck. I don't know of any translators for them in those facilities, which are by and large incredibly rural county facilities where the counties have contracts. There are no federal holding facilities, so the marshals sign contracts with little Mayberry jails, these little, dingy county facilities whose primary source of funding are these contracts with the federal government. A portion of that population will be your low-level burglars and repeat DUI offenders who are locked up with people awaiting trial on federal charges. In these places, the guards barely speak English, much less Spanish.

This narrative makes clear that the office of the public defender plays a crucial role at this stage, but also explains why without adequate translation there are so many things that can go awry, particularly since the detainee's fears can lead him/her to exacerbate his/her situation by trying to find a way out. There are a number of different ways this can occur, as a lawyer indicated:

> I believe that for cultural reasons immigrants often lie in ways that they don't need to, because that's what they think that they should say, and it destroys their case. It has happened with clients of mine. If I interview

> them enough, I can pick up on this and help them before it's too late. But I have heard about people saying what they think they should say, from their community, for example, and it really screws them up. It's very hard to get someone to admit that they have been lying to you, and to get them on board, and to trust you.

This issue of trust rears its ugly head early on, and so the one ally that the detainee might have is undermined because of inaccurate preconceptions about his/her status within the judiciary system. Here, as a public defender indicated, we see the potentially nefarious consequences of the defendant employing norms from his/her own country to think about his/her current situation:

> Immigrant clients, like many clients, think that we're part of the system, not much different from the prosecutor, and we're just trying to shuffle them through. Sometimes they distinguish between public defenders and lawyers when they say, for example: "I want a real lawyer". The sad thing is that in my perspective they'll get worse representation, especially when they are actually paying, because it'll be the worse lawyer that can be afforded, and there's no way that a paid lawyer will put the time in. The problem is that the news we have to tell them is so bad that they just cannot believe that we're just doing our job. We're the bearer of bad news who cannot do anything about it. I also understand that in Mexico, your success in court depends on the prestige of your lawyer. If they have had a contact with the legal system, then they come to a public defender without any faith that someone who comes for free can be effective. I certainly don't think that's the situation here.

The question of paid versus unpaid lawyers, and the respective quality of each, was a frequent refrain in these interviews. From my own experience with public defenders in the United States, the misconceptions about "free" lawyers are completely wrong-headed, for reasons articulated by a public defender:

> Access to justice issues interested me in law school. There is of course a huge segment of the population that doesn't have access to the justice system, and the only way they can have access is either through legal aid lawyers on the civil side, or public defenders. Through some of my work in law school, and prior to law school, it seemed like working as a public defender would be a good way to help people have a place at the table within the justice system. This seemed like something that would be an interesting opportunity for me to do. I don't really have any lofty reasons for doing it, I just think that it's a necessary role to play, and it's personally satisfying for me.

Despite his modesty, the point here is that this lawyer joined the office of the public defender instead of going into private practice because he wanted to help people who might otherwise lack proper legal representation for reasons that go far beyond professional responsibility. A former public defender offers further detail as to the types of parcours that bring serious and committed people to work as public defenders:

> I had a guy who asked me yesterday, he was lost, and he needed his permit. So I go up, and it took me twenty minutes to walk him through the process of getting his driver's license. But there was one case that was still pending, and he never went to court on it, so it was a formal thing, to get the court to waive it, or throw it out and be done with it. So afterwards the guy was trying to put money in my hand as we walked out the door, and I said: "No, no; for the years I spent in Central America, when they took me in, they fed me, they took my hand and walked me to where the bus was going to stop, so no, I'm not going to charge you for twenty minutes of helping some guy push some paper". My feeling is that I really owe it to those folks. I was in some fairly hairy situations in Nicaragua and Guatemala, where I could just as easily be dead in the jungle somewhere, but wasn't, because people took care of me. But I can't do it for nothing all of the time. I take kids over to municipal court all the time, though. They have the same thing, some tickets but no license, no proof of insurance, because you can't get insurance without a license, and they had been caught speeding, or whatever the excuse the cop used to stop them. Occasionally I would just group them together, four or five at once, because it's easier on me to take care of it, and then I'll give them a ride home when they're done, like five guys. They say afterwards: "What does this cost?" and I say: "Twenty bucks between all of you, for gas". But then I get a call six weeks later: "My brother is charged with murder". So I invite them in and they say: "What will this cost?" and I say: "Fifteen thousand, easily", and they say: "But you did my other ticket for $20!"

Public defenders generally articulated some version of this in the course of their interviews, making a convincing case for them being the right kinds of legal professionals to help undocumented immigrants, even over and above the question of cost. But the prejudices against public defenders, rooted in home country norms about class or gender, is just another way in which claimants can make bad decisions based on preconceptions:

> I think that generally people from Mexico are skeptical about the fairness of the justice system, and they have a sense that the person who has the most money wins. To become a lawyer there is often a class and status thing, and so lawyers, even more than in the US, tend to be upper class Mexicans. So they play into this system where people who have more

> money, win. We pursued three years and a thousand hours of litigation time for a client who was fired for trying to organize a union at his plant, and we lost on legal technicalities. At the end of it all he was saying: "I knew we would lose because I'm poor and the company's rich, so I never understood all along why you all thought we would win". That was at the end, the articulation of his final frustration. Through the middle he believed that the judge was paid off, and he believed that we were paid off. We brought boxes of pleadings and research and put it in his trailer to show him that we had been doing evidence, and other work on his case. It's hard. People have a reasonable narrative based on past experience.

These preconceptions often play out in ideas about the role of women in the host society, as a public defender explained:

> I think the main reason they do not trust me is the same reason my other clients don't, which is they are sitting in jail in little orange suits and I magically appear as if someone rubbed the genie bottle and I say: "Hi! I am here to help you!" That initially sounds really good, but then I start talking about them spending 8 years in prison, or something else equally bad, and they start thinking she said she was here to help me, but now she says, "I am really screwed. They do not know me. They do not know anything about me. They did not pay me. Their family did not talk to me". I think that part of this is a cross-cultural thing. When I go to court, I very much try to look like a lawyer, because I find it very much eases my interactions with my clients. There are public defenders who sort of look like public defenders, and I think that they have a harder time with their clients, particularly with people of lower classes who tend to sort of see identifiers and say "that looks like a lawyer". I think that may be even truer with my Hispanic clients, when I am wearing a suit and pantyhose and high heels.

These kinds of issues are particularly important in criminal cases involving domestic abuse, statutory rape or other gender-related violations that, as we've seen, make up a significant portion of the criminal charges against Latin American immigrants:

> Sometimes, like when I was working at Metro [police department in Nashville], I would get assigned a rape case. The client's lawyer is a woman, and the investigator is a woman, and he looks at us and says: "I'm lost here. I'm gonna lose. I'm accused of rape, and a woman is going to represent me? And my investigator is a woman? That's it. I'm done". I'm not going to say that we experience that kind of thing a lot, but it does happen, and I've experienced it right here in this office. We had a client who was a very macho figure, and he was pretty angry, an angry person. I

told the lawyer, "I think we have a problem because we are women, and I think he feels like because we are women, we can't be capable of defending him". Unfortunately, he fired us, saying he wanted another lawyer. He got another woman. At some point I saw her, and she said, "He fired me too! I think he needs a man". I've had that a few times. It doesn't happen very, very often. But yes, it happens with Latin Americans.

Another frequently mentioned issue is that undocumented immigrants, particularly Latin Americans, are accustomed to working with "notarios" in their countries of origin. A common scenario is that a Latin American inmate is assigned a public defender, he doesn't trust him, or especially her, and so seeks out a good male "notario" instead, as a public defender described:

> Notary publics from my understanding in Mexico are people you go to in order to get things notarized, but *notario* can also mean attorney, someone with legal experience. Obviously here, notaries are just notary publics. There are a lot of businesses that advertise this notary service, and people think that when they go there, they are talking to an attorney, when in fact it is just a notary. There are a lot of these businesses that do a little bit of everything for you: they will file your taxes; they will help you do paper work; and they just help facilitate things. But there is a lot of crookedness. People in a lot of businesses here offer to guide you through the criminal justice system, and sometimes they will charge $600 to $1000, sometimes more than attorneys, to just simply walk you through the process and interpret for you. Sometimes, people think that those people are lawyers. I think that the people are not saying they are lawyers, but they are also not saying they are not lawyers.

These gray areas cloud the many processes that unfold from the moment when an undocumented immigrant leaves the front lines and enters into the system. Almost every aspect of this process is foreign to most people, and this foreignness is gargantuan for poor, illiterate, unilingual Latin American farmers who have come to the United States and are working illegally, just as they are for poor illiterate Bangladeshi citizens who have crossed over the border to work in India (Ghosh 2012). Our conception as scholars or residents of First World countries is that there's a neat, codified legal system, but this is so far from the experience of these people as to lead us into profound questions, beginning with the most basic one: what, in a system like this one, is law?

What is law?

I wish to begin then by thinking about the experience of migrants once they have been identified as having irregular status in a host country, and then entered into the "legal system". In order to do so, I'll briefly turn to legal philosophy, and moreover, to the seminal work by Hart (1994). I'm not referring to his work in order to ask if the countries we are examining here have "legal systems", because in each case they do, but rather I am looking for what constitutes a "legal system" that applies to people who are considered "illegal", undocumented or *sans papiers*. By separating off this particular area of law, I hope to ascertain if the compendium of (arbitrarily applied) rules and regulations pertaining to undocumented persons should indeed be considered as a part of a recognizable legal system, or, on the contrary, if they constitute an assemblage of possible outcomes that are better understood in terms of prevailing ideologies and political exigencies. I'll then extend this question by asking if, given how unevenly and inconsistently it is applied, the so-called "law" that pertains to undocumented people can be deemed to have qualities relating to fiction.

As far as the overall legal system goes, Hart offers the following criteria:

> There are two minimum conditions necessary and sufficient for the existence of a legal system. On the one hand, those rules of behavior that are valid according to the system's ultimate criteria of validity must be generally obeyed; on the other hand, its rule of recognition specifying the criteria of legal validity must be effectively accepted as common public standards of official behavior by its officials.
>
> (p. 116)

Assessing this statement in regards to many of the utterances made by interviewees, there may be grounds for questioning the status of the judicial system that is invoked to punish undocumented immigrants, particularly in countries that are home to substantial undocumented populations over long periods of time. The United States, for example, is home to upwards of 15 million people who live and work without proper documentation; India is home to at least 10 million undocumented people who have come from Bangladesh and millions more from Pakistan and Afghanistan (*HT* Correspondent 2011); Libya is home to an estimated 2 million undocumented persons from Sub-Saharan Africa; and South Africa is home to a substantial number of undocumented people that some sources peg at 10 million individuals who are often scapegoated for many of the country's woes.

Many of these undocumented immigrants can live and work in relative impunity despite their constant vulnerability, since officials can choose to turn a blind eye; or, these same people can be suddenly subjected to arrest and possible deportation, particularly if they have been found guilty of some other crime in the past. A public defender provides a horrendous story from the American context:

> We have a case where a guy who was here illegally and doing well started a lawn mowing business. He and his wife were out in Hermitage, putting flyers for their business in mailboxes, driving from mailbox to mailbox.

> Some woman saw them, and didn't like that they were fooling with her mailbox and called the police. The police pulled them over without any basis, and ran the guy, and found out that he was illegal and had been previously deported after a felony drug conviction. So he is now looking at five years in federal prison and then deportation. You [the public defender] can suppress the stop. The stop has to be based on a moving violation, or some other reasonable suspicion. What they were trying to claim was that they were trespassing, fooling with mailboxes. But even if they do suppress the stop, what are they suppressing? They now know that the person is here illegally, they can't let him go out and then try to catch him doing something else, because [the fact that he's illegal is] out there now. We didn't have any recourse, even though the stop was bullshit. There are people like him who are arrested for minor offenses, and then there are serious immigration consequences, especially if they have been deported once already.

This kind of bad luck story, in which the migrant is in the wrong place at the wrong time, can occur because individuals are, by their very existence on the host country territory, "illegal", and also because there's a lot of ambiguity in the legal system in regards to some of the terms used in this description and the broader question of how ambiguity underwrites many legal procedures from the "reasonable" grounds to a stop, all the way up to interpretation of the constitution (Molot 2000).

An interpreter recalls a similar story, driving home this sense of how fickle and unpredictable the prevailing system is:

> I remember a very sad case we had recently of a guy, a Colombian fellow, who just had a little gardening business. In Nashville, you may have noticed that most of the gardeners are Mexican. This fellow was actually Colombian, but he was distributing his little cards, his business cards for his nursery on a street where the FBI had set up surveillance on a house where they knew some drug deals were taking place. Because he looked Hispanic and he was putting his little cards out, he got caught on videotape, and they went and picked him up and found out that he was here illegally. If they find you in this country illegally once and deport you, it is a misdemeanor. But, if it is the second time, it becomes a felony itself even if there has been no crime. I believe he had been deported previously and so he was in jail with felony charges because of this. He did not have anything to do with drugs. He was a gardener. Sometimes what I see is just heartbreaking.

Even despite such examples, however, in most host countries there is a kind of tacit recognition from officials that undocumented persons serve essential roles and that rounding them up and deporting them is simply not worth the effort, and so they rarely enforce (officially sanctioned) regulations. So what does this mean in terms of the "legal system", if it's an official structure that doesn't usually enforce its own rules?

Hart's oft-quoted statement concerning the nature of a legal system is in this regard helpful: "The assertion that a legal system exists is therefore a Janus-faced statement looking both towards obedience by ordinary citizens and to the acceptance by officials of secondary rules as critical common standards of official behaviour" (Hart 1994, p. 117). Once again, depending upon the time, the place and the people involved, we can suggest that when it comes to undocumented persons, it's not clear exactly what role the citizens should be playing here: does "obedience by ordinary citizens" include denouncing people who are undocumented? Furthermore, we know from the many examples cited thus far that common standards of enforcement aren't applied to undocumented people. Officials all the way up to police chiefs and even the President of the United States actively defy existing immigration laws pertaining to undocumented migrants. Does this mean that there's no "system?" We have thus far suggested that the entire process is arbitrary, implying chance and power relations, and discretionary, implying choice, and that both can be connected to ambiguity in the laws. But does this capture the entire image of what we have constructed thus far? Or can we say that the law that is sometimes applied to undocumented people is a kind of "fiction", upheld by both sides of the undocumented equation?

Fictional law

There are several *Oxford English Dictionary* (*OED* 2014) definitions of "fiction" that may apply here: "Feigning, counterfeiting; deceit, dissimulation, pretense"; "the action of 'feigning' or inventing imaginary incidents, existences, states of things, etc., whether for the purpose of deception or otherwise"; "that which, or something that, is imaginatively invented; feigned existence, event, or state of things"; and "invention as opposed to fact". Each of these definitions applies, variously, to the "laws" that are invoked to justify actions taken against undocumented people. Indeed, when considered from the perspective of undocumented people in (say) the United States or India, the mishmash of laws, proposed laws and discussions thereof combine to provide a fickle and inconsistent grand narrative that feigns legitimacy, but is, in fact:

1. a misrepresentation of which laws will be applied to migrants;
2. a series of inventions aimed at legitimizing illegitimate actions;
3. a misrepresentation of laws applicable to undocumented people at a given time.

Each of these characteristics pertains to the realm of fiction, so it may be useful to imagine that in some cases the laws and regulations we have been describing exceed the classification of the arbitrary, and extend further along the continuum, towards fiction.

And so as part of my effort to chip away at the very idea of borders and border control, it is useful to suggest that sometimes law is a kind of fiction, in the way that it is interpreted, or in the issues it raises. There are many cases in the real world that occur in the name of a version of law and order that are as arbitrary as the discretionary conditions that lead to them being invoked in the first place. This is often the case, one might argue, because the vast majority of illegal actions pass unobserved, or unprosecuted, and that this doesn't (necessarily) mean that the law that renders those actions illegal therefore doesn't exist. But in the case of undocumented immigrants, there is no recognizable set of laws that are consistently applied, and this is exacerbated by the vast and often contradictory array of laws, proposals and statutes that could apply, and can thus be invoked whenever officials for whatever reason feel like it. Furthermore, more organized decisions to enforce these laws usually come in response to the wishes of those who want to rid the country of "foreigners" for ideological, rather than legal reasons, and the actions that are taken therefore could have been taken at any time in the past but weren't, further complicating the undocumented immigrant's understanding of the legal apparatus.

And so the idea that there is a body of law that is applied to undocumented people to regulate their actions is, to follow one of the *OED* definitions, a feigned state of affairs, and undocumented people suffer from the ambivalence, ambiguity and discretionary application of law because, on the one hand, there is a body of law that can guarantee rights to people who are in the country illegally (rights to medical care, or education, or social services), while, on the other hand, the law can also promise terrible consequences if those negative elements regarding illegal immigration are brought to bear against the claimant. The definitions of fiction also give pause because they suggest, in terms like "feigning" and "deceit", that there may be some reason why law is in this case comparable to fiction. At the risk of sounding conspiratorial, I might add to our discussion the possibility that authorities that persecute and prosecute undocumented people do so fully aware that their actions will usually inflict suffering upon only a small proportion of the overall undocumented population. Furthermore, in many cases the real powerbrokers in a country are large corporations or other non-state actors, and it's well known that they may have very different interests. For instance, employers generally benefit from maintaining the marginal status of undocumented people in their employ because of the cheap, ample and necessarily non-union labor they provide (Chavez 2013; Schwartzman 2013). From this standpoint, the loud screaming about crackdowns and the draconian laws that are invoked against undocumented people can in many cases look like foils for the public to consume. And the occasional suppressions can easily placate or appease the local population when necessary (such as during election races), even as the laws that could be applied to the broad population of undocumented people are reserved for a small proportion of that population.

The problem with this argument, of course, is that it's not relevant for the thousands of people who are arrested and deported each year; it applies only as long as the undocumented people remain free and relatively unfettered in their actions. It's an interesting point, though, if only because it suggests that those in power to enforce, or not, these laws aren't as ignorant as the laws and proposals suggest they are. Any study that takes into account longevity and time considers the fact that it is generally the first generation of undocumented people that suffers, particularly in countries that have birthright. Efforts to strip children of these rights are rampant, of course, and some have succeeded (although it's unlikely that the law ensuring people born on US soil are Americans is likely to change). And President Obama's surprise decision last summer to use his executive authority to halt the deportation of some immigrants who were brought to the country illegally as children raised the ire of Republicans, but more importantly from our perspective is the fact that it's another way in which the draconian laws against undocumented people come to be mitigated or ignored. In short: more fiction.

This unequal application of law, the high levels of discretion at every level of the process and the degree to which local, state and federal laws can contradict or annul one another on particular issues make this particular legal system of potential interest for the realm known as "literature and law". Reference to this area helps us to situate the arguments here because its very existence has made us more aware of how law is represented in fiction, and how legal cases can be analyzed as regards categories of fiction, and with theories elaborated to study fiction. It is further motivated by the fact that lawyers and literary types who have developed interests in the law-literature overlap have concerned themselves with epistemological issues as they relate to the recognized "canons" of work, with the authority of interpretative strategies, and with the knowledge claims made in the realms of literature and of law.

So-called "literature" and the so-called "law"

The literature and law movement has been remarkably progressive and useful for pedagogical, theoretical and juridical reasons, and some of the most interesting and sophisticated work in literature has been undertaken by literature and law scholars, including Peter Brooks, Wai Chi Dimock, Richard Posner, Richard Weisberg, Robin West and Theodore Ziolkowsky. Nevertheless, there have remained gaps in which types of law or certain examples of fiction are chosen, which unduly limit the application of useful literary categories or theory to law, and the types of law deemed appropriate for consideration through literary or literary theory lenses. The range of genres usefully engaged could be expanded variously, of course, because one can cross any number of disciplinary lines by adding the "and", and produce valuable insights, particularly when one of the subjects considered happens to be literature: literature and religion, literature and philosophy, literature and anthropology, literature and language studies, literature and sociology, literature and ethics, literature and politics, literature and medicine – the list of existing programs or articles in each of these realms is vast. There are variations as well, such as the sociology of literature, or the politics of literature, or the ethics of literature, which extend this idea of cross-pollination. And given the vast array of subjects that can be treated by literature, one can easily envision papers or even courses on such combinations as literature and horticulture, literature and cooking, literature and architecture, or even literature and undocumented immigrants. But in the case of literature and law, law maintains its power and authority even if the law we're dealing with is arbitrary, as Thérèse Murphy (1996) aptly notes:

> If Disney World is a place where dreams come true, then law's world is the stuff of nightmares. It is a place full of facts, stripped of fantasy, fun and feeling. A place where the professional voice overwhelms all others and the virtues of precedent blithely trump those of justice. However, whether despite or because of this, law's public face retains an unassailable vibrancy. Its triumph is such that non-law or "law and" disciplines emerge as the also-rans. Their hyphenated worlds appear dingy when compared with the forthrightness of law. They are also beset by a grubby earnestness. We sense that these "other" disciplines seek empathy and, unlike law, have no stomach for absolute truth. With them, there are no certainties, there will be no resolution. This makes the choice between law and non-law and an uninspiring one.
>
> (p. 57)

Our example of law relating to undocumented immigrants challenges this tendency because in this instance law seems rather weak, dingy, fickle and fleeting, categories more usually associated with the hyphenated word to which Murphy refers here.

To provide some focus, and to suggest that it's not always as unequal or clear-cut a binary as Murphy describes, I would also suggest that literature and law is powerful in spite of the hyphen because the hyphen can also serve to remind us that law can bear characteristics associated with literature, and vice versa. For example, there are a plethora of legal themes in literature (crime, confession, revenge); there are many theories of narrative, language and fiction which have emerged in the literary realm and that can be applied to law (narratology, dialogism, reader-response theory) or that emerge from law and have great value in literature (evidence, examination, cross-examination, interpretation, judgment); both literature and law deal with questions of judgment and discernment; some legal texts can be considered inside of specific literary genres; there are overlapping themes of genre, canon, authority, representation, interpretation and evidence in both realms; there is a strong interest in stylistics, argumentation and rhetoric, which provides grounds for valuable cross-fertilization and discussion; and, my own hobby horse, there is the question of narrative "construction" which offers intriguing links between how we "construct a productive other" in legal settings, and how an author engages in similar issues when he/she creates a character in a fictional setting (Barsky 1994).

And so just as law students and practitioners in legal fields can benefit from the work undertaken in literary settings, students of literature can derive significant value from concrete legal examples. Furthermore, we are reminded through fiction that hard and fast approaches to subjective issues – be they "scientific", legal, formal, structural or otherwise – are easily challenged by literature when it arrives at the hearing, lampshade on its head, dancing, drinking and being the "trouble-fête" it plays so well. Fiction reminds us that proclamations in the third person (i.e. the undocumented immigrant experiences incarceration as...") can be challenged by actual interactions in the first and second persons (i.e. "I suffered because I was unable to communicate with my jailer..."), and that claims to monopolize the Truth can all be subjected to the subjectivity of real situations in which legal systems can become, as in this case, a collection of unapplied or even inapplicable norms, statutes and regulations.

But self-congratulatory work on the power of this overlap can be challenged by some difficult questions about the epistemological status of the two realms. If we say that there is much to be learned from literature and law, we presumably know what we mean by each of these categories, even as we recognize the institutional qualities of both. Here the waters are muddied, generally on the side of the literature, because the category we call "literature" is historically recent, epistemologically unstable and ever-changing. Even if, or perhaps because, the focus tends to be, or should be, upon the arbitrarily assigned category of "literature", I'd like to focus attention upon the more indubitable side of the equation, the letter of the law, to show that in certain cases, particularly those involving extreme levels of judicial and administrative discretion, the idea of the "law" can be considered as unstable as the idea of "literature", especially if the focus is upon the language employed in both (Dore 2006). It would be as reasonable in certain cases to point to (say) Kafka's *The Trial* as it is to invoke the federal statutes relating to deportation to explain why someone is doing 15 years in a federal penitentiary. For both instances, it's instructive to see what some of those who are writing about literature and law consider as their respective corpuses, their definition of "law" and their literary definitions. What follows, therefore, is a survey of approaches to the question of what constitutes law, a survey that is by no means exhaustive, but nonetheless is instructive as a way of delineating this other realm of fictional law.

What constitutes "law"?

The most-cited text in law/literature circles is Richard Posner's *Law and Literature* (1998) which offers what one might most expect in terms of institutional descriptions of "scholarship" from the two realms of literature and law:

> [U]ntil very recently both legal scholarship and literary scholarship were autonomous fields defined by a specific, narrowly circumscribed, and non-overlapping body of texts (the literary canon in the case of literary scholarship, and, in the case of legal scholarship, texts ranging from statutes, constitutional provisions, and opinions to articles and treatises – all written by lawyers) that were to be mastered by the application of a specific, narrowly conceived methodology. Literary texts lay outside the field of vision of the legal scholar, legal texts outside that of literary scholars. A recent blurring of the lines that separate different academic disciplines, and a growing professionalism and intellectual ambition in "soft" fields such as literature and law, got legal scholars interested in parallel fields, including literature, while literary scholars, as I have mentioned, have become interested in nonliterary texts, including those of law.
>
> (pp. 4–5)

These recurring references to "fields", blurred or otherwise, are institutionally inscribed, however, and therefore tell us little about what is to be considered therein except what is already considered as constitutive of it. This is perfectly useful for discussions of the literary canon or the corpus of case law, but it doesn't help very much in the question of how to talk about what we mean by "law", and therefore where the law/literature division could or should become meaningless.

One place to turn for clarity is to a very interesting overview of hermeneutic issues related in particular to the US Constitution, found in Levinson and Mailloux (1988). The preface names a key problem by calling attention to the (obvious) fact that "the meaning of texts is a central reality of any legal system", and that therefore all one has to do in a "mature legal system" is undertake interpretation and application of (written) documents "ranging from the wills of discrete individuals to the constitution of a modern nation state" (p. ix). Choosing which document applies to any given legal situation is of course part of the story we need to tell here, but presumably such a decision can be made, which lends at least preliminary validity to whatever interpretation ultimately emerges. But what if there are conflicting documents between municipalities, states and federal entities? Or what if a local government believes that a federal law is counter-productive, and thus encourages its front-line employees to ignore that federal law in the interest of promoting good government? Or what if there's such a level of discretion in regards to a particular area of law enforcement as to call into question the whole idea that there can be some kind of choice of which law to apply because the real question is whether or not to even enforce the law?

When put in this way, Fried's (1998) assertion in his "Sonnet LXV and the 'Black Ink' of the Framer's Intention" that the rule of law is premised upon the idea that "legal texts have meaning" as regards precedent, intention or whatever else is an equally valuable discussion to have in regards to immigration law; but the resulting well-worn dichotomy between those who look to foundational texts "under the banner of original intent" and those who believe that "interpretation must express a free response to contemporary conditions, mores and temperaments" (p. 47) cannot help us much if the original text(s) that subtends the debate is vague or disputed. This points to another level of "interpretation", but it pertains to the circumstance in which the text is invoked, rather than the text itself. Many discussions of literature and law, focused as they are on such issues as interpretative norms, varied methodological approaches and rhetorical politics raise a similar set of concerns because they already (legitimately) have some degree of investment in a particular set of applicable legal texts that will be applied. The fact remains, however, that no matter how questionable the meaning or varied the interpretation of some case file, statute, will, constitution, ordinance, writ or contract and no matter how similar or different the "legal language" used in any of these texts is to ordinary language or literary language, we can at least point to the text and assert or reaffirm the claim that it is part of the, or a, body of law. This isn't helpful if the choice of whether to even consult the text is a purely ideological, practical or ethical one.

In his contribution, entitled "Objectivity and Interpretation", Fiss (1998) helpfully reminds us that interpretation in literature and in law involves a "dynamic interaction between reader and text", and that "the idea of a written text, the standard object of legal and literary interpretation, has been expanded to embrace social action and situations, which are sometimes called text-analogues" (p. 229). It is particularly useful in this context to pursue the notion that "the appeal to interpretative analogy stems from the fact that interpretation accords a proper place for both the perspective of the scholar and the reality of the object being studied" (p. 229) because, in the realm of laws applicable to undocumented persons, the realm of discretion can go so far as to the question whether the text is a legal one and, if so, whether this text should be applied to the case at hand. It's also a very useful insight if we substitute (say) police officer for scholar in Fiss's example, but this isn't where he heads; instead, he ultimately assumes both the invocation of the text, be it what it may, and the stability of the legal texts in question. He refers derisively to "nihilists" who believe that "the text is capable of any number of possible meanings" because, as he claims, "legal interpretations are constrained by rules that derive their authority from an interpretive community that is itself held together by the commitment to the rule of law" (p. 248). This may be semantic, but it's a significant idea to which I think many people adhere, no matter what their perspective on these issues: law exists, and so does an interpretative community that is charged with the task of interpreting it, or even challenging it. With reference to this domain, though, there's a lot of room for maneuver in even figuring out what the applicable law is, and on what basis, and who at the end of the day can be deemed the interpretative community.

A humorous anecdote that gives pause as regards the text to which the judge is referring occurred in an interview I did in with a lawyer representing an undocumented immigrant who was pulled over for drinking and driving:

> All this goes back to the basic problem that DUI or alcoholism were treated as criminal issues, until I came up before a judge who had just gone through a very bad episode. I knew that he had some treatment, so I said: "You know, judge, this young man has never had treatment. And all of the charges are alcohol related". So the prosecution immediately fires back: "Oh here we go again, let's blame the alcohol, let's blame the drugs"! The judge looks at me and says: "The prosecution doesn't understand that alcoholism is an illness!"

In this little moment we are witness to a veritable paradigm shift, from law to medicine, from incarceration to treatment, in the same way that "driving while Mexican" (implying undocumented) can be just driving, getting from home to the workplace. A lot of this has to do with the presuppositions of the adjudicators, in this case the judge, who has set notions about the people with whom he is dealing that can have a bearing upon how fair the trial proceedings are, as is clear from this description from a lawyer:

> There's a mix of judges. I had a local judge here in general sessions' level, the entry level of the system. It was not my case. I was just standing in the courtroom. I hear a conversation come up, and the prosecutor says: "Judge, this Hispanic is an illegal immigrant and he claims not to speak any English." So the judge says "How can he not speak English if he's out there selling drugs?" So I perked up and said: "Judge, there's always that pesky presumption of innocence thing". And the judge says: "I understand, I'm not saying that he can't!" So I say "Really? It sounded that way to me. Shall we take a poll of the audience here? What the hell are you talking about?" But there are some judges who work with you and try to understand.

The reasoning applied by the judge is preposterous, and it offers a window into how decision makers in the field of law might consider what it actually means to be foreign to the host country. His default was to suggest that the claimant is lying, in evidence in regards to the question "How could he sell drugs if he doesn't speak English?" And his discretion, to (say) insist, or not, that there be a federally certified interpreter in the courtroom, is affected by his bias regarding how much English this claimant needs, and whether or not he/she possesses the appropriate linguistic skill.

Working with interpreters in a legal context

When present for the hearing, the skilled interpreter can play a crucial role at this juncture by bridging the complex linguistic gap, described by a federally certified interpreter:

> You have to be proficient of course in both languages. You have to have legal terminology down, you have to have knowledge of phrasings in the court, the way things are transmitted and conveyed and you have to be very quick to pick up dialects and different regional differences in Spanish, usually. It takes a lot of training to do that. I am aware of linguistic issues and cultural issues and certainly can read also the socioeconomic variables that go into the court room, different personal and interpersonal relationships and what's going on, and how certain people like to be treated, or need to be treated to feel like they are being respected, and so forth.

Even when a lawyer has access to a skilled interpreter, there is another rarely mentioned issue relating to how best to employ his/her skills. To this point the question has been how to interpret the text, or the testimony, but there is also the question of translating from source to target language, which also requires specific skills both on the part of the interpreter and the lawyer employing his/her services. On the interpreter side, a federally certified interpreter provides details:

> The goals of a professional interpreter are lofty. When you are waiting for a court procedure to begin, your conversation with that defendant is really minimal or nonexistent. You are basically a transcriber of sound, and while they may reach out and want to have some contact with you because they know that you speak their language and you feel empathy and so forth, you have to curtail your relationship to what you are there for, which is to be an objective and completely accurate conveyor of information from one language to another.

These "lofty" goals are difficult to realize, and many of the qualities that make for good interpretation even go beyond rich competencies in the source and target languages and into deeply complex realms like phrasing and tone:

> It's challenging to achieve these lofty goals of professional interpreting. Doing the actual work well means accurately interpreting and conveying

> exactly that which was said, maintaining a level of dignity, and treating the client with respect ... I am regularly tempted to phrase things in a way that's more sympathetic, and that would make [the lawyer] raise another question, because I can't just [provide an opinion]. I'm sure several times I have given into the temptation, but that does run counter to my professional commitment ... Now, there are ethics for a good interpreter, but obviously you are not a machine. Obviously there is tone of voice, and there are all kinds of layers to what you do. They [those involved in federal certification] really drill these things into you, and I think this is valid. And so you have to interpret the tone, and everything else. So for example if someone speaks harshly, you speak harshly. That hasn't happened to me a lot in the courtroom, but in the medical situation it has, where a doctor is being a total asshole. I will speak in a very disparaging way, and then after I am done [interpreting] I might roll my eyes at the patient, acknowledging that I can't believe he said this kind of thing, which is probably skirting the line of professional ethics. But by that time, the client probably knows me enough to know [what I'm doing]. So at the risk of saying that I fudge a little bit, I guess my humanity gets in the way, obviously. It is tempting to do that, but I think it is really my job as an interpreter not to interfere. My commitment is to be ethical, and to stay out of the way, but sometimes this is difficult.

In this example, phrasing and tone provide crucial nuance, but so too does body language, in this case the rolling of the eyes. This is a crucial area for the transmission of information beyond source and target languages, as a federally certified interpreter indicated:

> Body language affects the listener, and the cultural differences in body language I think can have significant effects. For example, if a Latino or Latin American person does not make eye contact but instead looks down, it is probably more a sign of respect than it is of guilt. We on the other hand would assume that not making eye contact creates suspicions. The cultural differences can have an ill effect on the situation of the immigrant, or the defendant, in terms of their relationship with law enforcement or even with court personnel. I am not involved in the process of assessing the person's credibility. I am just interpreting. So if [the lawyer] asks me whether I think they are credible or not, I would simply say: "I am sorry, that is not really an interpreter's role to make that kind of evaluation".

One way of thinking about this is as a dialogic process, and so lawyers who wish to derive maximum benefit from the interpreters should be trained to respect the boundaries of interpretive norms, for reasons explained by a federally certified interpreter:

> I am mostly a conduit. In fact, it is against the code of ethics of an interpreter for me to be an advocate if I am working in the legal setting. If I want to work in the medical setting, there is a little more room for actually advocating on the part of the client.... Sometimes they are very, very happy to have you there and they just start telling you their whole life story and you have to say, you have to answer the questions. You cannot talk to me. Please do not talk to me. Please talk to the attorney or the probation officer or whomever I am with, not to me.

Every lawyer, law-enforcement officer and judge with whom I conducted interviews was in favor of growing the number of interpreters and translators described in 28 U.S. Code § 1827 – Interpreters in Courts of the United States. One way to effect this objective would be to teach law students about the value and importance of interpreters because, as a federally certified interpreter explained:

> If it is an informal setting, or if the attorney does not understand the interpreter's role, then it is more complicated [for everyone]. We have four federally certified interpreters here in this area, which is very unusual for a small city. My colleagues have done an excellent job in training the attorneys around here, because the attorneys have to know what interpreters can do and what they cannot do, and how to use them properly. That makes all the difference in the world. One fellow that I work with cannot seem to get it through his thick head that we are not lawyers. We are not here to explain anything. And, we are not their personal friends. We are not supposed to befriend anyone, actually, or else our function is suspect, our whole role is not reliable. So it's a lot harder to work with those people. Depending upon the setting and the lawyer, the parties [to the hearing] can start to understand that things go perfectly when both the lawyer and the client start to forget that the interpreter is there. [In such cases] they look at each other, and talk to each other, and sometimes they even will not give the interpreter time to talk. They understand so well, and are communicating so well, that they talk over you, and then it all falls apart. But that does show that it was working very well.

The principles and the parameters of proper interpretation thus described are very stringent, and when interpreters are trained to this level of professionalism, they are expected to leave their allegiances at the door and carry out their assigned linguistic tasks with complete impartiality and resist the temptation to bond with the client. This is difficult, as an interpreter explained, because "people who speak the language that I interpret tend to want to see me as an ally". Since the interpreter is the only other party to the hearing who speaks the source language, "the clients want to trust that person, and turn the interpreter into a friend, someone who will tell officials their side of the story. People on the other side, like the attorneys, court personnel, are different".

This level of professionalization is comparatively rare, partly on account of how stringent the training is, but partly as well because the role of the certified interpreter hasn't been accorded the prestige it deserves and the interpreter him/herself lacks lack status (Katan 2009). This is a very interesting point because if translators and interpreters were respected in the way that (say) lawyers or doctors are, then they could be called upon to challenge prevailing assumptions about foreigners. I think that it's fair to say that it's the ill-informed who support the barrage of "English-Only legislation" in the United States (*New York Times* Editorial 2012), minutemen on the US-Mexican border (http://minutemanproject.com) or even the movement towards particular languages in Europe (Phillipson 2003) or in Africa (Vorrath 2011), and there's no professional group of translators who can explain the implications of these trends in the way that (say) the American Medical Association or the World Health Organization can in regards to health trends. Undocumented immigrants are often made more vulnerable by misinformation that could be challenged by professional associations, which could help ward off the nefarious effects of ranting call-in radio show xenophobes, or purposeful construction of hateful pronouncements against particular linguistic groups of the type we saw in the buildup to the Rwandan genocide.[1] Even when such efforts fail, they can still instill within the most dangerous segments of population the idea that the "foreign language", like the foreigner who speaks it, is going to undo the fabric of the nation, an ongoing discussion in places like Québec, Catalonia and Ireland.

A microcosm of this process occurs with each act of interpretation in court, and the nuances of this transaction have to be considered as we attempt to fully represent how the process unfolds within the legal system. An interpreter notes:

> It really varies a lot, in terms of whether the attorney is experienced or not with working with interpreters. A lot of attorneys find it difficult to adapt. Sometimes they just totally lose their common sense the minute they are in an interpretive situation. They assume they are not going to understand, and more than that, that they are not going to be able to evaluate the client they are working with. In fact, interpreters cannot do cultural mediation. [Nonetheless], in an attorney-client conference, if I have a sense that something is really missing and the clients are expressing a lot of doubt to me, I *might* say, before we get started: "I am taking my interpreter hat off right now in order to give you a little piece of advice. With a person who does not speak your language, and for whom you have to use an interpreter, you can employ all of the same techniques you would employ when speaking to an English-speaking person in order to verify what he is understanding. So, if he says that he is understanding

[what is being said], then I am not allowed to express an opinion about [whether or not I feel this to be true]".

This same interpreter offers some interesting comparisons between what people do in ordinary speech situations, and how to adapt the same procedures to interviews in foreign languages:

> How would a lawyer verify comprehension with an English speaker? He might say, for example: "Repeat back to me what I said, and tell me what you just understood?" The presence of an interpreter should not make a difference, but it does psychologically. The second thing that makes a difference is that messages are not necessarily as clearly transmitted as they seem, since interpretation depends upon the interpreter's degree of understanding of the message in the first place. Certainly in court, but obviously out of court as well, you can clarify things by asking more questions. In courtroom testimony, however, it is a lot more critical. The prosecutor brings the defendant in with his attorney. They just throw them together, and interrogate them about all the aspects of the crime, other players in the crime, and also try to get them to implicate other people. So, in those situations, especially where language is being used in a trickier way, the presence of an interpreter can, I think, be deeply problematic.

She also makes clear that some of the tactics that a lawyer might employ to assess the veracity of testimony can interfere with the work of the interpreter if he/she is not privy to the lawyer's tactics:

> Interpreters rely on understanding meaning in order to get a message across. If the meaning is not clear, or if the prosecutor is purposely trying to trick the witness, or to lead him into a certain situation, it may not work in an interpreted version [because of the nuances of the language]. An interpreter may feel like: "Oh my gosh, did I make a mistake last time? Because now [the prosecutor] is asking the same question, but he is obviously expecting a different answer". In such cases, as an interpreter I can feel that I've been put on the spot.

In certain cases, this means that the lawyer has to ensure that the interpreter is working with the appropriate utterances or texts, to ends that serve the case. In an example offered by a public defender, we come to realize how complex this task can be:

> I have a case where I represent a guy, and I think that he's the less culpable of two people who were stopped. A guy was driving from Dallas TX to Nashville, and there was cocaine in the car. He was driving with his

brother-in-law. After one of the proceedings, the interpreter said to me that my client's wife wanted to speak to me, and that she [the interpreter] was willing to interpret. So we're in open court, and it's recess, and there are lots of people around. My client and the co-defendant are within earshot. My client's interests are not at all consistent with his brother-in-law's, and we're basically going to testify against the brother-in-law. And my client is incredibly upset with the brother-in-law, because he feels like he was duped into participating in this transaction even though he had no idea that there were drugs in the car. He thought that they were going to Dallas to work. I'm saying to the interpreter: "I don't want to do this, we can't do this", and she is saying, directly translating to the wife: "I don't want to do this, we're not going to do this". The wife is like: "What the hell? We have an interpreter, and I want to ask you about my husband's case!" So I'm trying to tiptoe around the issue. I don't want to say anything. So I am trying to make stuff up, like: "I don't want the interpreter to become a witness to the proceeding". But what does that mean? Nobody understands what that means. And then the interpreter gets pissed, because she's saying: "I don't know who you think I am, but I'm not dealing with this". And the interpreter has no understanding [of the legal implications of what she's doing]. She doesn't know that we're going to testify against the brother-in-law.

These types of situations create the potential for a kind of "cross-pollution", as a public defender notes:

> Just because you send an interpreter to court does not mean that he can go back and listen to the defendant talk to his lawyer. He can go translate for the DA and then come into the courtroom. That is a kind of cross pollution that I think is maybe the biggest problem we are dealing with now. It is a real hard one to get anyone to understand because, by and large, my experience is that our judges do not speak more than one language and so they do not understand. They think an interpretation is an interpretation.

In short, on the front lines we need translators who can help convey the message by providing contextual and complementary information to the host country official; after the arrest, we need skilled interpreters who are familiar with the source and target languages *and* we also need to have lawyers who know how to work with interpreters. Furthermore, as the previous quote suggests, we also need interpreters who are sensitive to legal issues, as a lawyer indicated:

> Using a court interpreter is an incredibly awkward way to interact with clients. The interpreter is just repeating verbatim what you're saying, and verbatim what the client is saying, and that's the role that they have

> to play. They cannot become a witness to the proceeding, which would happen if they start gleaning information from the client that is not solicited. So I understand that they have to play that role. But it's difficult, because you start to speak in a kind of stilted manner. I just find it incredibly uncomfortable. With interpreters who are knowledgeable I am more comfortable letting them help with the relationship, and speak more extemporaneously, not just saying exactly what I have said. But either way, it's a very difficult way to interact with clients. You're presumably building this relationship of trust, but I just find it incredibly difficult, and I haven't learned exactly how to do it. For example, we had an interpreter with a client a few weeks ago, and I said to her: "Will you ask Mr. X if he has read his statement of rights?" And she just repeated that statement right to him, word-for-word. And I'm just sort of saying: "Would you please just ask him?" It comes to resemble a childlike interaction that is extremely frustrating. Afterwards the interpreter said to me: "Someone must not have trained you very well". I have had no training on how to interact with an interpreter, and I said: "You are making this extraordinarily difficult for me".

The entire act of presenting and translating information that is valuable to the case becomes by these descriptions extremely multifaceted, and far more complex than what we generally consider when talking about the conveyance of information in a trial. In fact, even in the literature and law movement, which does consider a host of narrative and linguistic questions, there is very little discussion about translation and interpretation across linguistic, cultural or even class lines, and, moreover, there isn't any acknowledgment of the subjective elements of the lawyer-interpreter-client-judge interaction that fully accounts for what is being described here.

Notwithstanding the distinction between translation on the front lines and interpretation in the system that I've insisted upon here, there remains amongst experts a divergence of opinion about how the expertise of the interpreter should be brought to bear in formal legal proceedings. A federally certified interpreter suggested in an interview that in spite of her general support for remaining impartial to the proceedings, there are circumstances when exceeding this mandate could be crucial to the proper transmission of information:

> Attorneys, for example, want to see me as a person who can be their assistant, and give additional cultural information, which is prohibited. I may give some linguistic hints, like if I know that someone comes from a country where the word "trial" means something quite different than it does here. For example, in Mexico the word that we use for *trial* is *el proceso*, which means *the process*, which starts with the arrest and ends with resolution. It is a lengthy and totally written process, [different from] the

> short oral debate thing that we call a trial, where there is an oral presentation of evidence before a jury. Likewise, the jury exists, but only recently have they started using juries in Mexico. So here in the US, the attorneys typically will tell the person what his rights are, and what the process might involve. They then set a date for a jury trial, but they might not go on and say what a trial means, or that the defendant has a right to a trial before a jury. And so if the attorney is not elaborating on the process, I might say to him: "It would be wise to verify what this person understands by the words 'trial' and 'jury', because even though those words exist for him, they may mean something different from what you intend, or else they may be devoid of meaning totally. And so I would suggest an explanation". I will go that far during attorney-client meetings, but not in court, ever.

This example suggests that a defendant may not even understand the nature of the process into which he/she has been drawn, and even a well-intentioned lawyer may not think to provide useful details that bear upon the case. As a general rule ignorance of the law is no excuse, but the very concept of law, and the mechanisms that specific settings offer as means of obtaining justice, can vary tremendously and without proper information clearly conveyed, the defendant can be at a significant disadvantage.

Judges and interpretative communities

One way to avoid the aforementioned problems would be to train immigration judges to speak target languages, or, at the very least, to be sympathetic to the challenges of interpreting. In response to a question about the viability of having judges hear cases in the language of the claimant, an interpreter said:

> I think it would be helpful, although you can never tell. Generally, I think it would be helpful because the cultural understanding would be different, I think, and the judge would appreciate difference in other ways, magnified ways, and also it would just keep tabs on whether something were being done accurately enough.

At the same time, however, a judge who speaks the language of the claimant may be biased against certain clients, or may exercise personal bias about the migrant's credibility. And so the argument that you always need highly qualified people can in fact lead to arbitrary or politically motivated bias against certain populations.[2] So we go from "how to interpret the law" to "how to interpret the defendant" to "how to use the skills of the interpreter", to "how best to train judges". Given how important the narrative is to justify the claim or defend the client, one would hope that there'd be some kind of training made available to ensure that the *right* story is told to the judge and jury, and that some agreed-upon law, enforced by a recognizable and well-understood process, would be upheld during the hearing. By this point, there are so many variables that a degree of arbitrariness has crept in, and this in the most formal part of the entire process.

To return to Murphy (1996), it may be valuable to return to the kinds of naïve observations she mentions as being typical of those posed by first-year law school students, such as those silly "But is it Law?" inquiries. As Murphy points out, the answer to the question: "What is Law?":

> ...rarely seems worth the hassle, given the irritating inevitability of the ensuing tussle. Thus, faced with the "But is it Law?" question, real options usually appear slim on the ground and vocal allies few in number. This makes for predictable, and depressing, outcomes. The misunderstood and hounded either retreat, despairingly, to seek out the commiserations of other "non-lawyers," perhaps to fight another day or they are co-opted by the "lawyers", comforted by dreams of inside attack or, more realistically, by the enhanced promotion prospects which come as reward for "hard law" expertise. Sometimes, these skirmishes stir up talk of dangerous supplements, bottom-up theory and outsider jurisprudence, but through it all, law school life goes on much as before.
>
> (p. 64)

The realms within which a legal "business-as-usual" approach can be challenged are those in which issues of exclusion or marginality are raised and discussed. Feminists, for example, can and should ask these questions, according to Murphy; using their lead, we need to start trouble, and we must:

> neither entrench nor melt the sex/gender binary pair and its terrible entourage: we need simply to fuzz them a bit and wait for the sparks to fly. Using Medical Law and Law and Literature, I think that we might be able to create just the right degree of controlled chaos.
>
> (p. 77)

This is important because speaking from outside of the usual interpretative community may eventually shift the sense of the "sayable".

On the other hand, Murphy's approach dreams of changing the hierarchy rather than wondering about the validity of the whole enterprise, and about the danger of relying upon some version of discretion to get there. Stanley Fish is wise to such eventualities, and to the broader issues at stake; as such, he places the community, which for Fiss only offers "authority", at the very center of the enterprise, therefore properly placing the subjective in the center of the whole process. I'll ultimately extend his argument beyond the scope of either the "text", as described in Fish (1982) or the "interpretative community", described fully in Fish (1990), by suggesting that in some legal instances, no such "community" exists to even look at the text, either because the text is ambiguous, or because it's not clear which, if any, text should be invoked because of the broad array of possible violations and the different texts that could be applied to each. For the moment, however, it's valuable to take Fish's views of Fiss's work under advisement, since they do inch us forward towards an extremely arbitrary law.

In commenting in this same volume upon Fiss's sense that rules "act as constraints on the interpreter's freedom and direct him to those meanings in the text that are appropriate to a particular institutional context" (p. 251) Fish writes:

> If the rules are to function as Fiss would have them function – to "constrain the interpreter" – they themselves must be available or "readable" independently of interpretation; that is, they must directly declare their own significance to any observer, no matter what his perspective. Otherwise they would "constrain" individual interpreters differently, and you would be right back in the original dilemma of a variously interpretable text and an interpretively free reader. To put the matter another way, if the rules tell you what to do with texts, they cannot themselves be texts, but must be – in the strong sense assumed by an older historiography – documents. Unfortunately, rules are texts. They are in need of interpretation and cannot themselves serve as constraints on interpretation.
>
> (p. 252)

This is useful in regards to our discussion, and the "interpretively free reader" provides a wonderful sense of what we might mean by discretion, even in regards to the text that the interpretative community chooses to employ for the case. The issues surrounding the interpretable text play directly into the issues of sometimes conflicting and usually unenforceable laws that are put forth in the varied settings that bear upon undocumented people. As valuable as this is to the question of how the status of interpretation relates to the text, however, it is in fact an understatement of just how subjective the whole process can be when the idea of "discretion" is extended to the point of becoming the overriding factor at each and every "judicial" and administrative level, including the decision of which, if any, "rules" apply and who, if anyone, will enforce them. Even at the more formalized levels of the process discretionary decisions are made that can have important effects upon the case (Wadhia 2010, 2011, 2012) and the front lines are nothing if not fickle. Nevertheless, Stanley Fish, more than anyone, brings us along the desired road towards oblivion by proposing that there can be no formalist approach to law because meaning is not, and cannot be, latent in a text. The meaning ascribed to the text depends upon which interpretative community is brought to bear upon the text, which suggests that the performance of the law is in some cases as important as the facts of the case. The best way to understand the Fish approach, and one which he in fact endorses by his own prefatory remarks, is to take any of the essays and discern its consequence in terms of this performance, what he calls the "practice" of law because "no matter what it's putative topic each chapter reduces to an argument in which the troubles and benefits of interpretative theory are made to disappear in the solvent of an enriched notion of practice" (Fish 1990, p. ix).

Dworkin (1985) adds another component to the argument when he describes legal practice as "not only when lawyers interpret particular documents or statutes, but more generally" (cited in Ledwon 1995, p. 29). Fish's interest in this idea stems from Dworkin's approach to legal interpretation, but he also makes some useful observations about the law per se when he refers to the fact that "propositions of law" can be considered to have either a descriptive quality ("no will shall be valid without three witnesses"), or a prescriptive quality (when, for example, the proposition is an expression of what the speaker wants the law to be, such as an affirmative action statement). Dworkin (1985) suggests that:

> propositions of law are not merely descriptive of legal history, in a straightforward way, nor are they simply evaluative in some way divorced from legal history. They are interpretive of legal history, which combines elements of both description and evaluation but is different from both.
> (p. 30)

What emerges in this essay is a sense of a legal chain, whereby:

> each judge must regard himself, in deciding the new case before him, as a partner in a complex chain enterprise of which these innumerable decisions, structures, conventions and practices are the history; it is his job to continue that history into the future through what he does on the day.
> (p. 40)

There is much that Fish likes, and dislikes, in Dworkin's ideas, but for our purposes the basic critique is that while trying to work through an approach which doesn't fall on the side of abstract law or pure description, Dworkin lands up with an effort to describe law as practice that nonetheless misses Fish's ever-repeated thesis that:

> interpreters are constrained by their tacit awareness of what is possible and not possible to do, what is and is not a reasonable thing to say, what will and will not be heard as evidence, in a given enterprise; and it is within those same constraints that they see and bring others to see the shape of the documents to whose interpretation they are committed.
> (Fish 1990)

This certainly brings a degree of ambivalence to the practice of law beyond the practice itself, a fact that is blurred in highly discretionary realms because the "community" of like-minded legal practitioners that Fish invokes doesn't always exist in such highly discretionary realms; so any law invoked therein is as fickle and unpredictable as the statute, law or pronouncement that is invoked for the case in question. We could suggest that legal action against undocumented people isn't even necessary because they are, as the nomenclature goes, already "illegal" in spite of the rights that all people have under international law.[3] As such, whether they are charged with any crime or not, whether they are charged with the same crime as another "illegal" or a different one, or whether they are punished, it's all coming from the same basic point of departure, which is that undocumented people are, by their very existence, already "illegal". Moreover, the question of what crime they come to be charged with is ultimately far less important than whether the option of even consulting the realm of immigration law is exercised.

In addition to the "What is Law?" and "Who is in the 'interpretive community' that will adjudicate whichever set of facts is presented?", we also have this relationship between law and time. Law gives an impression of internal coherence and relative stability, but this is another illusion. The existence and nature of actions deemed judicial are linked to the time it takes to (say) get someone out of custody, and so it depends on whether the undocumented person is held long enough as to whether or not he/she comes to feel the heavy weight of the law. In other words, every moment an undocumented immigrant spends in a legal space, for whatever reason, increases the chances of him/her being charged with something, as a lawyer pointed out:

> The thing about it is that it's not unusual. Look, there's a guy in jail whose got a criminal charge, and I go in and tell them I don't care where you come from, I don't believe in illegal human beings. All I need to know is, do you have papers? If they don't have papers I go straight to the clerk and ask what it's for, driver's license, speeding, DUI. If it doesn't say: "Hold for I.C.E.," then we're going to work something out to get him the hell out of here now. They don't want to plead you out for a sexual assault, because that's moral turpitude, so you're screwed with that one. But even if it's not that, it's not unusual that you call the next day and find out that he's still not out, and now there's a note on the file: "Hold for I.C.E." So some of those evil bastards understand, and wait until after they come back from court, and then they call the INS. So your best plan has just gone all to hell.

Arbitrariness and discretion in time

This idea, that the chances of a discretionary decision being rendered (pre-lawyer, one would assume) increase in time, creates a whole new area of power-inflected arbitrariness to worry about, particularly when people aren't given meaningful access to counsel, or even support from friends or family, which is often true in immigrant cases. Before the undocumented person is charged, he/she usually has no idea if he/she has any rights under the host country's legal system:

> If they can make bond quickly, they do not face the immigration issues. If they cannot make bond quickly, there is more likelihood of someone from the DA office calling Immigration, or the sheriff department calling Immigration. There is no rhyme or reason to it. I have had clients who have been serving sentences for involuntary manslaughter who never got an Immigration hold on them, and then people who just happen to be there more than 2–3 days, they get the Immigration hold, so there is really no rhyme or reason.

The crucial factor here is time. It's not just that the more time someone spends incarcerated the more procedures can be initiated against him/her, time is also linked to accessing legal counsel, interpreting or translating crucial information into a hearable form and, moreover, securing the funds required to make bond. As these variables come into play, this process, like so many others in our society, comes to be dependent upon socioeconomic means. An interpreter notes that:

> I saw certainly the disparity between being able to pay bond money and not. That is the big culprit of the socioeconomic divide. Once you can't, you're basically screwed. You are at the mercy of the court system. People have languished nine months in court to combat a charge that was likely untrue, and they were incarcerated the whole time.

Once incarcerated, it's often difficult for undocumented people to reach out to those who might help them secure representation and material resources. And even if they do have someone to contact, most undocumented people don't know where to find useful legal assistance and, if they insist upon a lawyer instead of a public defender, they may not have the resources to pay for useful guidance. And third, the friends and loved ones illegal immigrants call are themselves afraid of being apprehended, so they resist coming to offer any assistance. A minister who works with undocumented people said:

> Money makes such a huge difference because with mandatory minimums, if a kid gets stopped for drugs and the mandatory minimum says there is going to be no negotiation, then once this charge goes down and they are convicted, the judge has absolutely no discretion. But if he has money and a good lawyer, he can get kicked out of the system before he gets to the conviction. That's where the negotiation

> happens. People without power and money have no way to do the front-end negotiation.

At this point it's worth calling next upon one of, or perhaps the founding theorist of the law/literature enterprise to make sense of all this. In his landmark book (1992), Richard Weisberg offers a very promising distinction at the outset which in fact helps trump the issue of "field" of law by suggesting engagement in "the delightful task of associating two major human enterprises: establishing justice and telling stories" (p. ix). His subsequent elaboration of terms (and his attacks on Richard Posner's approach) lead him to describe the fields in terms of respective tasks, which usefully bypasses the epistemological issues I'll discuss below. According to Weisberg, when we consider the lawyer's work, the way that they "talk, the way they rule, the way they figure out what has occurred – these pursuits represent for the literary artist an analogue on the level of coercive reality to their own more private but equally verbal pursuits" (p. x). Here, the problems of discretionary, arbitrary or fictional law remains, but all of this uncertainty is shifted over to the lawyer, who must determine where the law that he/she is trying to work through is located.

Marie-Christine Leps (1992) takes on the question in a usefully divergent way by asking not about the law, but about the composition, definition and articulation of the "criminal" in the 19th century. This approach towards the recognized "nature" or reality of the criminal helps us to realize that the "criminal" is a category that shifts in regards to "the relation between the status of a discursive practice (as scientific, informative, or entertaining discourse), its mandate in the social production of knowledge, and the limits of the sayable" (p. 3). What we can say about the criminal, and on what basis, is a fascinating corollary to the question of how fictional law produces criminals, and how in a particular social discourse universe this could somehow be legitimized – on the basis of stereotypes, fear mongering or "scientific evidence" – if only to allay the conscience of the society supporting such actions. Formalistic approaches to law or rigidly prescriptive ideas of what constitutes the criminal are hereby understood in a properly fluid context, an approach that certainly applies to, say, criminalized migrants in our own era.

This is useful for our purposes because a problem we're facing now is to figure out who is acting in a criminal fashion. The tremendous power handed over to law enforcement, combined with ignorance of rights, means that the "outsiders" to the host country don't really know what the legal standards are, and what they should be led to expect if apprehended. They may not be "criminals" when they are stopped on the front lines, but with the passage of time and missteps, they can be transformed into criminals and, along the way, they can waive the rights accorded to them as such. One example is driver's licenses, or (in certain cases) driving certificates that are given to people who cannot demonstrate that they have legal status in the country. The rules for procuring the right to drive often shift, and an investigation into the effects that this is having led to yet another layer of discretionary action, in this case an investigation against the reporter who wrote the news story about these regulations:

> There was a project in the law school here to look into license issues for immigrants. They got quoted in a story for the *New Sentinel*, a big story about all of the difficulties in this driver's license issue, especially the continually-changing goal posts as to what you need to get a license: today it's a water bill, tomorrow it's a certified letter from God.

A few months after the story appeared, "the FBI knocked on her door. She calls me and I said 'you tell them I'm representing you and go the Hell away'". Without this advice even she, a law school researcher, can come to feel like a criminal even though, as this lawyer tells it, the real crime is committed on the other side of the judicial line. This reflects the ambivalence felt within the legal system itself, where, on the one hand, officials want to make life bearable for undocumented people by (say) allowing them the right to a driver's license, but, on the other hand, make it clear that these undocumented people should not only not have the right to drive, they shouldn't have the right to be in the country.

All of this ambiguity leads to the kind of confusion we have been describing, and to a host of queries; what messages are we sending to people if as "illegals" they can "legally" procure a driver's license, "illegally" procure employment, "legally" marry and have a child who has birthright, "illegally" enroll that child in a school and then perhaps gain pardon somewhere down the road for having entered the country illegally in the first place (Johnson 2012)? Furthermore, given the huge numbers of undocumented people all around the world, what can we say about their experiences as "outsiders" and, moreover, how can these narratives find a sympathetic ear?

Caring and the narratives of the outsider

A number of texts that are addressed to issues of feminism and excluded voices in the courtroom and the justice system are valuable for this discussion because they challenge "the methodological norms of legal scholarship" (Heinzelman and Wiseman 2012, p. 44), while sometimes arguing against (negative) discretion with (positive) discretion. In some ways, this book could be conceived of as a critique of arbitrary or discretionary decision making or actions, or, on the contrary, it could (and often is) an argument in favor of positive discretion that advocates for non-enforcement of unjust laws. This leads us to question what is meant by justice in cases dealing with the extreme margins of society, like undocumented people or homeless people or those who are not given voice, for whatever reason.

Coughlin (1995) addresses this area by discussing:

> alternative methods and languages that will include their distinctive perspectives' in the hope of repairing "the partial accounts of outsiders" lives embedded in conventional scholarship and, ultimately, to supersede the type of self-effacing "objectivity" exemplified in current legal theory and practice.
>
> (p. 1230)

All of this is to be achieved through the telling of outsiders' stories, with the assumption that "storytelling...has a radical transformative potential" (pp. 1230–1). The assumption is that if outsiders such as irregular migrants are given the chance to speak openly they will challenge the traditional narrative boundaries that exist within and beyond the legal domain. There are two obvious obstacles to this objective in the realm of undocumented people: their "illegality", and the likelihood that they will not possess either the appropriate forum or the linguistic abilities in the host language that would be necessary to present competing stories within the social discourse. Furthermore, the idea that life stories or autobiographies can have a redemptive value depends upon whether a viable outlet exists for their narration and diffusion, as in, for example, the (growing) realm of books containing "immigrant voices"; more importantly in the legal realm, certainly in the short term (before "outsider stories" have an effect upon the social discourse), this assumes that these outsiders will not only be given the right to speak, but that they will also be "heard" (Bourdieu 1990).

In cases of migrants who have found themselves on the wrong side of the discretionary fence, this aforementioned ability to create an utterance that can be "heard" within a community of adherents speaking an authorized language is far from obvious, and, interestingly, this is true on both sides of the power equation. Wal-Mart executives would probably prefer open borders, but officials in that company aren't likely to campaign for them, just as workers would prefer to work legally in different countries, although unions representing them are unlikely to support such an effort either. What we are left with is an upper level of power with contradictory aims: to appease corporations who desire open borders while at the same time pandering to an occasionally xenophobic block of voters whose fears and rancor in the face of (say) high unemployment figures or Ebola outbreaks can verge on the hysterical.

This whole complex, contradictory enterprise is made manifest by a rough-and-tumble group of administrators working nightshifts in prisons, desk shifts in jails or patrol shifts in police cars who, if the donuts aren't fresh, the night is too long, the noise is too loud or the *O'Reilly Factor* too convincing, just might decide to make all of the worst night-time phone calls to Homeland Security, ICE or the FBI, those little gestures that can wreak such havoc. There are multiple reasons why this call might be made, including the belief on the part of certain incarceration officials that doing so is a way to protect themselves from retribution later on. By acting on the basis of this fear, we might suggest that they are "caring":

> About the people in the jail making a discretionary decision as to whether or not they are going to call [immigration officials], or all that kind of stuff. I'm sure that does go on. I can't speak for every jail, that's for sure, but the way that I had always trained my folks is that they are obligated to call. Here's why: If a guy comes in and he is illegal, and they know it, but they're not going to make a call because again it's a small little thing, no big deal. But when he's released, if he happens to kill someone, or some kind of a thing, they are going to find out that he was just in jail two days before. Now we're in trouble because [they will ask]: "Why didn't you call? It's the procedure".

To "care" is thus a crucial but complex term for this area of work because like the discretion that may compel or allow us to care, it can be a double-edged sword when exercised. Robin West (1999) speaks directly to this issue of caring in her very humanistic work that demands not only a better approach to specifically female persecution, but a whole new approach to justice. West refuses the Kantian insistence upon the primacy of a blind figure of justice that, in an unbiased, uncaring fashion, simply weighs the facts of each case as though they were so many widgets with values prescribed by an overriding (and of course fundamentally masculine) economic system. Along the way, she also launches upon a number of anti-postmodern tirades so as to demonstrate as clearly as necessary the nefarious qualities of any approach which, by obliterating the idea of a stable and situated subject, refuses any discussion of essentialized (female) experience, and thus opens the door to the worst kinds of abuse. This is a provocative and powerful notion, but its focus on an ethic of "care" can be undermined by the very discretion she favors. West's sense of this ethic is that:

> If it is true, as relational feminists claim, that the act of caring for others to whom we are connected in some way is central to our moral lives, then our capacity for care should be at the center of our understanding of our public and legal, as well as private and personal, virtues, and specifically that it should be central to the meaning of "legal justice".
>
> (p. 23)

On the other hand:

> For most of our history, however, our capacity to care has not been regarded as necessary to the capacity to do justice (indeed it is more

> typically regarded as antithetical to it) and the result has been a deformation of both the private ethic of care and the very public ethic of legal justice.
>
> (p. 9)

Furthermore, we might argue that the problem in the realm of undocumented people is the very fact that people "care" about people who are acting "illegally", just as we might claim that the problem in reproductive rights or sexual orientation or proclivities is that people "care" about other people's private lives. We tend to like "care" when it is directed in the direction we favor, just as we don't mind discretion as long as it ensures that it will be exercised in favor of that in which we believe, like providing leniency in sentencing. A lawyer provides a sense of this issue:

> Immigrant clients, like many clients, think that we're part of the system, not much different than the prosecutor, we're just trying to shuffle them through.... The problem is that the news we have to tell them is so bad that they just cannot believe that we're just doing our job. Until recently, when they changed the sentencing via a case in the Supreme Court, making it very discretionary again, at least for a time. Before that we were going with the grid, within eight months. They simply cannot believe it. They say: "I did five years before I was deported for that crime, and now you're telling me that they're changing my sentence from one to five years? I already served out the time for that crime". They say: "This is the biggest mafia in the world". We're the bearer of bad news that cannot do anything about it. A lot of these crimes have no defense, and all the guidelines were very high, like five or more years. Our ability to get them better sentences is almost non-existent unless you can get the whole case thrown out on a suppression issue, like an illegal stop. Otherwise there's not much you can do. I also understand that in Mexico, your success in court depends on the prestige of your lawyer. If they have had a contact with the legal system, then they come to a public defender without any faith that someone who comes for free can be effective. I certainly don't think that's the situation here.

In this case whether or not the public defender or even the judge "care" about the migrant, they cannot help to remedy the unfair minimum sentencing regulations herein described. An investigator who does work for immigration lawyers stated that:

> I just think that the punishment is just too severe. The punishment for illegal reentry after the commission of a felony is very severe. It's just very severe. I think you might need to be treated case by case because sometimes you might have a felony, like, for example, they count points

> for each conviction, right? But suppose you have a felony conviction of cocaine that you were dealing, say half a gram, or whatever, to make it a felony, whatever the minimum amount of cocaine is a felony. Okay, and so you might have somebody who was dealing like five kilos. When they count the points assigned, it's the same number of points. I think you would have to do this case by case.

"Case by case" is precisely West's point here, but even in this example it could cut both ways. To allow for discretion is also to hope that the determination would be done with the kind of respect and compassion that West envisions.

The other way in which West's approach is undermined in the current juncture is by demonizing everyone who commits certain crimes. The best example of this is the categories of crimes that have been instituted as work-arounds to national justice systems, such as the "War on Drugs", "terrorism", "illegals", and any action that involves guns. "Illegal" people by virtue of their foreignness are deemed to be smuggling drugs across borders, engaging in some kind of international terrorism and, naturally, packing heat. These are the actions most associated with undocumented people, and they also happen to be the categories that bear the direst consequences. A lawyer drives the point home:

> If someone is caught with a gun, unless we can get it suppressed based on a constitutional violation, our job becomes basically holding that person's hand as he is sentenced to five or seven or ten years in federal prison for something that could have been avoided.

What becomes apparent when we examine the crimes punished most vociferously is that the cards are generally stacked against poor people because they are the ones who are out past midnight in public places, in the same way that the cards are stacked against Latin Americans in particular because, as one public defender notes, "the great majority of clients I have are not your stereotypical gangbangers who are using the gun in a threatening manner. The guns are just part of the fabric of that community". Once again, West's idea of "care" can be turned against these people, as the local population demonstrates "care" for "me and mine" by turning away those criminal illegals.

Beyond the cultural dimension, there are also the many ways that being poor, marginalized or fearful can lead to inappropriate actions, as a public defender notes in regards to one of his Guatemalan clients who, interestingly, suffers the consequences of having learned habits typical of the host country:

> I have a guy who was sentenced in November who was in his second year of college, a 26-year-old guy who had been in state prison. He has a family, he was the only member of a parent-teacher organization for his daughter's school, and he got caught with a gun. It was a very strange

> set of circumstances. The police came to his house, actually his sister's apartment, in response to a loud music complaint. He didn't even realize that the music was loud. The apartment complex is in a bad neighborhood, it was around Christmas time, and there had been home invasions. There's this conventional wisdom that around Christmas time robberies and home invasions increase because people are looking for money and different stuff to give away as gifts, or to pawn. Whether there is any empirical evidence backing that up I don't know, but there's a perception that around Christmas time robberies increase. So there's a bang at the door, he doesn't know who it is, he goes to the door and says: "Who is it?" He sees nobody, because the officers are standing by the wall, out of range of the peep hole. He repeats himself two or three times, and finally he thinks: "Someone wants me to open the door to rob me". So he goes to bedroom, gets a gun that the sister has in the bedroom, puts the gun in his waistband, flings the door open, and there's a police officer there. He's now doing forty-six months. And it could have been worse.

This example is remarkable in the way that it recounts a story of someone who has integrated into his environment, and become aware of local norms, which arguably leads him to act in a "caring" way by ensuring that his home is safe. Since he has learned the wrong messages from the social discourse around guns in the United States, the only solution is education on the front lines, as prevention, says a public defender:

> I think that it's critical to have outreach in communities where guns are part of the fabric of that community, and to say: "I don't know if you're aware of this, but when you pled out to some small crack charge when you were nineteen years old, you cannot have a gun, to protect yourself, your family, or anything. You cannot use a gun". I think we'd be doing a great service to lower income communities if we got out and explained that to people, because fathers, sons, and brothers are going away for crimes that they've already served time for. If the crack charge, or indeed any drug or gun charge, happened in Mexico, it still counts, as does previous deportation, so the law about guns, otherwise relatively straightforward, can come to be modified completely in particular situations.

There may be a better way to "care" for people, which is to develop a greater degree of understanding and empathy for their plight. This ensures that people don't care in the abstract, as in caring about your country and doing so by keeping out foreigners, but instead "caring" in the way that we might care for a nanny or a housekeeper or a babysitter we like and trust. We often hear stories about people who are against undocumented immigrants, with the exception of the people who they employ to do work in their homes. This comes out of a caring in proximity; you care about someone, or you are emotionally invested in someone, simply because you know him/her (a phenomenon often studied in medical settings, cf. Konczal and Varga 2012; Lewis, Valentine and Waite 2014; Meloni et al. 2013).

Interpreters as caring mediators

In the previous chapter I outlined the criteria for good translation on the front lines, and a lot of the positive discretion for which I advocated could be subsumed into this category of caring. There may be a way to practice this kind of caring in a formal judicial setting as well, even with the more rigid linguistic criteria set forth by federal certification. Although interpreters are constrained by professional norms, they can still provide subtle, non-linguistic contributions to interactions between the host and home worlds if only by setting the client at ease. A public defender explained:

> I actually think it helps because it is someone who seemingly has a background potentially similar to his or hers. I think that is someone they tend to be drawn to, someone who speaks their own language. They always seem to like the interpreter way more than they like me. Working with an interpreter really, really helps, even in situations where my clients will say they speak English, and, on a basic level, I can communicate with them. Bringing in the interpreter not only enhances the communication, but I think it improves the whole relationship. It is a person to trust. It makes them feel more comfortable, and I think that it facilitates the whole process, and enhances it for everybody.

So much of this mediation relates to trust, which is the central quality that contributes to the claimant's ability to tell the appropriate story, as a lawyer suggested:

> It is not so much the culture as the language. They trust someone that speaks their language more, and I do not think it is really a cultural thing. As you know, the Hispanic culture is very divided within itself. I think it is more of a language thing. They are just happy that someone can speak their language and explain things to them and they can explain their story to the court.

On the other hand, there may be drawbacks for some lawyers, who feel that the presence of an interpreter can become an impediment to building an appropriate relationship with the client:

> Building a relationship of trust and understanding is probably the single most important thing that can be achieved, whether English- or Spanish-speaking. And it's so much harder doing that using an interpreter,

> because there's proof positive that there's this linguistic and cultural gap that compromises one's ability to advocate on behalf of the client, there's no question about that. It makes me look at the case differently. You hate to say that the cases in which you become more emotionally-invested are the cases where you're going to work harder, but I think that this is probably what happens. I think that it's harder to become deeply invested in a case when there's a huge gap.

This could be an argument for making foreign language training an integral part of the law degree, and to training lawyers to achieve a near-native ability in the language(s) of their eventual clients. This may be an argument as well for employing investigators or researchers from countries of origin for law firms engaged in immigration work, so that they can help the attorneys understand the cases to which they are assigned, and also help develop a trusting relationship between lawyer and client:

> Almost none of [my clients] trust me at the outset. I feel that in virtually all of my cases. I've come to expect this, for all of the reasons that we have discussed. It's critical to develop the relationship not only to have clients who trust and have confidence in you, but because at the end of the day, they are going to plead guilty because there is no defense, and an early guilty plea is one of the few ways to guarantee a sentence that's going to be lower than it would be after a conviction and a trial. A lot of what we do in that context is mitigation, sentence mitigation, trying to put forth evidence about the client's background and family, and that requires a lot of trust for the client to open up to us, to give us access to the family.

Lawyers who can communicate in the language of their clients have a much better insight into their cases, and promulgating language teaching in law schools could help provide jobs for immigrants in the host country. A former undocumented immigrant who now works as an investigator provides a sense of her value for the clients:

> I think that my role in their case is not only as an investigator, but I am their contact person. If they have any problems at the jail they call me. Or if they want me to tell the family or call the family I can call the family. I can call Mexico. I can call El Salvador. I may wind up calling Colombia.

The difficulty in the current juncture is finding people who have sufficiently proficient linguistic and cultural competencies. A public defender describes the obstacles:

> It's never simple, there's always gender and race and country of origin, all of these different things playing in. So it's important to be sensitive

> to them, and to have people that have the capacity to understand these issues. But I don't think you can find any one person who could mediate all of those things. The thing I would say is that it's important that the organizational structure of an institution be evaluated for its cultural capacity. Are your offices comfortable to people? Does your system of intake allow people to bring their problems? How do you deal with English proficiency? and so on.

Cultural competency also includes the ability to recognize the challenges that the client faces on account of his/her level of education, the milieu from which he/she comes and his/her knowledge of the host country. A lawyer describes this issue:

> Did they go to 10th grade in this country or did they get to high school in their country? And what does high school mean in their country? You have to also figure that out. Not just that they are able to talk to you, but that they might not even be that educated and even in their own language, and so they cannot understand what has been said in any language. I have represented a lot of people who only went to grade school, and then dropped out of school to help their family or for whatever reason. And so that is another thing you have to figure out for communication. So it's not just whether or not they speak English.

One of the ways in which the client's education level or home country cultural milieu is manifested is through the use of slang, which can be very localized:

> There are some people who did not even finish grade school in their country and cannot read their own language, so sometimes it is hard to get them to grasp the legal concept and the processes. There is that, and then there are lots of people who speak Spanglish, and use a lot of slang. My own Spanish is from 1960, and then you have people who have more modern slang than I do, and also there are a lot of words that have become Spanglishized. Like, I have heard people refer to the word for type will say *typeya*, which is not a real word.

In addition to local slangs, there are also regional differences, from country to country, and from class to class. A Latin American public defender noted that:

> There are different linguistic issues. I cannot understand Puerto Ricans for anything, anything. Sometimes Salvadorians slip into a slang that is so difficult that I just have to say: "Hold on!" And sometimes with my Cuban clients I have to say: "Would you please quit speaking Cuban and speak Spanish!" They all laugh. They all actually know what I mean, and they sort of clean up their language and get it back to more standard

> Spanish for me. So there is some dialect stuff, and then just sometimes my abilities are not quite up to the speed or the vocabulary that someone is using.

Spanglish and slang when misinterpreted can lead to disaster, in both Convention refugee hearings and immigration hearings, as a lawyer indicated:

> In Spanish if you have brothers and sisters, you would say the word *hermanos*, which is male. Then it got all confused because the interpreter said: "I have 5 brothers". Later on, it came out that he [the client] really had 3 brothers and 2 sisters. And then she [the judge] thought: "Well, he is lying". I said: "No, ma'am, he is not lying". That is a problem with literal interpretation, so even though that is a minor point, it affected his credibility with the judge.

Beyond the purely linguistic issues, a public defender provides an example of what an appropriate intermediary can do, even after the claimant is in the system:

> We have an investigator in our office that is from the Dominican Republic. She is really our only connection to the families. A court interpreter is not going to meet with the family, that's not a service they provide. So without someone internally who can speak Spanish, and more than speak Spanish, can identify with the cultural background, I don't know what we would do. We have a person in the office whose primary role is to do outreach with the families. That becomes a facet of her investigation of what's going on. If we think that he might be less culpable than a co-defendant, or might not be giving us the whole story, then we generally go to the family to try to figure out what is going on.

The role of this investigator is similar to the kind of "translator" for whom I've advocated on the front lines because she is investigating around the edges, rather than interpreting in a formal setting. Without these intermediaries, the levels of trust and caring essential to the process of building a defense can get short-circuited. For this reason a public defender suggested the following:

> I try to impress upon them that they are going to be participants in their defense, and that it's necessary that they communicate with me effectively, because ultimately that is going to help them. I try to make it more of a relationship of equals, to get together and try to resolve this with them in the best way possible, and let us recognize that there are going to be barriers. But in order to do the best we can do, we are going to have to work to get past those.

There is an area of literature and law that relates to the above-mentioned processes of drawing out appropriate narratives and live stories, and it relates to the crucial category known as confession.

Crises and confessions, in literature and in law

The final set of law and literature texts offers some suggestions as to where we might be headed, either with the fiction that relates to law, or with the fiction that law can become. One approach is Brooks' (2000) discussion how a confession can be as "problematic" as fiction:

> To do its job – to pass judgment – the law needs to insist upon traditional notions of responsibility, including responsibility for acts of confession. Yet what we learn about confessions from literature, from the religious tradition, and from the psychotherapeutic culture, suggests that where confession is concerned, the law needs to recognize that its conceptions of human motivation and volition are particularly flawed, even perhaps something of a fiction. Hence its heavy reliance on confessions in criminal justice creates a certain unease.
>
> (p. 5)

Motivation for undocumented people who are asked to narrate some aspect of their life story is notoriously difficult to understand because what they say has everything to do with what they think that the official wants to hear. Furthermore, confessions of guilt, true or not, are often uttered by migrants who are just anxious to sign any kind of declaration in order to put an end to their interaction with authority, giving up crucial rights:

> It's still an open question as to how long it is taking people to get into that national loop, and what rights they are giving away before that happens. There's a fairly developed legal rights education system going on in Florence AZ, and places like that, where they enter the National Immigration Detention Center system that will lead to their deportation. But if people are spending 30 to 90 days in Blank county before then, and being asked to sign voluntary departures, they are being asked to sign away custody to their kids, to make all these really important legal decisions without the advice of counsel and without any sense of what their legal rights are, that's very disturbing.

If literature helps us understand the complexity of human motivation and volition, then it's all the more valuable in this realm, in which the motivation is complexified by the legal status, the fear and the cultural differences of the person doing the confessing.

One area that Brooks couldn't imagine, given his corpus, is the hearing in which a claimant offers a confession, or a plea, on the basis of information he/she doesn't understand or information that is incorrectly translated. A lawyer provides an example:

> I was in Dayton County, where they had the historic monkey trial at the historic courthouse. I was on the side of this Hispanic kid who was charged with vehicular homicide. While on his way to work he fell asleep, crossed the center line, hit someone, and killed him. I went down there to represent him. I'm sitting there, and there are lots of Hispanic folks because it's farm country. They were looking for someone to translate, and so someone says "Go get Paco, somebody said Paco is around". Paco had done eight months in jail and had become the darling of the sheriff and the judge, so they went to go get Paco. I'm not saying anything, I'm just from out of town, visiting, I'm going to hang out here to see what's happening. So I go up and stand next to Paco while he's translating, and I'm just saying: "Don't mind me, I'm just standing here". So the judge says to Paco, "You understand son, you have the right to go to trial". Paco translated this as: "You don't want to go to trial, you'll get more time". The judge says "You have a right to have a lawyer with you today". Paco says, "You can have a lawyer, but that means that they are going to continue it, and you don't want to do that, best thing you can do is plead guilty". So I finally got the judge's attention and said, "Ah, pardon me judge, I'm not so sure Paco is doing a real good job translating!" It may be a problem, it may not be a problem, but that was what was passing for translation. And I don't think it has changed, even though there are new rules, of where you have to have someone who is trained. But the rule is, if you don't have a certified translator, then you have to have a registered translator. And if you don't have a registered translator, you can have uncle Joe. And if you don't have uncle Joe, you can have Paco. It just keeps coming down until Paco gets right back into court.

This phenomenon has shifted in the American context subsequent to a Supreme Court case in the United States (28 V 119 § 1827) that now stipulates that "the Director of the Administrative Office of the United States Courts shall establish a program to facilitate the use of certified and otherwise qualified interpreters in judicial proceedings instituted by the United States". This follows many of the recommendations proposed thus far, as regards courtroom interpreting, but the next paragraph keeps the door open to Paco:

> Only in a case in which no certified interpreter is reasonably available as provided in subsection (d) of this section, including a case in which certification of interpreters is not provided under paragraph (1) in a particular language, may the services of otherwise qualified interpreters be used. The Director shall provide guidelines to the courts for the selection

> of otherwise qualified interpreters, in order to ensure that the highest standards of accuracy are maintained in all judicial proceedings subject to the provisions of this chapter.

The "otherwise qualified" interpreter may be competent, or not, and may add Paco-style commentary, or not, and there may be someone present in the court to tell the difference. Or not.

The image here is one in which inadequate (linguistic) resources can destroy a life, and the life of the family to which the person is connected; and nobody except perhaps the interpreter will ever understand why. This is a preposterous level of arbitrariness because the presence, or not, of a federally certified translator could be the difference between a correct and an incorrect plea. An interpreter comments on the chances of such an eventuality, confirming many of our worst fears:

> Well, I realize there is a whole body of literature on interpreting and I have a colleague who has been instrumental in publishing a lot about that. I think it has changed for the better in terms of people being aware of some of the issues of interpreting, how difficult it is to do it well, and how unfair it is to everyone without it, particularly the dependent. What has happened in Tennessee is typical of what has happened nationwide, where you have a law enacted so you have to scramble to get people to interpret. That is the positive side, that there is a growing awareness of what it takes to have interpreting and translation skills. The negative is that in that scramble, a lot of people are underserved. When I worked at the public defender's office there was, in spite of this lobbying, the fact that you were required to have a skilled interpreter. Metro had someone on staff who had a pager, and he was called from courtroom to courtroom all day long as needed to interpret, sometimes in the jails as well. This person was not qualified. He was reportedly bilingual, but he was not qualified. In fact, when he tried to get qualified, he failed the exam. And yet, he was called on for years. He is no longer there. It is really a pressing need, and I am just talking about Spanish, which is the majority of the cases. It is illustrative, I think, of how difficult it has become. It's a kind of a many-headed monster and unfortunately it is one easy target for the courts to say it is a problem with immigration. We have to spend so many resources getting an interpreter, and you can't get a good interpreter because we don't have enough of them. It just adds to the conflict and the tension.

The chances of having adequate interpretation in the post-front-lines realm are low, but, as with so many elements of our justice system, they can be raised if the migrant has the resources to pay for proper representation, or the knowledge to secure adequate translation. The deck is stacked against this possibility, however, in an era of arbitrary, discretionary and uneven justice.

Inadequate counsel in an era of shifting law

Just as disturbing in this age of arbitrary law is how complex are the laws that relate to undocumented migrants, and, moreover, how quickly they change. This has important consequences in terms of selecting the right legal counsel, according to a lawyer:

> Many, many attorneys in this area are unaware of rights immigrants have. There are people who appear to be undocumented who might have relief if they have lived here since before 1972, or they have grandparents who are citizens, etc. There's a list of five or six things, and people suggest that up to fifteen percent of people have this kind of relief. I was at one point looking for an attorney to find people to call for those in that situation, and I found an attorney. So I spoke to him and said: "If I have someone who is about to be deported can they call you about defenses to deportation?" He said: "Defenses to deportation? What is that?" So I am nervous people are giving up their rights; and the issue of kids is also important because there are many citizen kids with undocumented parents, and they're not getting good counsel about what their options are in those situations.

Perhaps the vast contradictions, instability and blatant injustices will lead to a radical upheaval and new hope for undocumented immigrants? Theodore Ziolkowski (1997) offers an interesting perspective on legal upheaval in which he provocatively suggests that: "Justice gazes most often into her literary mirror when she has been disheveled by the winds of social and political upheaval". Can this be applied to the case of undocumented immigrants? There is an important corpus of literary texts and autobiographies that describe first-hand the experience of undocumented people, and it may be one of these that rises to the level of collective consciousness to effect this mirroring that Ziolkowski describes. For the moment, we can return to Kafka's frightening world of pure discretion against a backdrop of shifting, ambiguously worded laws enacted arbitrarily. It may be time to look into the prisons themselves to see what is being carved onto pages and into walls as 2 million people find themselves locked inside of the *Gates of Injustice* described by the likes of Alan Elsner or the *Gulag America* so powerfully rendered by Michael Dow. Despite being more codified at the level of sentencing, there's still ample discretion in that realm as well, as we'll see in the next chapter.

Notes

1 The Montreal Institute for Genocide and Human Rights Studies provides the transcripts for the radio broadcasts that led up to the Rwandan genocide, as well as other important information that helps us make the link between language and praxis. Available at: http://migs.concordia.ca/links/RwandaRadioTranscripts.htm.

2 Colaiacovo (2013) confirms this: "This paper presents statistical analysis of over 68,000 refugee claims adjudicated by 264 members of the board from 2006 to 2011. It finds that the probability of acceptance is associated with individual members' characteristics including education, gender, and professional experience, when holding constant the claimant's country of origin, gender, and the year and regional office of adjudication. The findings suggest that the identity of the adjudicator affects whether or not an individual receives asylum" (p. 122).

3 This issue is often raised as regards healthcare and the right to treatment, as described in, for example, Kinney (2011).

Bibliography

Barrera, Mario and William I. Robinson (2012) "Global Capitalism and Twenty-First Century Fascism: A US Case Study", *Race & Class* 53.3, pp. 4–29.

Barsky, Robert F. (1994) *Constructing a Productive Other: Discourse Theory and the Convention Refugee Hearing*. Amsterdam and Philadelphia, PA: John Benjamins.

Bell, C. and J. Morison (eds.) (1996) *Tall Stories: Reading Law & Literature*. Dartmouth, NH: Dartmouth University Press.

Bourdieu, Pierre (1990) *Language and Symbolic Power*, Introduction by John Thompson. Cambridge, MA and London: Harvard University Press.

Brooks, Peter (2000) *Troubling Confessions*. Chicago: University of Chicago Press.

Chavez, Leo (2013) *The Latino Threat: Constructing Immigrants, Citizens, and the Nation*, 2nd edition. Stanford, CT: Stanford University Press.

Colaiacovo, Innessa (2013) "Not Just the Facts: Adjudicator Bias and Decisions of the Immigration and Refugee Board of Canada (2006–2011)", *Journal on Migration and Human Society* 1.4, pp. 122–47.

Coughlin, Anne M. (1995) "Regulating the Self: Autobiographical Performances in Outsider Scholarship", *Virginia Law Review* 81.5, pp. 1229–340.

Dimock, Wai Chi (1997) *Residues of Justice*. Oakland: University of California Press.

Dore, Florence (2006) "Law's Literature, Law's Body: The Aversion to Linguistic Ambiguity in Law and Literature", *Law, Culture and the Humanities* 2.1, pp.17–28.

Dworkin, Ronald (1985) *A Matter of Principle*. Cambridge, MA: Harvard University Press.

Fish, Stanley (1982) *Is There a Text in This Class? The Authority of Interpretive Communities*. Cambridge, MA and London: Harvard University Press.

Fish, Stanley (1990) *Doing What Comes Naturally*. Durham, NC: Duke University Press.

Fiss, Owen (1998) "Objectivity and Interpretation", in Levinson and Mailloux (1988), pp. 229–50.

Fried, Charles (1988) "Sonnet LXV and the 'Black Ink' of the Framer's Intention", in Levinson and Mailloux (1988), pp. 45–51.

Ghosh, Palash (6 February 2012) "India's 'Mexican' Problem: Illegal Immigration from Bangladesh", *International Business Times*. Available at: http://www.ibtimes.com/indias-mexican-problem-illegal-immigration-bangladesh-213993. [Accessed: 15 January 2015]

Hart, H. L. A. (1994) *The Concept of Law*. Oxford: Oxford University Press.
Heinzelman, Susan Sage and Zipporah Batshaw Wiseman (eds.) (2012) *Representing Women: Law, Literature, and Feminism.* Durham, NC: Duke University Press.
H T Correspondent (14 November 2011) "More Illegal Immigrants from Afghanistan than Pakistan", *Hindustan Times New Delhi.* Available at: http://www.hindustantimes.com/india-news/newdelhi/more-illegal-immigrants-from-afghanistan-than-pakistan/article1-769063.aspx. [Accessed: 15 January 2015]
Johnson, Kevin R. (2012) "Immigration and Civil Rights: State and Local Efforts to Regulate Immigration", *Georgia Law Review* 46, pp. 609–39.
Katan, David (2009) "Occupation or Profession: A Survey of the Translators' World", *Translation and Interpreting Studies* 4:2, pp. 187–209.
Kinney, Eleanor D. (6 May 2011) "Realizing the International Human Right to Health for Noncitizens in the United States", *Notre Dame Journal of International Comparative & Human Rights Law*, pp. 94–113.
Konczal, Lisa and Leah Varga (2012) "Structural Violence and Compassionate Compatriots: Immigrant Health Care in South Florida", *Ethnic and Racial Studies* 35.1, pp. 88–103.
Ledwon, Lenora (1995) *Law and Literature: Text and Theory*. Abingdon, Oxon: Routledge.
Leps, Marie-Christine (1992) *Apprehending the Criminal.* Durham, NC: Duke University Press.
Levinson, Sanford and Steven Mailloux (1988) *Interpreting Law and Literature*. Chicago: Northwestern University Press.
Lewis, Hannah, Gill Valentine and Louise Waite (2014) "Multiply Vulnerable Populations: Mobilising a Politics of Compassion from the 'Capacity to Hurt'", *Social & Cultural Geography* 15.3, pp. 313–31.
Malecki, Michal (2014) "The New Europe: Freedom against Aliens and Minorities", *Territoriality and Migration in the E.U. Neighbourhood, International Perspectives on Migration* 5, pp. 111–24.
Meloni, Francesca, Monica Ruiz-Casares, Cécile Rousseau, Alexandra Ricard-Guay and Karine Vanthuyne (2013) "Health Workers' Perceptions of Access to Care for Children and Pregnant Women with Precarious Immigration Status: Health as a Right or a Privilege?" *Social Science & Medicine* 93, pp. 78–85.
Molot, Jonathan T. (2000) "The Judicial Perspective in the Administrative State: Reconciling Modem Doctrines of Deference with the Judiciary's Structural Role", *Stanford Law Review* 53.1, pp. 1–110.
Murphy, Thérèse (1996) "Bursting Binary Bubbles: Law, Literature and the Sexed Body", in Bell and Morison (1996), pp. 57–82.
New York Times Editorial (10 August 2012) "Mr. King's English-Only Bill", *New York Times*, p. A18.
Nykänen, Eeva (2012) *Fragmented State Power and Forced Migration: A Study on Non-State Actors in Refugee Law*. Leiden, Holland: Brill.
Oliver, Guy (2011) "Police Blame Illegal Immigrants for Crime", *IRIN Humanitarian News and Analysis.* Available at: http://www.irinnews.org/report/88303/south-africa-police-blame-illegal-immigrants-for-crime. [Accessed: 15 January 2015]
Oxford English Dictionary (*OED*) (2014) Online edition. Available at: http://www.oed.com/view/Entry/69828?rskey=2p5QHE&result=1#eid. [Accessed: 15 January 2015]

Phillipson, Robert (2003) *English-Only Europe? Challenging Language Policy.* Abingdon, Oxon: Routledge.
Posner, Richard (1998) *Law and Literature.* Cambridge, MA and London: Harvard University Press.
Schwartzman, Kathleen (2013) *The Chicken Trail.* Ithaca, NY: Cornell University Press.
Sharma, Rashmi (2011) "Gender and International Migration: The Profile of Female Migrants from India", *Social Scientist* 39.3/4, pp. 37–63.
Vorrath, Judith (June 2011) "Political Trends in the African Great Lakes Region", United States Institute of Peace. Available at: http://www.usip.org/sites/default/files/Political_Trends_Great_Lakes.pdf. [Accessed: 15 January 2015]
Wadhia, Shoba Sivaprasad (2010) "The Role of Prosecutorial Discretion in Immigration Law", *Scholarly Works* 17. Available at: http://elibrary.law.psu.edu/fac_works/17. [Accessed: 15 January 2015]
Wadhia, Shoba Sivaprasad (2011) "Sharing Secrets: Examining Deferred Action and Transparency in Immigration Law", *University of New Hampshire Law Review* 10.1. Available at: http://ssrn.com/abstract=1879443. [Accessed: 15 January 2015]
Wadhia, Shoba Sivaprasad (2012) "The Immigration Prosecutor and the Judge: Examining the Role of the Judiciary in Prosecutorial Discretion Decisions", *Penn State Law Legal Studies* 2. Available at: http://papers.ssrn.com/sol3/papers.cfm?abstract_id=2033803##. [Accessed: 15 January 2015]
Weisberg, Richard (1992) *Poethics and Other Strategies of Literature and Law.* New York: Columbia University Press.
West, Robin (1999) *Caring for Justice.* New York: New York University Press.
Ziolkowski, Theodore (1997) *The Mirror of Justice: Literary Reflections of Legal Crises.* Princeton, NJ: Princeton University Press.

Chapter 5

Incarcerations, public and private

> Where do they get the idea that putting someone in a box had anything to do with rehabilitation? I mean, that is a profoundly stupid idea.
>
> (A public defender interviewed for the project)

> We don't want to talk about the issues of prisons and how prisons are basically cruel places. And it's not a cruel place because you don't have enough room, you don't have enough food, you don't have whatever. It's a cruel place because if one group of people has absolute power over another group of people, you have abuse. Period. No matter where you are. And no matter what the institutional structure is. And that's human nature. That is the evil in humans.
>
> (Community organizer)

Pre-trial (Struve 2013) and post-trial incarceration and detention for immigration-related offenses (Aas and Bosworth 2013) are international phenomena that have both seen spectacular growth in the past few decades, and the blurry line between incarceration and detention practices has caused considerable concern about how migrants can be criminalized simply because they are on the territory of a host country. Even people who have fled a country of origin in order to claim Convention refugee status in the host country, and who do so under ensconced international legislation set forth by the 1951 Geneva Convention (Barsky 2001), have found themselves in detention in conditions akin to those endured by criminals in prisons. Recent work by Bosworth (2015), Bosworth and Turnbull (2015) and Bosworth, Hasselberg and Turnbull (2015) catalogues the growth of immigrant detention and incarceration as a means of punishing those who cross borders illegally, and instilling fear into those who are considering doing so (Ham and Pickering 2014):

> Immigration detention is not new. However, states have been most active in pursuing immigration detention policies and expanding practices since the late 1990s. At present, most countries utilize some form of detention

> as part of their immigration and border control policies, although the structures, functions, and purposes vary. What most countries share, however, is a predominant focus on "unauthorized" migrants—those "irregular", "illegal", "alien", or "undocumented" persons who lack formal immigration approval to enter and remain.
>
> (Bosworth and Turnbull in Ham and Pickering, p. 3; see also Wilsher 2012)

Using examples from Australia, Canada, the EU, the UK and the United States, Bosworth and Turnbull describe how incarceration as a border control measure strives to ward off would-be migrants (Martin and Mitchelson 2009; Mitchell and Sampson 2013):

> As the use of detention for immigration purposes continues to rise among countries of the western world, questions about its purpose, justification, and legitimacy can no longer be ignored. The growing "use of penal tactics to manage international conflict and migrant and refugee flows" present important lines of inquiry for scholars of punishment and others interested in the expansion of penal power under conditions of globalization. Similarly, the racialized and gendered nature of immigration detention reveals interconnections between migration, criminal justice, and entrenched legacies of colonialism and imperialism in contemporary border control efforts and responses to mass mobility.
>
> (Bosworth and Turnbull 2015, p. 3)

Majcher and Senarclens (2014) discuss the implications of current practices regarding immigrant incarceration in Europe, with some important implications and recommendations. The authors note that from a theoretical perspective:

> pre-removal detention under the EU and Swiss legislation may not only be employed as an administrative tool to prevent absconding. Rather, it may also include deterrent purposes that are traditionally restricted to (punitive) criminal sanction. Arguably, immigration detention should no longer be described as a merely administrative tool of immigration control. In fact, in practice it is often used as a deterrent to facilitate migration control.
>
> (p. 4)

This is a crucial point, since it distinguishes between the objectives of the various legislations in the different countries, and the practices that follow in their wake. Arguably the gap between legislation and practice creates another space into which arbitrariness or discretion can crawl. Furthermore:

> Immigration detention thus constitutes a disciplinary and punitive instrument designed to shape the conduct of a category of migrants in terms of both immigration and crime control objectives. In that respect, it shall be considered not only as a measure to enforce removal but more generally as an apparatus designed to "discipline and punish" migrants considered "unwanted" while they cannot be expelled.
>
> (p. 4)

This leads to an intertwining of procedures that come to be directed against those who migrate legally (such as asylum seekers) and illegally; and the fact that both groups can be detained fuels further concerns about the criminalization of migration, and the concomitant growth of public and private detention and prison complexes.

Although practiced with some degree of variation worldwide, the incarceration and detention of migrants is a gargantuan phenomenon, especially in the United States. The range of rationales employed to check immigration status and then to incarcerate migrants who are in violation of migration laws is vast, but play out very differently depending upon the context. A lawyer draws attention to the unevenness of the practice, even within a single state:

> In Davidson County the [former] police chief himself has said that if it's not a deportable offense, then they will not report the person's incarceration to the Department of Homeland Security. The flip side of that is that you've got local law officers who are trying to check the immigration status of everyone they walk up to on the street, not only people with whom they're involved, but people they find who look brown. So the practices are running the gamut, both at the official policy level, and at the implemented level.

As a result of there being no rule of law upon which to rely, law enforcement can come to be transformed into a predator in a game of cat-and-mouse, with various forms of incentives for participating. A number of experts who were interviewed for this project describe the immigrants not as mice, but as "indentured slaves", a jarring term that points to crucial issues discussed in Brysk and Choi-Fitzpatrick (2012), Murphy-Aguilar and Tiano (2012) and Rodriguez (2011). An interpreter working on the Canada-US border provides an example that from her perspective reflects the overlap between slavery and undocumented immigrants:

> Immigrants [in upstate New York] lived in constant fear of incarceration. In fact, they lived almost like indentured slaves because of it. We lived right on the border with Canada and because – and I do not know if this happened since 9/11 or if this was always the case – there is a 20 mile stretch from the border inland all along the border where the border

> patrol has a lot more freedom to invade property and to pick people up and search for people. A lot of the civil rights that people have outside of that stretch of 20 miles are not applicable there. So, the guys hide out. They hardly go out of these farms.

If the officer does apprehend the immigrant and chooses to make an arrest, then the detainee enters a correctional system that simply cannot handle so many inmates, and certainly lacks the facilities to deal with issues specific to foreigners. Even in spite of Obama's 2014 Executive actions to forestall deportation of certain groups of undocumented immigrants, there is still enormous pressure on the detention and incarceration systems in country grappling with the logistics of keeping 2 million+ people behind bars. Furthermore, it could be argued that the uncertainty and the (continued) lack of status even for those who might qualify under particular programs such as Obama's Executive Order is itself a form of segregation from the rest of the population. Bauder's (2014) previously cited "Commentary" doesn't use the term indentured slave, but referencing the work of Aliverti (2012), Balibar (2000, pp. 42–4), De Genova (2005), De Giorgi (2010), Guenther and Heesters (2000) and Ngai (2004), he does describe a new kind of disenfranchised worker:

> The undervalued economic contributions made by illegalized refugees and immigrants are further undermined by the unequal treatment by the state, which provides them with limited or no access to social welfare, employment insurance, or health care. Although illegalized refugees and immigrants work and live among citizens, sit on the same subway cars, and send their children to the same schools, illegalized refugees and immigrants are denied the status that would formally recognize them as members of society. Scholars of criminology use the term "hyper-criminalization" to describe the process of illegalization. They point out that the invocation of criminal law in cases of refugee and immigration offences serves mostly as a threat rather than to actually prevent the offence or persecute the offender. Criminalization and illegalization are forms of "punishment" that effectively discipline the affected population. For example, the realization of their own "deportability" as illegalized refugees and immigrants has helped create docile workers and fearful subjects. As unwanted refugees who are denied legal protection, as workers who are experiencing disproportionate exploitation, and as persons who are subjected to social and political exclusion, illegalized refugees and immigrants have become the "modern proletarians".
>
> (p. 331)

The growing numbers of foreign and undocumented inmates add another level of complexity to the incarceration issue (Hernandez 2008), leading to heightened tensions amongst the inmates and between the inmates and the guards that are played out on a daily basis over a range of concerns relating to inter-cultural communication, race relations, the carrying-out of religious rites, access to appropriate culinary conditions and relations with their families. Bosworth and Turnbull (2015) note that:

> For critical race scholars, immigration detention helps constitute the nation along racial lines. In this view, the detention of primarily non-white migrants in postcolonial contexts refines and reproduces the "whiteness" of the citizenry and the state, while naturalising the illegality of non-white, non-citizen others. Indeed, the racial and ethnic make-up of detained populations in countries such as the UK and US speaks to long-standing connections between empire, colonialism, and imperialism. For example, in the UK, the detention estate has large populations of ex-colonial subjects from Bangladesh, Pakistan, India, and Nigeria (Home Office 2013). In the US, Mexican nationals comprised 67 per cent of the total number of detainees, followed by Guatemalans (9 per cent), Hondurans (6.3 per cent), and El Salvadorans (5.5 per cent). Importantly, immigration detention is also a gendered phenomenon, with male migrants making up the majority of those who end up in detention.
>
> (p. 93)

The issues surrounding mass incarceration were already serious in the 1990s, but they have exploded, according to Alberti (2010) and Simanski and Sapp (2012), in part on account of the post-9/11 application of tenets set forth in the 1996 Antiterrorism and Effective Death Penalty Act (AEDPA) and the Illegal Immigration Reform and Immigrant Responsibility Act (IIRIRA). In *American Gulag*, Mark Dow (2005) notes that these two Acts massively expanded "the categories of crimes for which immigrants who had become legal residents were 'deportable' and subject to 'mandatory detention.'" Furthermore, these laws "eliminated the INS's discretion to release certain aliens and require that it detain large numbers of legal resident aliens without setting a bond" (p. 9). The effect was that from 1994–2001, the average daily detention population in the United States more than quadrupled, from 5,532 to 19,533 (and by 2013 they nearly doubled again).

Dow (2005) also reiterates, from the US standpoint, that lines have been blurred between criminals and other detainees held for immigration issues:

> Today [2005] the immigration agency holds some 23,000 people in detention on a given day and detains about 200,000 annually. The prisoners are held in the INS's service processing centers; in local jails; in facilities owned and operated by private prison companies such as the Corrections Corporation of America (CCA) the Wackenhut Corporation,

> and the Correctional Services Corporation (CSC); and in Bureau of Prisons facilities, including federal penitentiaries. Wherever they are held, INS prisoners are "administrative detainees"; they are not serving a sentence. (p. 9)

A crucial point made in Dow's book relates to the many draconian changes that occurred on account of 9/11, and the upshots thereof for issues relating to incarceration. And Obama, a former law professor, has maintained rather than challenged these practices, further ensconcing them into standard practice.

The other worrisome trend that has developed since 9/11 is that the time spent between arrest and trial has grown in the United States, and so even individuals who are innocent of the criminal charges still spend considerable time in detention or jail. A public defender notes that:

> Clients are going to be sitting in a county jail probably at least a couple of months to a couple of years before their case even gets to court. They may or may not have a bond set, depending on what they are charged with, and they may or may not meet with a lawyer, if they can afford a lawyer. If not, they can have a lawyer appointed. They start in General Sessions Court, where they can have a probable cause hearing or settle the case. If it is something serious, they are likely to have a probable cause hearing. Their case then gets sent over to the Davidson County Grand Jury that reviews it. They are just going to sit there in jail for 3–6 months. If they cannot make their bond at this point, they just sit there. They may see a lawyer during that time but they may not. Once the Grand Jury returns an indictment, then they go to criminal court. They then plead not guilty. They have to reconnect with their lawyer. And then they see if they can resolve their case, or if they need to go to trial. If they need to go to trial, it could be anywhere from 9 months from when they came into custody, to, like, years.

Another public defender notes that even when a prisoner has representation, there are huge obstacles to him/her being able to discuss the case because of the logistics of where he/she is imprisoned before trial:

> All of our non-citizen clients are most likely detained while they're awaiting a trial, which is unusual for the state system, but in the federal system, a whole lot of people are detained before trial. It has been quite a while since the Federal system has been like this. If the defendant is not a citizen, he'll be in jail until his trial. So they put them in a jail around here, some are held here in Nashville, the rest are out in Kentucky or in Springfield Tennessee. During the pre-trial proceedings, we go out and see them, and talk to them through a glass thing, with wires and stuff so we can't see people's eyes. It's a really inadequate way to communicate

> with a client. The marshal system is such that they bring them in, after a two-hour drive to Kentucky, but then we have lousy experiences talking to them. So you spend four hours driving there, round trip, to meet them, for this experience.

As a result, many undocumented immigrants awaiting trial rely upon counsel that is readily available, persons who are known in lawyers' circles as "jailhouse lawyers", a subject on which interviewees were quite divided. One community organizer suggested flat-out that:

> Jailhouse lawyers aren't bad, they're good. They help the Latino population. People look down their noses at them, but they get stuff done. And in point of fact, institutions have tried to curtail activity of jailhouse lawyers because it is also a money making deal, since they get paid by inmates.

This comment was the exception to the rule as regards this topic, with other lawyers and public defenders insisting that there is no way for an inmate to discern whether or not the person helping him/her is offering correct information for his/her case. A representative comment came from a public defender:

> There are jailhouse lawyers serving longer sentences and who provide our clients misinformation about the ways that laws affect them, based upon very generous interpretations of the law, and sometimes on misinformation. That creates problems for us, because it erodes our ability to have a relationship of trust.... I'm seeing more reluctance on the part of my Spanish-speaking clients to do something as simple as sign a form, because somebody said, "Don't sign any waivers. Don't sign anything!" In some cases, it's a waiver for speedy trial rights, something we need the client to sign to conduct investigations, prepare a trial defense, and they simply don't want to sign based upon some information that someone has told them.... If there's a Spanish speaking person from your country or from a similar cultural background who says: "Don't sign this form, whatever your white English speaking lawyer says, don't do it, it's not right", then they won't sign. I can totally understand, if I was incarcerated in Mexico and there was another English speaking person there that looked like me, I'd be more inclined to believe that person.

This is an interesting example because it is indeed the case that undocumented immigrants do sign forms that they will come to regret, usually on the front lines, including for example signing away the custody of their American born children. Here again, the kinds of arbitrariness and discretionary decision making practiced by law enforcement on the front lines continues to resonate post-arrest, where residues of arbitrariness and discretion remain, but in different forms. And if the lesson learned by migrants is to distrust authority on the front lines, they might sabotage their own cases by refusing the advice of Counsel.

For individuals with high-level reading skills, and the kind of time required to peruse legal texts, there is a court-mandated access to law libraries (Schouten 2004) that seems to be violated throughout the state and private systems, according to a lawyer:

> There's a Supreme Court law regarding access to the courts that requires that they have a law library, but it's so antiquated in most of these facilities that there's no meaningful access. That's when word of mouth comes in lieu of access. And most of these guys have limited educational backgrounds anyways, they just get someone who has been there for a while, and this is who the inmates speak to. There are no real resources, from what I've seen.

It would make sense to furnish relevant legal resources to prison libraries because the criteria for detention is related to the risk of flight, and because there's a virtually automatic link between this risk and the fact that they already entered the country illegally, it's almost impossible to keep defendants out of jail before their trial. A public defender noted the different ways in which defendants can be detained:

> The vast majority of my clients are incarcerated awaiting trial. After indictment you have the right to a detention hearing. In most federal cases the government will move for a pre-trial detention, and then will have a hearing, and it is our burden to show that the client is neither a risk of flight nor a danger to the community. In many federal cases there is a presumption of one if not both, so we lose most of those hearings, and our clients are incarcerated. They have seventy days before trial, and in most cases we have to ask for continuance because it's hard to prepare a defense in seventy days. Three quarters of my clients, and all Spanish-speaking clients are in prison. They have a detention hearing, but ICE has a detainer, as soon as they discover they are here illegally, and even in some cases when they are here legally. So were we to prevail at a detention hearing, they would go into immigration custody and would lose any time that they had accrued towards their sentence. They would also be taken to these ICE facilities, often in Louisiana. So we have no meaningful ways to have contact with them prior to their trial, so we generally just waive those hearings, and they go into protective custody immediately. It would be impossible for us to show that someone who was here illegally was not a risk for flight, even if we knew that to be the case, it would be hard to convince a federal magistrate judge that this person is not a risk for flight. But even if we were able to accomplish that, and the person was

> released pending trial, there would be a detainer placed on that person and they would be taken to an immigration holding facility.

Again, in spite of the hope that has been offered by Obama to several million undocumented people in the United States, there are still huge deportation numbers and many more millions of people who won't qualify under the proposed (temporary) amnesty; and in order to placate those in government who feel that any kind of amnesty or pathway to citizenship is wrong, it's likely that there will be more crackdowns against those who are inadmissible under the new rules. These crackdowns have further raised the burden placed upon immigrant detention centers, and this trend upward is forecasted for the future unless significant changes are made at the national level:

> The Department of Homeland Security (DHS) requested approximately $2 billion in funding for immigration detention for 2014, which runs October 1, 2013 to September 30, 2014. This funding level would support Immigration and Customs Enforcement (ICE) with funding to maintain a detention capacity of 31,800 people in nearly 257 facilities[1] on any given night, including operational expenses, at an average of $5.05 million per day.... The House of Representatives has made clear that it intends to fund immigration detention at levels that exceed the request from the Administration, specifically $5.6 million per day spent on immigration detention and 34,000 daily detention beds for FY 2014.
>
> (National Immigration Forum Staff 2013)

The net effect of wide-ranging legislation, such as Operation Compliance in the United States or similar legislation worldwide, has been to create uneven treatment of immigrants and asylum seekers on the basis of the availability of individuals to adjudicate the claims, and a shortage of places to house the growing numbers of persons in detention (Hernandez 2008). This penury of space is creating a lucrative incarceration business in the United States, as a lawyer describes:

> If somebody is taken into custody in Morristown, for instance, they will be in the Justice Center, which is the local jail, whether they are taken in by city, or by county police. They can be held for up to forty-eight hours on a solely immigration hold.... They are supposed to transfer the person to one of their [the Immigration Department's] holding facilities. They have one county jail in each county area, and they pay 85 dollars per night to have people kept there. The jails like this because it's business. Then they are transferred to Blank County, and then to the national detention center loop, either Louisiana, or Denver, or somewhere like that.

The entire system is built upon an impersonal sense of simply putting people away, and with the shortage of space to house them, inmates are finding themselves further and further away from their families and other sources of support, as a lawyer notes:

> As far as visitation, families, undocumented or otherwise, are less likely to visit, because it's an incredibly daunting experience, even for me. For instance, in Bowling Green, KY, it's a fifteen-minute visit. And Bowling Green is ninety miles away. So you get your family, you go in, there's very restricted hours, you get signed in, you have to produce an i.d., and if you don't produce an id you don't get in. By the time you jump through all of the hoops, the reward is a fifteen-minute visit through a mesh screen. I had a guy sentenced a few weeks ago, and his girlfriend had no means of transportation. He's at a processing facility in West Tennessee, and she's now in Nashville. So his girlfriend wanted to see him, and we got there at nine at night, and visiting hours are from nine to nine fifteen, and her i.d. was expired. She doesn't have a driver's license, and her i.d. had expired three years ago, and they just said: "You cannot come in". Fortunately, we were able to get her in, but it was difficult. It's an extraordinary obstacle just to get to Bowling Green Kentucky, and it's just exacerbated for Spanish speakers, because it's not like the guard at that facility is going to say: "Hold on, let me get a translator to come and help you, and to address all of your cultural issues". Kentucky is a scary place, even for me.

Once the migrants are detained, the suffering grows exponentially, sometimes leading to worsening mental health conditions. In one case, a family feud growing out of the incarceration occurred, leading to an Hispanic prisoner being cut off from everyone he knew on the outside. A priest who knew of the case told me:

> I think that his feelings of alienation and isolation have really grown. That has been a really difficult psychological thing, to go for days and days without speaking to anyone. And he's two-and-a-half-hours from here. I think that he's having an emotional breakdown. He is not doing well. And it's hard for us to say if he has had previous mental illness. We have tried to get something on his history, but to get anything on him given that he's here illegally is difficult. He didn't have health insurance. At least with English speaking clients there are obvious sources for health issues, and we get them to sign a release, and we get treatment, evaluation, and a whole health history. They might even have undiagnosed conditions. So this guy I'm telling you about seems extraordinarily depressed, but is he more depressed than anyone else would be alone for days in Kentucky? Or are there serious psychological issues, and do we need to get him evaluated?

Just as we saw with the law libraries issue, there is a penury of essential resources, and so here again, even if the facility did provide someone to undertake a requisite psychological evaluation, could it be done in Spanish, with appropriate intercultural understanding? And even if it did, which is unlikely, there's also a very serious problem of keeping sensitive information private, and allowing for the diffusion of useful information to the right sources. One public defender even resisted the idea of cultural mediators in the prisons because she feared that in certain instances they might undermine claimants' cases for reasons that correspond to what a lot of lawyers and public defenders say about jailhouse lawyers:

> Having a cultural mediator, well that is scary to me. I would not want someone in the jail talking to my clients. No way would I want that to happen. I do not want them to have anyone that they trust more than me. If they trust someone more than me, then that person is going to know things that I should know.

The solution would be to insist that the cultural mediators be present for intercultural communication issues that arise in medical treatment or interactions between inmates and figures of authority, but not to act as legal advisors:

> They do not have enough access to language people. The prisons, for example, have very few people who speak any Spanish. The infirmaries, in particular, are not staffed with anyone who can speak Spanish. They only use interpreters where they are required to by law. Nobody wants to use an interpreter where they are not going to be sued because they didn't do so. That's the way it works for the most part. I feel that this is a real problem in prisons, lack of language access. So immigrants end up helping each other. But that is not good, that's not the way to do it, because there is no privacy there. Issues are shared, and there is no trust, and a lot of time there is misrepresentation that goes on, intentional misrepresentation, because of ill-will. There is a real problem with just using a buddy, because the person who helps you may not be your friend.

A significant portion of what has been described thus far points to the indomitable fact that inmates won't receive the assistance they need, when they need it, and whatever assistance they do get will likely come from an unreliable source. This is another contributing factor towards the unevenness of treatment inside the prisons and detention centers because there are no set standards for health, access to useful legal counsel, interpretation services and cultural concerns within or amongst host countries. There has been considerable discussion about these issues in Canada as well, and it's an important destination for Convention refugees and other classes of migrants (Mire 2013). And even if most Canadian facilities are state-owned, they rely upon private firms to provide many of the services inside the facilities, and that can have a bearing upon crucial judicial concerns such as visitation or consultation with Counsel (Cannon and Flynn 2009). Immigrant detention of immigrants has opened new doors for private firms, generating considerable interest and serious pressure on governments all around the world. This is a deeply divisive issue that was invoked by most of the informants to this research, including one of the founding executives of the private prison industry, whose opinions will mark the next section.

Private versus public prisons

A leading private prison corporation, the Corrections Corporation of America (CCA), was founded by two graduates of Vanderbilt University and its head office remains in Nashville, giving Nashville the distinction, deemed by many as ignoble, of being one of the capitals of the private incarceration industry. This provided me with unexpected access to industry experts and to local activists who are concerned by an unsavory industry in their own backyard. An executive in the industry remarked on his engagement in the industry, and many of his comments are helpful in sketching out how and why private prisons have become mainstream in the United States and beyond:

> I was approached by a private corrections company, in 1986, and it was strictly in its infancy, as you can imagine, at that time.... We were visited by any number of representatives from foreign countries and many other American states, including prominent senators and representatives from various states who just wanted to see how this thing could possibly operate. We had convinced the state that we could actually operate this thing fairly well, and about that time, 1987 or 1988, we are getting up there. In 1989, there were other companies that were coming into the business, and they were getting contracts in Texas, Alabama, Tennessee, California, and a number of other places. It was still very much in its infancy.... The company [for whom I worked] was growing, and, at the same time, other companies were growing too. There was no major boom just yet. Shortly thereafter, probably 1993 or 1994, there were some 25 companies that were actively engaged, and had at least one contract with a government entity to operate their correctional facility. The economic factors at that time were pushing for privatization, and governments were not wanting to spend 100 million dollars to build a new facility, and operate it, and all of that.

This is the crucial point, and one that he emphasized throughout the interview: when a government decides to build a new prison, it needs a significant amount of cash in order to build the infrastructure, and it needs to have the resources to hire, train and equip the workforce required for such an operation. This outlay on the front end provided the impetus for companies to move into the business of incarceration, despite opposition from major parties to the decision:

> We had great opposition in those days from the American Bar Association, from every union of course that would have anything to do with correctional facilities. A lot of academia was also quite adamantly opposed to it. We have kind of moved through that era now. There were many legal issues at that time, and we were in court all the time. Almost every contract was challenged as to its constitutionality.... As we stand here, in the last five years, all those small companies got eaten up by the big ones, which I guess resulted in the field narrowing down to about six big companies. The legal issues dropped off. There were some positive things that were coming out in various articles, and from various groups. A lot of the conservative groups, especially Republican groups, were very supportive and, again, we had a number of foreign countries interested. Australia was one big one, as well as England, France, Spain, South Africa, and other countries are dabbling in it. As it stands now, there are five or six prominent companies, and some are public companies, and they are doing quite well. The good news for private corrections is now they have a history, and they have learned pretty much how to operate correctional facilities. They have brought in excellent administrators from public corrections, both Federal and State, some very, very prominent names, good folks, educated people.

With the precedents set, and the legal hurdles overcome, private prison corporations could use their resources to build a base by offering government officials who might be on the fence about important expenditures on facilities the possibility of paying on a per-prisoner basis. The lure is powerful because private companies can set up the entire operation, and then, like a hotel, charge the government a fixed amount per inmate. All they have to do is undercut projected costs to the state:

> You cannot go into a state and charge them $40.00 if it cost them $39.00. That would never work, obviously. The idea is you have to do it for less. Now, the state of Texas has legislation, you have to do it 10% less, and other states have picked that up. The trick is to find out whether the state is going to give you an accurate figure of what it really cost them. Let's say it's $45.00. Then you know you've got to come in somewhere under that. If you say $44.00, you are still saving them $1.00 a day per 1,000 times 365. That's lots of money for just a one-dollar savings. Now if your bid is higher than somebody else's, does that mean you're out? No. That's what lobbyists are all about. They are going to say: "Hey, I know my guy's a high bidder, but he's got the best reputation, he can do the job".

The real question then becomes, what does a private prison offer, in comparison to a public one? This is where the private prison executive was adamant about the potentially useful role that private prisons could play, and even if his point sounded a bit like the National Rifle Association (NRA) claim that it's not the guns that kill people it's the people that kill people, it was still a crucial insight. He broke down the costs of incarcerating people into the range of goods and services that were required, including basic fixed items like cells and beds and sinks and showers, and services such as guards, cooks and cleaners. Given the size of some corporations, most notably the CCA, there were considerable economies of scale to be had that may or may not be available to states or the federal government. This executive believed that private industry is better at (say) the bidding process than the government is, an idea that is consistent with the American perception of government waste and inefficiency.

The obvious result of all this is that private incarceration is a growth industry. Lee (2012) provides some of the numbers, and they are staggering. There were 128,195 state and federal prisoners housed in private facilities as of December 2010, an increase in private facilities of 37 percent since 2002. For our purposes, it's particularly notable that 33,330 immigrants were being detained in 2011, many in one of the 66 facilities owned and operated by the CCA ($1.7 billion: total revenue recorded by the CCA in 2011) or in one of the 65 facilities owned and operated by the Geo Group, Inc., the United States' second largest private detention company ($1.6 billion: total revenue in 2011).

Much more significant than the supposed relative efficiency of private versus public prisons, however, was the executive's adamant belief that if something is wrong with private facilities, the fault lies not with the corporations that run them, but with the lawmakers who contracted them in the first place. Any contract can include stipulations about what constitutes reasonable practices within the industry, and in his opinion governments have insisted upon the facilities being secure, rather than emphasizing the importance of educational facilities, access for lawyers and healthcare officials and an environment conducive to rehabilitation. As a consequence, private facilities are for the most part set up to warehouse people, and the corporations who run them have placed little stock in resources that could help inmates, families and legal representatives with the many issues that arise in incarceration and detention because there was never any incentive to do so. As a result, private prisons have all of the problems associated with public prisons, only worse.

Virtually every lawyer, public defender, interpreter and advocate that I encountered has been deeply critical of the private prison industry, and the litany of lawsuits, assaults and violent actions recorded in private prisons provide some background as to where this criticism comes from (Currier 2012; Lee 2012). In all of the interviews there was only one positive upshot to incarceration in a private facility: the court maintains jurisdiction over the prisoner. The fact that this difference exists speaks yet again to the importance of having good counsel because, like all other judicial realms, the one that oversees incarceration for immigration violations contains significant loopholes for those who are well advised. A public defender accustomed to such dealings described it as follows:

> Now for the pros and cons of CCA versus the Department of Corrections: when an inmate goes to the Department of Corrections, the court, in essence, loses jurisdiction over the case. The judgment becomes final. The court cannot say: "I am going to suspend the rest of your sentence". If you go to CCA on a 6-year sentence or less, anytime within 45 days of your sentencing day, your lawyer can file a motion on your behalf asking the judge to suspend your sentence. Lots of times, the inmates [can participate in] programs in CCA, like a 9 month program, when you are serving [up to] a 6-year sentence. You do the 9 month program, say a drug program, and if you are in there for drugs, I can march you right back in front of a judge and say: "He is done with a drug program judge, let him out on his sentence and let him do the rest on probation". Most times, the judge says yes. That is the upside to CCA.

These kinds of programs may become more popular as governments impose regulations upon private firms that are aimed at rehabilitation. The need is glaring, according to a public defender:

> The way that we incarcerate and sentence people convicted of federal offenses is totally misguided. There's an emphasis on punishment, with no emphasis upon rehabilitation. I think that one of the reasons that people gravitate towards these faith-based programs is because the prisons lack the resources to provide any meaningful substance abuse treatment. All of the policy arguments you've heard show that by simply incarcerating people for extraordinary periods of time, nobody wins. They're not any more rehabilitated on the back-end than they were on the front-end, and in many cases, their families and communities suffer so much because they are incarcerating people who would be working, people who would be contributing to lives of families, who would be a source of support and stability. A lot of the people we are incarcerating are not the worst of the worst, and they wouldn't be a detriment to their communities. So I think that the system as a whole as it applies to migrant inmates, and English speaking citizens is not effective, not humane, it is just not humane.

The wealth of evidence that the current system is failing inmates and societies alike has provoked discussion in the public arena. Damon Hininger, the chief executive of the CCA, stated in an interview with the *Wall Street Journal* (Barrett 2014) that "government clients are increasingly concerned about the long-term costs of housing inmates and are pushing CCA and other private operators to save them money by reducing recidivism, the number of inmates who are released only to do a repeat turn in prison". As a consequence, Hininger "plans to expand the company's prison rehabilitation programs, drug counseling and its prisoner re-entry work in cities around the country". The article notes that if the CCA were to do so, it would be a "significant shift" from its profitable business of incarcerating people, a business that has made it "the fifth-largest correction system in the country, after only the federal government and the states of California, Florida and Texas":

> "This is a watershed moment for our company and we hope it will be for our entire industry", Mr. Hininger said. "We are determined to prove that we can play a leadership role in reducing recidivism and that we have every incentive to do so. The interests of government, taxpayers, shareholders, and communities are aligned. We all just need to recognize that and commit to that."

This "alignment" of interests seems a tad disingenuous, as Hedy Weinberg, the executive director of the American Civil Liberties Union of Tennessee, indicates:

> "It must be a challenge for CCA to implement programs that could reduce recidivism when that runs counter to the private prison model itself", she said. "We can only hope that CCA's interest in such programs indicate a shift away from its previous stance that 'reductions in crime rates' are a 'risk factor' for business and toward a completely new business model that does not rely on ever-growing mass incarceration."

To bring Weinberg's comments to bear upon interviews that were undertaken with the private prison executive, we can surmise that CCA's "interest" in such programs would need to be ensured through proper regulation, and not just incentives or assurances by its Chief Executive Officer that there is suddenly some good financial reason for them to act more responsibly towards the inmates and the larger community.

When we head into the community of lawyers, public defenders and interpreters, the candid wrath against private incarceration companies is made manifest:

> How much do they hate my client? If they do hate him, and he is a problem, how long are they going to make me sit here before they bring him out? Is he going to be shackled? When I have to wait an hour to see my client at CCA, do I want to go see him? No. You never know how long you are going to have to wait. I hate going there visiting them. If I know I am going out there to visit someone, and this is hypothetical, if

> I am going to visit someone who I know the guards don't like, and who is a trouble maker or is someone that they perceive is a trouble maker, who asks too many questions, I know I am going to have to go out there and wait this long. And then because it is this guy, I have to wait a little longer, and you see what I mean. I think it's because immigrants are not embraced, and also because prisons are not run by the most sensitive people. It just can bleed into all of these other things. I have gone through phases where I just wanted somebody to sue the shit out of CCA, because it is my opinion that they make you wait so long that they interfere with right to counsel, not just by access, but by making everybody wait every time we go out there.

Here the issue relates to the right to counsel, an issue that was frequently invoked, and the tactics used to restrict this right have other very tangible effects upon the quality of the inmates' lives. A public defender describes the CCA experience with reference to the time that everything takes, and the quality of those carrying out tasks inside the prison:

> That CCA facility is just terrible. Everything is really slow. They do not have the best employees, and they have high officer turn over. They have rude people working there. If you have a bond that is high, they put you in maximum, solitary confinement and lock you down. You are presumed innocent but they are locking you down, 23 hours per day if your bond is over a certain level. If you are a lawyer and have a person in lock down, you have to go through all of these different gates. You might have to visit with your client in the laundry room because that is the only place they have for you to talk. They will leave the door open for security reasons so you cannot really have a good conversation. I mean, you really have to pitch a fit when you go out there and say: "No, you have to shut the door!" The other thing about CCA is that they might be on count, or shift-change, or mealtime, and they are not going to let you in. They have mealtime 3 times per day, and they have count every couple of hours. I have been known to ask the judge's clerk to put my client on the docket for no reason at all just to bring them to court so I could see them there.

The "counting" that occurs every two hours is a symptom of the previously described emphasis upon security over rehabilitation, and the quality of the staff may have something to do with the nature of the job, and the egregiously low wages. A public defender adds as well the plethora of arbitrary and shifting rules that are constantly introduced, imposed, revoked and changed:

> The private prison is horrible. There is just no other way to put it. They are awful, obscene. They are a business. I cannot get in to see a client in under one hour. You and I could leave here and I could be inside visiting

> my client on death row in under one hour. That would include driving there 30 minutes. {In private prisons,} you cannot get in. Every time I come, they have a different dress code. Somehow what I wore to court does not meet their dress code, so I end up digging in my trunk trying to find whatever it is that they want me to cover, which is every part of my body that they find offensive, in order to get in. You cannot make an appointment to come there. They tell me I have to have an appointment, so I call and they say I don't need one. I arrive, and they say: "You do, you have to have one". "Can I make one?" "No, you have to leave to make one". So I have to go outside. I can go outside the door, and I call on my cellphone. I can see the woman I was just talking to pick up the phone, and I say: "May I make an appointment?" and she says: "Why yes you may. When would you like to come?" and I say: "Now, if I can". And she will say: "No, you cannot come for another twenty minutes". I have many people preferring to take a longer sentence and go to TDOC as opposed to staying at the local facility that is a private prison.

On this point even the executive who works for a private prison company concurred:

> One of the things about the private sector at this point is that they're attracting people from all points in the United States, and so the visitation thing becomes a real problem. Now with immigrants, of course, it's exacerbated even more. It's abysmal. It is terrible. This is one of the problems that these private corrections companies have. They build these small visitation areas because you see, if you are going to have out-of-state people, they're not going to have a lot of visitation. Now it means that you contact attorneys and you say: "Now, don't come over here at breakfast, lunch or dinner. Don't come at visitation. Don't come while the guy is in GED class". "Well, my god, when can I come?" "Always call ahead, make sure you call ahead and we'll have the guy ready and all that." Well that sounds good from the prison's standpoint, but for the attorney, who's got a harried schedule anyway, and he's trying to fit things in, it doesn't work at all. And when they get out there, my god, you practically have to be strip searched to get through, and then when you get in there they can't seem to find the guy because he's somewhere, and you sit there for an hour waiting for your client. Attorneys hate coming to these places.

The image that emerges on the basis of these critiques is not just security, it's control, it's not just the runaround, it's the arbitrary imposition of authority against the very individuals that the state employs to assist people who have been charged with, or convicted of, crimes. A public defender puts it in stark, Foucauldian terms:

> In these privatized facilities the emphasis is on discipline and authority and control. I don't know that these guards have any interest or ability to communicate with these inmates on any meaningful level. Most of the rank-and-file are people who were laid off from their jobs, who might have high school educations. I don't think that the emphasis is placed on communication. The CCA facility has a gift shop with little CCA polo shirts, and they have cocktail tumblers. And on the other wall, they have high tech weaponry, helmets, and batons, – not for sale – but that's where the emphasis is.

All of these observations and critiques apply of course to the incarceration system as a whole, and the comments serve as important warnings to states and countries that are contemplating the commissioning of private firms for the purposes of incarcerating criminals. But the situation is even more dire for immigrants because so much emphasis is being placed on warning other immigrants that they shouldn't enter a country illegally.

Majcher and de Senarclens (2014) extend this discussion to the European context, and suggest that in order to confront the many issues that grow out of this domain, "pre-removal detention should either be restricted to purely administrative measures, or its penal character should be explicitly acknowledged in order to afford stronger procedural protection to immigration detainees", and "detention should be allowed only on the ground of the risk of absconding, which should be clearly defined and not be deduced from the irregular status of the non-citizen concerned", and detention should not exceed one month. Finally, "If immigration detention were used as a purely administrative measure to prevent absconding, the authorities would be more inclined to replace it more often with less coercive and cheaper 'alternatives to detention'" (p. 16).

Improving basic conditions

Many of the lawyers and public defenders, aware that these kinds of systemic changes aren't likely to occur in the short term, offered valuable suggestions as to how to improve the existing detention and incarceration systems. Most of these recommendations fall under the rubric of commonsense, and like the rest of this research project, the suggested amendments could be applied to virtually any host country. For instance, a crucial issue for all of the lawyers, public defenders, investigators, interpreters and family members was access to the incarceration facilities. Given the widespread availability of Wi-Fi, internationally, many lawyers and public defenders argued for expanding the use of video conferencing through such services as Skype. A public defender makes reference to this realm in regards to legal consults, but we can imagine it expanded to include online visitation rights:

> The other one is the simplest thing in the world, and they are doing it everywhere, and that is video-conferencing. What there is in the courthouse, and it already exists, is a television and a [hookup]. The attorney sits there, and the warden has the inmate come to this room, and he sits there, and they talk.... They don't have to transport anybody. They don't have to spend their money coming out there, and finding a place to park, which is almost impossible. It's just all those little mundane things that all of a sudden turn into major issues. They don't even want to come out for visits, that's what I have found.

Expanding online communication could also overcome the many issues relating to telephone calls, particularly between inmates and their families:

> The phone companies that have contracts with these facilities charge ridiculously excessive amounts of money. It's a collect call, from a prison outside, so it's around eighteen dollars for the first three minutes. It's something that people would be outraged by if they knew. So there's no way for any of our clients to make these calls. It's all a lucrative market for phone companies, and we have looked into this before, with very little success in terms of challenging this. And most of the facilities don't let inmates use calling cards. A couple do, which certainly defrays the cost, but if you're making a straight collect call.... Our office is taking a hit because our clients are calling collect, so we encourage them to write letters. It's a huge expense for our office.

Then of course there's the issue of privacy, as a public defender bemoaned: "On the telephone, you never know who is listening. You know that in the prison they have all of the phone calls taped, even though they are technically not supposed to listen, they still do. And I think mail is too slow. There is no really good form of communication for someone who is incarcerated."

Communication and visitation aren't small concerns, and if the mail is slow and monitored, if telephone calls are expensive and taped, and visitation is difficult, where does it leave the inmate? An interpreter elaborates:

> The problem is that many of the institutions that they are in do not have decent visiting, and the situation with incarcerated immigrants is that family members often live at considerable distance from where the prison is and do not have financial means to travel.... For example, people who have been caught crossing the country with drugs, and the case comes up here in Nashville, but the family is in California maybe. Well if they are put in a place like Springfield or Bowling Green, which are the kind of places where we generally put our prisoners, their visiting time may be 15 minutes a week. No one is coming from California for 15 minutes. Now they might if they can get somebody to transfer them to Mason....

> So the conditions in the jail, itself, do not favor family interaction unless the family is close at hand and close emotionally with the prisoner. The situation is too restrictive.

One way of leveling the playing field would be to build relationships between the governments of host and home countries, and a way of doing so would be to involve the consulate from the home country from the moment of the arrest all the way through to the incarceration. The government from the home country could provide interpreters, advice and counsel, in addition, perhaps, to books and other materials suited to helping the inmate productively pass the time. Most of the lawyers and public defenders offered mitigated support for this idea, but had areas of resistance. One lawyer invoked the oft-mentioned concern about confidentiality and attorney/client privilege, while voicing his support for consular assistance with keeping the inmate's family abreast of his/her situation:

> We have gotten people involved from their consulate's office. I have not found this to be really helpful, but they have gotten involved and were looking into the issues. The consulate was able to help me with things unrelated to their defense. My experience was a little awkward because they also wanted to go and meet with the client and talk about the case and I kind of had an issue with that. They cannot hide behind that attorney/client privilege with stuff they are talking to you about. I do not want the client necessarily making admissions to the consulate about stuff that went on, because the client is not savvy enough to know what can be incriminating. If someone caught wind of the consulate going in they could potentially talk to the consulate and subpoena the consulate and get all the confidential information. The consulate to me was kind of this potentially useful tool, but potential mess as well. The consulate again was, like I said, really good about keeping the family updated, keeping contact with them, and letting them know the status of the case.

Another public defender suggested that "the consulate should be more involved at the parole hearing level", and should also be in touch with immigration officials to ensure that the person is deported upon completion of his/her sentence, so that the incarceration isn't dragged out unnecessarily and to ensure that inmates have advocates on the outside. More substantively, an investigator suggested an array of roles for consular officials:

> The consulate's involvement might be at the family level, because they cannot help them get out of jail. What they could do, like for example with Mexico, is that they could serve their time in Mexico, and that could be arranged by the consulate. We don't even have to be involved. What I think we would like for them to help us with is contacting people, and

> getting information from Mexico or documents from their country, like a legal document that we might need here. Also, if something is happening at the jail and they are being mistreated or whatever, you know that they have this number that they can call and then somebody can call and say, "I'm calling from the Mexican consulate or the Honduran consulate and this inmate, so and so, is having problems. We want to investigate that".

An interpreter provided other substantive ways for the consular staff to be involved in ways that recall the recommendations about "soft law" in previous chapters:

> Mexico is more involved than probably any of the other countries, and I think that they should be involved even more than they are. I think that all countries should be, because, the enforcement of international treaties is important. I think that there should be a provision of legal consultation and referrals to get attorneys. I think that providing reading materials and visits from community volunteer groups who would be interested would also help; anything that can get a community and individuals involved with people who are in a prison or jail is very useful for maintaining a certain level of civil socialization. It is very, I think, extremely alienating to be in a jail or a prison, no matter who you are, and for foreigners, it happens sometimes there is no one else who speaks their language. It does happen, and I think that has to be horrible.

The "horrible" part is the sense of isolation and despair, which can lead to serious issues relating to mental health, an area that merits a prolonged discussion in itself, as regards inmates and, moreover, migrant inmates, as a lawyer indicated:

> A much higher percentage of the native population is on some form of medication than my immigrant population. My immigrant clients, and I don't know if this is a diagnosis issue or if this is a cultural distinction in terms of mental illness, but we have a lot of guys, native guys, who are in the jail who are taking stuff for depression, but very few of them are immigrants. My experience with the immigrants is that they are crazy, crazy, crazy, like undeniably crazy, eating their feces crazy, or else they are totally fine. There is not a lot of the bipolar, little mood swings, some depressive tendencies, or in-between stuff, whereas in the native population, most of the people being medicated are being treated for their bipolar disorder or depression.

In light of the details provided in this book, it seems appropriate to end a chapter on incarceration with depression and despair. Virtually every observation or insight provided by the informants to this project considered that incarceration for migration offenses is senseless and counter-productive, and that in fact incarceration for non-violent crimes is an invitation for unnecessary criminalization of the population. And that the current system decrees that people who have served their sentences must then be deported, necessarily, is the proverbial icing upon a poisonous cake that is served up after a host of malevolent actions committed on discretionary and arbitrary grounds.

And yet despite it all, these public defenders, lawyers, investigators and interpreters continue to advocate on behalf of their clients, hoping that someday a more lasting solution will be proposed and adopted. In the next chapter I'll discuss one such proposal that could provide temporary amnesty for a few million undocumented people in the United States. I'll then conclude on a more optimistic note, describing a world without the arbitrariness, the fickleness and the violence of borders, a world that isn't utopian, in the sense of being unattainable, and is in fact in accordance with prevailing beliefs and existing legal instruments that pertain to the movement of peoples, worldwide.

Note

1 *2DHS FY 2014 Budget Justification*, p. 43.

Bibliography

Aas, K. F. and M. Bosworth (eds.) 2013, *The Borders of Punishment: Migration, Citizenship, and Social Exclusion*. Oxford: Oxford University Press.

Alberti, G. (2010) "Across the Borders of Lesvos: The Gendering of Migrants' Detention in the Aegean", *Feminist Review* 94, pp. 138–47.

Aliverti, Ana (2012) "Making People Criminal: The Role of the Criminal Law in Immigration Enforcement", *Theoretical Criminology* 16, pp. 417–34.

Balibar, Étienne (2000) "What We Owe to the Sans-Papiers" in Guenther and Heesters (2000), pp. 42–3.

Barrett, Devlin (12 September 2014) "Prison Firm CCA Seeks to Reduce Number of Repeat Offenders: Company Pushes to Reduce Costs Associated with Recidivism", *Wall Street Journal*. Available at: http://www.wsj.com/news/article_email/prison-firm-cca-seeks-to-reduce-number-of-repeat-offenders-1410561176-lMyQjAxMTA0MDEwMzExNDMyWj. [Accessed: 15 January 2015]

Barsky, Robert F. (2001) *Arguing and Justifying: Assessing the Convention Refugees' Choice of Moment, Motive and Host Country.* Aldershot, Sydney and Burlington, VT: Ashgate Press.

Bauder, Harald (2014) "Why We Should Use the Term 'Illegalized' Refugee or Immigrant: A Commentary", *International Journal of Refugee Law* 26.3, pp. 327–32.

Bosworth, M. (2015) "Immigration Detention, Ambivalence and the Colonial Other", in Eriksson (2015).

Bosworth, M. and Sarah Turnbull (2015) "Immigration Detention and the Expansion of Penal Power in the UK", in K. Reiter and A. Koenig (eds.), *Extreme Punishment*. London: Palgrave.

Bosworth, M., I. Hasselberg and S. Turnbull (2015) "Imprisonment in a Global Age: Rethinking Penal Power", in Y. Jewkes, B. Crewe and J. Bennett (eds.), *Handbook of Prisons*. London: Sage.

Brysk, Alison and Austin Choi-Fitzpatrick (eds.) (2012) *From Human Trafficking to Human Rights: Reframing Contemporary Slavery*. Pennsylvania Studies in Human Rights. Philadelphia: University of Pennsylvania Press.

Cannon, Cecilia and Michael Flynn (September 2009) "The Privatization of Immigration Detention: Towards a Global View", *Global Detention Project*. Available at: http://www.globaldetentionproject.org/fileadmin/docs/GDP_PrivatizationPaper_Final5.pdf. [Accessed: 15 January 2015]

Currier, Cora (2012) "Land of the Free: The Best Investigative Reporting on U.S. Prisons", *ProPublica*. Available at: http://www.propublica.org/article/land-of-the-free-the-best-investigative-reporting-on-u.s.-prisons. [Accessed: 15 January 2015]

De Genova, Nicolas (2005) *Working the Boundaries: Race, Space and "Illegality" in Mexican Chicago*. Durham, NC: Duke University Press.

De Giorgi, Alessandro (2010) "Immigration Control, Post-Fordism, and Less Eligibility: A Materialist Critique of the Criminalization of Immigration across Europe", *Punishment & Society* 12.2, pp. 147–67.

Dow, Mark (2005) *American Gulag: Inside American Immigration Prisons*. Oakland: University of California Press.

Eriksson, Anna (ed.) (2015) *Punishing the Other: The Social Production of Immorality Revisited*. Abingdon, Oxon: Routledge.

Guenther, Len and Cornelius Heesters (eds.) (2000) *Social Insecurity*. Alphabet City Series 7. Toronto: Anansi.

Ham, Julie and Sharon Pickering (eds.) (2014) *The Routledge Handbook on Crime and International Migration*. Abingdon, Oxon: Routledge.

Hernandez, David M. (2005) "Undue Process: Immigrant Detention, Due Process, and Lesser Citizenship", *ISSI Fellows Working Papers*. Available at: http://escholarship.org/uc/item/15b1h07r. [Accessed: 15 January 2015]

Hernandez, David M. (2008) "Pursuant to Deportation: Latinos and Immigrant Detention", *Latino Studies* 6.1, pp. 35–63.

Home Office (2013) *Immigration Statistics, January to March 2013*. London: Home Office.

Lee, Suevon (20 June 2012) "By the Numbers: The U.S.'s Growing For-Profit Detention Industry", *ProPublica*. Available at: http://www.propublica.org/article/by-the-numbers-the-u.s.s-growing-for-profit-detention-industry. [Accessed: 15 January 2015]

Majcher, Izabella and Clément de Senarclens (2014) "Discipline and Punish? Analysis of the Purposes of Immigration Detention in Europe", *Illegality Regimes*, a special issue of *AmeriQuests* 11.2. Available at: http://ameriquests.org/index.php/ameriquests/article/view/3964. [Accessed: 15 January 2015]

Martin, L. L. and M. L. Mitchelson (2009) "Geographies of Detention and Imprisonment: Interrogating Spatial Practices of Confinement, Discipline, Law, and State Power", *Geography Compass* 3.1, pp. 459–77.

Mire, Muna (7 November 2013) "Canada's Immigration Detention System may be Worse than Egyptian Prison", *Vice*. Available at: http://www.vice.com/en_ca/read/canadas-immigration-detention-system-may-be-worse-than-egyptian-prison. [Accessed: 15 January 2015]

Mitchell, G. and R. C. Sampson (2013) "Global Trends in Immigration Detention and Alternatives to Detention: Practical, Political and Symbolic Rationales", *Journal on Migration and Human Security* 1.3, pp. 97–121.

Murphy-Aguilar, Moira and Susan Tiano (2012) *Borderline Slavery*. Aldershot and Burlington, VT: Ashgate.

National Immigration Forum Staff (22 August 2013) "The Math of Immigration Detention", *Immigration Forum*. Available at: http://immigrationforum.org/blog/themathofimmigrationdetention. [Accessed: 15 January 2015]

Ngai, Mae (2004) *Impossible Subjects: Illegal Aliens and the Making of Modern America*. Princeton, NJ: Princeton University Press.

Rodriguez, Junios P. (ed.) (2011) *Slavery in the Modern World: A History of Political, Social, and Economic Oppression*, 2 volumes. New York: ABC-CLIO.

Schouten, Joseph A. (2004) "Not So Meaningful Anymore: Why a Law Library Is Required to Make a Prisoner's Access to the Courts Meaningful", *William and Mary Law Review* 45, pp. 1195–227. Available at: http://scholarship.law.wm.edu/wmlr/vol45/iss3/9. [Accessed: 15 January 2015]

Simanski, J. and L. M. Sapp (2012) *Immigration Enforcement Actions: 2011*. Washington, DC: US Department of Homeland Security Annual Report, pp. 1–7. Available at: http://www.dhs.gov/sites/default/files/publications/immigration-statistics/enforcement_ar_2011.pdf. [Accessed: 15 January 2015]

Schuster, L. (2005) "A Sledghammer to Crack a Nut: Deportation, Detention and Dispersal in Europe", *Social Policy & Administration* 39.6, pp. 606–21.

Stanton, Ryan J. (15 April 2012) "Undocumented Immigrants Losing Fight to Keep Children Who are US Citizens", *The Ann Arbor News*. Available at: http://www.annarbor.com/news/undocumented-immigrants-losing-the-fight-to-keep-their-us-citizen-children. [Accessed: 15 January 2015]

Struve, Catherine T. (2013) "The Conditions of Pretrial Detention", *University of Pennsylvania Law Review* 161, pp. 1009–79.

Wilsher, D. (2012) *Immigration Detention: Law, History, Politics*. Cambridge: Cambridge University Press.

Chapter 6

Conclusion: deportation, and return to the host country? Or open borders?

> I find borders sort or arbitrary and bizarre.... I find the whole idea morally repugnant. Particularly, it should not be a crime to try to feed your family.
>
> (Lawyer in Tennessee)

> Boundary enforcement as it is now applied inevitably feeds into the systems of exclusion that are antithetical to human rights, to liberalism, to anti-racism.... Immigration control is part and parcel of the system of exclusion and inevitably produces indelible differences, inequality, leads to uncertain circumstances of life and death and that's basically the same thing that racism is. We are telling people on the basis of where they are born, something they can't change: "You're not allowed to come here, or if you are allowed to come here, you are going to come here under shitty conditions and we are going to make your life hell". How different is that from Jim Crow? Simply because we do it on the basis of nationalism it's okay.
>
> (Activist scholar)

I wish to conclude with concrete suggestions of what we can do to improve the lives of the many millions of people who are marginalized and persecuted by virtue of their irregular immigration status, all around the world. To give some sense of the scale of this issue, Nanda (2011) reports that:

> According to the International Organization for Migration's (IOM) World Migration Report for 2010, international migrants, currently numbering approximately 214 million, compared with an estimated 150 million in 2006, constitute 3.1 percent of the global population. Perhaps 10–15 percent of all international migrants are irregular migrants, and an estimated one-third of all migration from developing countries could be in that situation.
>
> (pp. 356–7)

In other words, somewhere between 20 and 30 million people endure the instability, fear and precariousness that has been described in this book, and this number grew more than 25 percent between 2006 and 2010. I hesitate to offer any kind of Band-Aid solutions because they might be deemed to be contributions to "reforming" or "upgrading" the existing international regime instead of recognizing its profound internal contradictions and failures. Nevertheless, to help reduce the suffering of those who are or are about to be subjected to the whims of the current system, there are some efforts that could be made in advance of loosening border restrictions, en route to a universal policy of open borders.

Language issues

Throughout this study I have identified a range of linguistic issues that relate to migration, and suggested that each of the processes by which host country officials encounter, arrest, adjudicate and incarcerate migrants has a crucial linguistic element. By the same token, improvements to the existing system could focus upon linguistic matters, at least in the first instance. For example, host countries need to not only promote and value bilingualism and multilingualism, they also need to communicate the value of the diversity that immigrants carry in their wake. Part of this recognition involves the active promotion of teaching the languages of neighboring countries, and the recruitment and training of people in the fields of translation and interpreting. In the context of the Americas, for example, there would be enormous advantages to everyone learning English, French, Portuguese and Spanish, and benefitting from the rich and diverse cultures of the millions of people who live and work therein. For Europe, the Swiss model of language instruction in languages on its borders offers obvious benefits for all beneficiaries of such education. Examples of the value of multilingual education could be found for all of the regions of the world, and such work would be of benefit for political, social, research and even neurological reasons (Hobbs 2011; Markert et al. 2014; Skutnabb-Kangas and Heugh 2011).

Beyond language and pedagogy, and consistent with some of the proposals made by those lawyers who advocated for involving consular officials in the lives of migrants, the aim is to promote the United Nations, international agencies and non-governmental organisations' involvement in national and international efforts to educate people about common human values and norms. In November, 2010 in commemoration of the 20th anniversary of the Human Rights Convention, the United Nations High Commissioner for Human Rights, Navi Pillay, addressed the Global Forum on Migration and Development at Puerto Vallarta, Mexico (Pillay 2011). She called for:

> the strengthening of anti-discrimination measures everywhere. Racist violence and xenophobia against foreigners must be countered with all appropriate legal and administrative means, perpetrators must be prosecuted vigorously, and education that promotes our common human

values, teaches respect and tolerance – in short, human rights education – must be pursued with urgency.

These types of efforts gain traction through the work of such international organizations as the Global Migration Group (http://www.globalmigrationgroup.org), a UN inter-agency organization established in 2006 and comprised of 12 UN agencies, the World Bank and the IOM. The Global Migration Group (2010) issued a "Statement on the Human Rights of Migrants in Irregular Situations" calling upon:

> states, civil society, the private sector, the media and host communities to address the demand side of trafficking and exploitation, to work actively to combat xenophobia, racism and incitement to discrimination in national politics and in public discourse to protect all migrants, as well as to actively promote tolerant societies in which every person can enjoy his or her human rights, regardless of migration status.

Of note here is the emphasis upon "public discourse" as a means of promoting tolerance, and human rights instruments to address ongoing issues:

> Too often, States have addressed irregular migration solely through the lens of sovereignty, border security or law enforcement, sometimes driven by hostile domestic constituencies. Although States have legitimate interests in securing their borders and exercising immigration controls, such concerns cannot, and indeed, as a matter of international law, do not, trump the obligations of the State to respect the internationally guaranteed rights of all persons, to protect those rights against abuses, and to fulfill the rights necessary for them to enjoy a life of dignity and security.

These are pleas for new approaches that could be enacted against a backdrop of the international human rights regime, and even these relatively modest efforts could help shift the social discourse surrounding human rights, migration and diversity.

This kind of reorientation of policies based on universal values and international law could also help foster concrete efforts aimed at recognizing the value of diversity. To complement these efforts, officials at all levels of government would need to provide the kinds of material support required for such efforts, including vast programs aimed at promoting and valuing cultural diversity and international human rights. To bolster these efforts while ensuring adequate and appropriate interaction between individuals from the host and home countries, interpreters and translators would need to be hired to work throughout various levels in police forces, schools, hospitals and government offices. This would help raise the levels of training and competency in other cultures and languages, thus alleviating some of the horrendous suffering caused by purposeless acts of violence and repression. For those caught up on the wrong side of the steel fence rendered by Martin Wong in "Closed", the cover image that adorns this book, such initiatives would at least provide some ability to communicate outside of the horrors of their own troubled minds. And an interpreter added that states need to valorize foreign language studies, which would help facilitate communications and "by extension, this would value the diversity that immigrants bring culturally to our city, to our nation". The current system doesn't value diversity when it invests so many resources into the detection, arrest, detention and deportation of undocumented people, as is currently the case. This is a worldwide phenomenon, and since many countries look to the United States and the EU for both good (and bad) practices, the recent American legislative and executive exercises relating to border security are worth examining in detail.

Recent border legislation

We can begin by looking back to recent US legislation such as the "Border Security, Economic Opportunity, and Immigration Modernization Act" (Congress 2013) or, by way of comparison and contrast, the "Task Force for the Mediterranean: Actions on Migration and Asylum in the EU" (TFM) (European Commission 2014). Both of these proposed pieces of legislation failed to address the kinds of fundamental issues confronting undocumented peoples because they reinforce, rather than undo, the systemic obstacles placed before migrants. These obstacles aren't intrinsic to US or EU societies, and are indeed found in countries as different from the United States as Bangladesh, Burma, India and Thailand (Cornelius 2004; Datta 2004; Kraler 2012; McNevin 2011; Pickering 2011; Zanfrini et al. 2008). A review of current challenges in Bangladesh, India, Nepal, Pakistan and Sri Lanka provides a sense of why this is the case:

> Various surveys and studies (e.g. Barbora et al., 2008; Theime, 2006) reveal that migrants are disadvantaged relative to the native population in terms of employment, education and health. While their contributions are often key to the survival of families and communities back home, those who move and those who remain face many vulnerabilities. For the person who moves, language barriers may limit their choices and reduce their capacity to negotiate a better livelihood and distance from family often leads them to seek alternative support, which may lead to risky behaviours. At a programmatic and social level, government policies and programmes and cultural factors uphold discrimination and hinder migrants' access to services. Their legal status adds to their vulnerabilities as laws and policies may prevent them from accessing health and social services.
>
> (Samuels and Wagle 2011, p. 1)

In the EU example, the TFM has shifted responsibility away from the host countries rather than smoothing the flow of people that will inevitably come to EU shores by relaxing visa restrictions, lightening the burden placed upon those who are trying to migrate legally, bolstering humanitarian admission and improving the quality of life for migrants in the EU. An Amnesty International (2013) press release quotes Nicolas Beger, Director of Amnesty International's European Institutions Office:

> The European Union urgently needs to change its mindset and approach to migration control. No matter how high member states try to build their walls, no matter how often they shift responsibility to neighbouring countries, and no matter how often they try to turn a blind eye, people will still be compelled to leave their country. And so, more lives will be lost off Europe's shores.

Instead, Amnesty advocates for "a protective migration policy with increased search and rescue, safe routes for refugees, and one that does not rely on outsourcing migration control to countries with deplorable human rights standards and records".

Within the American context, on June 27, 2013 the US Senate passed the Border Security, Economic Opportunity, and Immigration Modernization Act, and on 3 July, the Congressional Budget Office (2013) and the staff of the Joint Committee on Taxation reviewed its impact on a range of levels, related primarily to the US budget. The review found that had it passed the House, the Act would have changed how certain noncitizens who are currently unlawfully present in the United States would become eligible for social security and Medicare benefits. From a pecuniary standpoint, it would have led to the appropriation of $46.3 billion for expenses relating to the security of the southern US border and initial administrative costs, as well as $1.5 billion for an employment program for youth, it would have prohibited certain unauthorized work from counting towards eligibility for social security and Medicare benefits and it would have resulted in fewer unauthorized residents in the country than projected. That reduction in population would, according to the predictions outlined in the report, have reduced the taxes paid by, or on behalf of, unauthorized residents by $3.2 billion over the 2014–23 period. The review also predicted the Act would reduce the inflow of undocumented immigrants by between 1/3 and ½, but would also generate a 10 million person increase in the US population, mostly from Mexico, and that these changes would result in a decrease in federal budget deficits by roughly $685 billion over the 2024–33 period.

These figures provide some sense of the social and also financial consequences of a deeply punitive system of incarceration, deportation and marginalization of vast, undocumented populations around the globe (Petersilia and Reitz 2012). The continued tracking, arresting, investigating and then incarcerating and deporting of illegal immigrants has massive pecuniary implications and these funds could be directed instead to job creation and integration rather than creating more and more victims of the punitive system (Michalowski and Hardy 2014; Rothe and Kauzlarich 2014). By way of illustration, it's estimated that the apprehension, legal process and eventual removal of undocumented people from the United States costs around $23,000 per person, and nearly 290,000 individuals were deported in the fiscal year 2012 alone for a total cost of $6,670,000,000 (Asher and Wallace 2014). The same problem can be found on the outer edges of the EU, and in the UK, where the magnitude of the task is similarly huge. In 2013 alone, 50,741 people were removed from the UK, or else departed voluntarily after the initiation of removal. This represents an increase of 14.5 percent from 2012, and more than double the number from 2004 (Blinder 2014). Costly and elaborate tracking devices are driving people to ever more difficult border crossings, and we are seeing a growth in the number of border deaths as this trend increases (Orrenius 2014).

In spite of these figures, the reception of the review by the US population was divided, with the usual suspects lining up on either side of the debate. The defectors on either side, that is, Republicans who supported the Bill and Democrats who opposed it, reflect a political landscape that is increasingly crowded with Latino voters, particularly in certain regions in the country; but the schism is also tied to historical arguments made by nativists, trade union activists and the English-only type, xenophobic voters, variously present in different regions of the country. Surprising, at least from my perspective, was the dearth of information regarding the life that is being imposed upon a group of people who represent 5 percent of the total US population, equivalent to the totality of Asian Americans in the United States (InfoPlease 2015), or the effect that this new law would have on them and their families both in the United States and back home. In short, the response to the Bill, modest as it was in terms of addressing the current crisis, could only be described as representing the most xenophobic elements of a deeply divided American populace.

Obama's Executive Order

In accordance with the Republican Party (GOP) approaches to human suffering, John Boehner and the Republican Party chose to let this Bill die without ever being brought to the floor of the House for debate. As a result, Obama issued an Executive Order (EO) that reflects some of the intentions of the Senate Bill:

> The Obama administration has made historic improvements to border security and immigration enforcement, leading to "record" numbers of deportations that surpass the performance of earlier administrations. In December 2012, John Morton, then-director of U.S. Immigration and

> Customs Enforcement (ICE), announced that his agency had removed nearly 410,000 illegal aliens that year. Major news outlets, pro-amnesty lawmakers, and other Obama administration allies heralded this apparent milestone as evidence that the border and illegal immigration were now under control.
>
> (Vaughan 2015)

Even the Obama Administration itself doesn't pretend that this issue is "under control", and in fact the enormity of the current situation, involving an estimated 12 million undocumented people, led to Obama's November 20, 2014 Executive Order, which he described as follows:

> [E]ven as we focus on deporting criminals, the fact is, millions of immigrants in every state, of every race and nationality still live here illegally. And let's be honest – tracking down, rounding up, and deporting millions of people isn't realistic. Anyone who suggests otherwise isn't being straight with you. It's also not who we are as Americans. After all, most of these immigrants have been here a long time. They work hard, often in tough, low-paying jobs. They support their families. They worship at our churches. Many of their kids are American-born or spent most of their lives here, and their hopes, dreams, and patriotism are just like ours. As my predecessor, President Bush, once put it: "They are a part of American life."
>
> (Obama 2014)

Allying himself with Bush on this matter is politics, of course, likely aimed at those who would like to challenge the EO on the grounds that such renegade proclamations exceed the President's mandate. The reference to Bush may help pundits recall Bush enacted a similar Order during his time in office. But in the longer term, the EO was likely directed at a block of voters who, come election time, could make the difference between a Republican and a Democratic president, particularly given the large number of Hispanic voters in the so-called swing-states. Obama explained the amnesty in terms that could best be described as realist:

> Now here's the thing: We expect people who live in this country to play by the rules. We expect that those who cut the line will not be unfairly rewarded. So we're going to offer the following deal: If you've been in America for more than five years; if you have children who are American citizens or legal residents; if you register, pass a criminal background check, and you're willing to pay your fair share of taxes—you'll be able to apply to stay in this country temporarily without fear of deportation. You can come out of the shadows and get right with the law. That's what this deal is.
>
> (Obama 2014)

The rhetoric is for accommodation and legality, but the emphasis here is *temporarily*; this EO offers the possibility of a three-year stay, bringing the matter back after the next US federal election. More politics and more uncertainty in a system filled with arbitrariness and discretion.

This EO, with its relatively modest scope and limited time frame, drew the expected wrath and ire from politicians and large segments of the population. And on December 16, 2014, Federal District Court Judge Arthur J. Schwab handed down a decision in the sentencing phase of a criminal case in which he ruled that the Obama EO that will allow for millions of illegal immigrants to remain in the country (temporarily) is unconstitutional. One of the many problems with this widely reported ruling was that the Judge was never asked his opinion on Obama's EO, and the issue wasn't raised during the hearing because it wasn't in any way pertinent to the case. Ungar (2014) commented:

> This was a criminal matter and the Executive Order specifically, and with great clarity, prohibits anyone who recently came across the border illegally to avail themselves of the benefits of the E.O. Considering that this defendant had plead guilty to doing precisely that—recently coming across the border illegally—there really wasn't any reason to worry about either the constitutionality nor the applicability of the Executive Order.

In making his ruling and adding this commentary, Schwab became the first federal judge to provide an opinion on the EO, and as such he managed to garner considerable press in what promises to remain a contentious issue for the years that remain in the Obama Presidency. The proclamation is, however, totally unrelated to the case. The defendant in question would not have had any recourse under the EO because under Obama's plan amnesty would never be granted in such cases. In response to the Schwab ruling, the Justice Department noted: "No party in the case challenged the constitutionality of the immigration-related executive actions and the department's filing made it clear that the executive actions did not apply to the criminal matter before the court".

Schwab's comments came as little surprise, first because according to Ungar he is a rogue judge who is often misusing his powers, but also because this issue and this EO are hot-button issues amongst voters. It is not the case, as those who oppose Obama on this claim, that this President has been particularly kind to undocumented immigrants. Even in spite of his June 15, 2012 decision *not* to enforce the removal provisions of the Immigration and Nationality Act (INA) against an estimated population of 800,000 to 1.76 million individuals illegally present in the United States, the Obama White House had been more active than any other in deporting people. Before looking to longer-term solutions, it's worth examining what this deportation process looks like from the inside.

Deportation

As we saw previously in regards to the debates about incarceration, or the criminalization of migrants, the interviewees invited to discuss issues surrounding undocumented immigrants had strong opinions about deportation. Most of the interviewees spoke of it in regards to policies of incarceration, and in certain cases advocated for placing the punitive burden upon the home country judicial system. One lawyer said, for example, "If your policy is to deport people here illegally, then do it. Don't bother with incarceration. If they have committed a crime, just send them back to their judicial systems." This approach would address other issues raised in regards how shocked undocumented people are by the brutality of the system, and how dismayed they are by how little can be done to help them once they enter the judicial system. A public defender stated:

> I think that most of them are aware of the global consequences of their actions, in terms of deportation. But most of them are surprised that they're facing significant prison terms prior to the deportation. Many of my clients say: "Okay, you have caught me, please deport me, can't we do this?" I think that there's a real lack of understanding. On a fundamental level it makes no sense, if the plan is to deport somebody, then the underlying philosophy is that they will punish this person to show that they shouldn't come back, but that's the hard point to make. If I were in their shoes I would find it ridiculous myself. I think that the understanding of deportation is there, but not that there are other related consequences.

Many of the interviewees used language like this, invoking empathetic notions like: "If I were in their shoes", an example of caring that is seldom invoked at the legislative level and yet another reason why this book is dedicated to them. It's also worth noting that one reason why many migrants believe that they will be deported, and not incarcerated and then deported, is that this was commonly the case pre-9/11. This leads us to an important truism: migrant communities are often misinformed about changes that occur to host country laws before it's too late. A public defender recalled:

> It used to be that often being an illegal immigrant and being able to be released to INS was advantageous in terms of your criminal case. That is to say, I could say to them: "Look, he is going out of the country anyway, why should we pay to incarcerate him here?" I am not talking about on a murder or rape but I am talking drug crimes, breaking into car crimes, even home burglary crimes. I could say: "We can just give him unsupervised probation and release him to the INS", and they would do that. They virtually will not do that anymore. There is a lot more of a belief, a

> sort of assumption, that people can get in, and that they will get in again, and that is a bad thing.

A lawyer provides an example of the consequences of such misunderstandings in regards to those who re-enter the country subsequent to deportation, an act that has been heavily criminalized in the United States:

> The federal government has really cracked down on people who have re-entered illegally. I had two of those clients. They are so difficult because they have gotten away with it for years. They have crossed-over, been sent back, crossed-over, been sent back, and all of a sudden you're telling them: "This time, they want to give you 10 years". They are just furious. It's a disaster. Like this one case I had, he ended up going through four lawyers and everybody was telling them the same thing, but he just could not believe it. It's just so hard to explain: "Yeah, all of the other lawyers you have had in the last twenty years were able to get you sent back and not do jail time, but me, I am getting you ten years". There is not much of a defense. I mean, all the government has to prove is that you were deported.

Linking this shifting ground to Obama's EO provides another important insight: at this point in time, if and when the new program takes effect, there's a lot of uncertainty within the undocumented migrant community as to who is eligible for temporary relief. Currently, a phone call to the United States Citizenship and Immigration Service (USCIS) office includes a recording that tells would-be claimants to hold on while details are ironed out, and to check back soon. From the perspective of research that emphasizes the discursive elements of migration, including the importance of gossip and rumors, such uncertainty is bound to lead to confusion and to incorrect advice offered by jailhouse lawyers, community members and even ill-informed lawyers.

This uncertainty contributes to the vast and complex system that is used to identify, entrap, arrest, incarcerate, adjudicate, deport and police the borders, a system that seems as fickle as it is brutal. An interpreter, also representing the majority of those interviewed, drew attention to the vast resources committed to these efforts, on both sides of the equation:

> The deporting doesn't solve the problem at all. I have two impressions I guess. One is, it is incredible the amount of resources that this government, my government, pours into laying down the law and prosecuting. It is ridiculous. On the other hand, it is also encouraging that the defense attorneys, while they are overloaded and have fewer resources than the prosecutors, are doing a really good job of doing everything they can to appeal, and so forth. But again, people are incarcerated for longer, and the state is spending a lot of money. We are spinning our wheels, it seems.

The threat of deportation can also be invoked from informal sources, that is, arising from accusations, legitimate or not, that an undocumented immigrant has committed crimes such as domestic violence. A translator offers a common scenario:

> I saw so many people who were accused of domestic violence. I think it is something in the police mindset that they acknowledge as a fact that there's a problem with Latinos with this kind of behavior, domestic violence. It's also an easy way to get someone in trouble, or to get back at someone. It's a vengeful act for a woman to call the police on her Latino husband who is drunk again, and it creates a lot of problems. With kids involved, it gets very messy and complicated, and with domestic violence charges it's very hard to extricate him from that situation. If he doesn't have any bond money, then he is really stuck. I think it's kind of a stereotype that Latinos are violent and abusive, especially Latino men.

The threat of notifying authorities in cases like this one cuts several ways. First, the fear that the breadwinner of the family will be deported can keep victims of violence or abuse from calling the police. Second, people bearing a grudge, for whatever reason, can either threaten to call authorities, or they can do so, knowing that the consequences will be almost certain incarceration, felony charges and deportation. As a result, certain community groups have advocated for a kind of localized vigilante justice system, whereby people who have been abused by a member of the group can call an enforcer from the community who will carry out some kind of punishment in lieu of calling local authorities. Each of these scenarios is deeply problematic, and each contributes to a resistance on the part of the migrants to participate actively in the host country society.

Taken together, the complex picture painted by the details of this book is one of fickle, discretionary, arbitrary actions taken against a profoundly vulnerable population that is bereft of substantive legal rights, or the means to use them. At the same time, this book describes millions of people, all around the world, who have exercised a legitimate right, firmly ensconced in international law, and practiced with virtual impunity by the wealthy and the powerful, to engage in border-crossing. Most of the people described herein are not only working for a living, they are also sending home remittances; and, because of their fear of authority, most of them live without the benefits of the social services that should be available to everyone on the national territory. Policies aimed at punishing those who live "illegally" or sending out warnings to those who are contemplating doing so create an atmosphere of fear and loathing, uncertainty and abuse.

There are no solutions to the undocumented immigrant situation that can hinge upon bolstering border protection or control, in my opinion; borders are always porous to some degree, and people will try to cross them illegally if the push or pull factors are strong enough. Furthermore, there is no legitimate scientific method to assess who has suffered from the kinds of persecution that can provide rights under such recognized international instruments as the 1951 Geneva Convention because there's no way to determine with any degree of certainty whether a claimant has experienced the kind and degree of persecution that would render him/her eligible for protection (Barsky 1994). In other words, there are no ways to adjudicate borders that don't simply favor the wealthy and well connected over the vulnerable or the disenfranchised, and, frankly, there's no reason to engage in such adjudication. The simple solution to the question of how to control borders is to stop thinking that we should, and to overcome the belief that people move around for purely criminal reasons. People who leave their countries of origin tend to do so to seek what all travelers want, like new experiences or adventures, or what all workers need, which is employment. People leave their countries reluctantly, in most cases, because they are leaving their homes, with all that this implies (Barsky 2001); but, if they want to, I have found no serious legal or ethical reasons why we shouldn't encourage them to do so, and facilitate both their travel and their integration in the host country. The solution, in short, is open borders.

Open borders

Despite the tenor and magnitude of the immigration debate worldwide, there is but a tiny proportion of individuals who have suggested that border controls between countries be loosened or eliminated. This is surprising because open borders warrants serious consideration as an antidote to the many failed approaches to border control, worldwide. I want to address these lacunae by promoting and discussing ideas of eliminating the dysfunctional borders that bind us, and seek to reinforce this idea by pitting them against a much broader discussion about the experiences of undocumented people, the *sans papiers*. Unlike the current plan to legalize the existing undocumented population and then enforce stronger border controls, as we saw in the failed Border Security Bill, an open borders policy actually addresses the underlying issues relating to the movement of people, while remaining consistent with such objectives as promoting free trade and reducing unemployment.

Those who have contributed to the open border discussion, such as Barsky (2001), Chomsky (2014), Hayter (2000), Juss (2004) and Riley (2008), help us to understand why it is that when the emphasis of lawmakers and law enforcement is placed upon illegality, or the absence of proper documentation amongst migrants, then the broader perspective on what more open borders might look like gets lost. For example, freer movement between Mexico and the United States would lessen the suffering amongst undocumented persons, as we've seen, but it would also provide Americans with (say) the opportunity to legally work as a lifeguard in Cancun, a guide in the mountains of Puebla or a journalist in Mexico City. By the same token, if Britain would smooth the movement between the UK and India, then undocumented Indian citizens could take advantage of the new opportunities, but so too could British citizens. How many Canadians would welcome the possibility of spending some portion of their lives working legally in Spain? The opportunities afforded by the EU to French citizens, who can spend time in Ireland learning English, working in completely new settings and enjoying a very different culture, are remarkable. Why wouldn't we want similar opportunities for Brazilians to work in Mexico, Dutch citizens to work in Japan or Indonesians to hire people from New Zealand? And just as the opening of borders offers new opportunities for citizens of host countries, so too would it provide undocumented persons who are trapped inside of host countries with the possibility of returning home.

With robust systems of detection and apprehension that are growing in sophistication as new technologies are brought to bear upon borders, many undocumented immigrants are terrified of returning home because of their fear that they will be captured en route. They have nonetheless taken this risk, and people will continue to run these risks, because people like to move around, and in many cases they need to move around. We need to find ways to accommodate this obvious need. A public defender noted that even when we factor in the criminal element, by far the minority of migrants, there's still virtue in having freer flow universally:

> I think that this system with illegal re-entry rules doesn't deter people, they don't think it's really going to happen. At the same time, I don't know what a deterrent would be. The kinds of people who tend to come back are going to be criminals anyway, or they're so desperate that they'll do a drug crime to make money. The other people have serious ties to the country, and they'll come back, because they have family or kids. They're going to come back, even if it means five years in jail. There's no other option. They need to loosen up immigration laws, and let people with real ties, let them come into the country, and regularize their status. The other people are criminals, so they're going to get busted anyway.

One way of moving towards lessening border controls is to consider it in regards to larger phenomena, such as the circulation of workers, goods or even water or air or animals across these man-made national borders. I think of open borders as an attitude that we can all develop, just as we have developed an attitude of free circulation of goods in "free trade" zones like AFTA, APTA, CEFTA, COMESA, G-3, GCC, MERCOSUR, NAFTA, SADC, SAFTA, SICA and TPP (to name but a few)[1]. If our attitude is consistent with approaches to free trade that envision the free circulation of workers and the goods that they produce, for example, then we can easily find that the EU, despite its many flaws, is a reasonable model. Then, if we go beyond workers, we might suggest that everyone should be able to freely circulate inside of their country of origin, and also have the right to leave any country, including their own, and to return to that country. This is an attitude that favors free movement of people, which has a long history, and many interesting elements (see, for example, the compendium of work assembled at http://openborders.info/immigration-and-trade). Incidentally, those very words describing leaving a country and returning to it are taken almost verbatim from Article 13 of the Universal Declaration of Human Rights, which states, quite simply, that "Everyone has the right to freedom of movement and residence within the borders of each State. Everyone has the right to leave any country, including his own, and to return to his country." These words are inscribed into the Declaration that was adopted by the United Nations General Assembly on December 10, 1948 in the course of a General Assembly meeting in Paris. Eight nations abstained from that vote, but not one dissented. One of the members of the drafting sub-committee was Hernán Santa Cruz of Chile, who wrote:

> I perceived clearly that I was participating in a truly significant historic event in which a consensus had been reached as to the supreme value of the human person, a value that did not originate in the decision of a worldly power, but rather in the fact of existing—which gave rise to the inalienable right to live free from want and oppression and to fully develop one's personality. In the Great Hall...there was an atmosphere of genuine solidarity and brotherhood among men and women from all latitudes, the like of which I have not seen again in any international setting.
>
> (United Nations s.d.)

Instead of upholding the general principle of free movement that this Declaration takes as a kind of founding principle, many, if not most, people support the kind of rigid and inflexible borders that have led to the current international crises surrounding undocumented or "illegal" people. But we can also look to positive developments that have occurred in the past few decades. An obviously relevant historical precedent for our purposes was established by the European Parliament (2004) that allows citizens of EU Member States to (relatively) freely relocate and work across the broad spectrum of EU countries. And while there's no telling what crime rates would have been like had borders between EU Member States been maintained, it's probably safe to say that reducing border restrictions hasn't made the situation significantly worse than it would have been (Eger and Schäfer 2012). One reason for this is because the border policing that is possible under an EU-style system still allows for measured and appropriate law enforcement. A photographer-scholar pointed out that we already have such border patrols within the confines of the United States:

> Allowing for freedom of movement doesn't mean that one could not police the US-Mexico boundary to the extent that we are worried about the possibility of people bringing in weapons or individuals wanting to do harm to people in the United States. There are ways to police the boundary without controlling movement of the vast majority of people. In other words, you could still have inspections of people that are coming into the United States. For example, on the California/Oregon border, if you drive in from Oregon, there was a border checkpoint run by officers from the California Department of Agriculture. They wanted to make sure people weren't bringing in fruit, because they were concerned about the various agricultural pests being brought into the state. That's a form of a boundary policing if you will, but it doesn't involve violating people's basic human rights. We could probably figure out other ways of addressing those security concerns independent of building walls and fences and basically denying the vast majority of people who want to come in to the United States the right to do so.

Most people have a knee-jerk reaction to the idea of dismantling borders between states as different as Canada, Mexico and the United States, or between countries as similar, but contested, as (say) Pakistan, India and Sri Lanka; but how shocking is this idea, really, when compared to today's free movement between Germany and France, or Italy and Romania, or Ireland and the UK, considering the history of the 20th century? In the context of North America it's ironic, in fact, that Americans would have or feign concern about borders given how many people cross them each year, and how vast they are:

> According to the U.S. Geological Survey (USGS), the length of the International Boundary line of the U.S.-Canadian border, excluding Alaska, is approximately 3,987 miles, while the length of the U.S.-Mexican border is estimated at 1,933 miles. The length of the Alaska-Canada border alone is 1,538 miles.
>
> (Beaver 2006)

The fact is most of these borders cannot really be controlled, and efforts in this direction (walls, tracking devices and so forth) are enormously expensive and cost inefficient. Furthermore, this entire tracking system has come to favor the wealthy border-crossers who have access to GOES, NEXUS and other costly systems. It will of course be argued that the EU system has proven a failure, in light of recent news about the euro and delinquent countries (Cyprus, Greece, Portugal); but in fact, this isn't necessarily a direct consequence of the EU border policies and, if the United States is any indication, the situation would likely be worse had the EU not been formed (Hermann and Mahnkopf 2010).

Anti-immigrant, isolationist, nationalistic or patriotic arguments also fly in the face of history, and ignore the early ideals of the Indian poet Tagore, Confucianism, the Islamic concept of the *umma* and the early ideas of a "world empire" touted by Alexander the Great, or "universal morality" upheld in Greek Stoicism. More recently, we can reference the ideal of "world citizenship" described by Erasmus and Kant, and a host of those very people now invoked to denounce free movement or free trade, people who in their lifetimes often touted both as part of their credo advocating freedom and promoting happiness.

In the American context, Thomas Jefferson in his instructions to Virginia delegates to the 1774 Continental Congress declared that:

> nature has given to all men [a right] of departing from the country in which chance, not choice, has placed them, [and] of going in quest of new habitations, and of there establishing new societies under such laws and regulation as, to them, shall seem most likely to promote public happiness.
>
> (Jefferson 1774, p. 435)

By invoking the EU, and the uplifting words of Thomas Jefferson, I aim to demystify and validate the possibility of at least imagining a world without national borders. This is a legitimate and all-encompassing approach to the abhorrent situation that imposes illegitimate, undue and disproportionate suffering upon people exercising one of the most fundamental rights of human beings, and one of the most common traits of living beings of all sorts: free movement, and the promotion of "public happiness".

Note

1 ASEAN Free Trade Area (AFTA), Asia-Pacific Trade Agreement (APTA), Central European Free Trade Agreement (CEFTA), Common Market for Eastern and Southern Africa (COMESA), G-3 Free Trade Agreement (G-3), Gulf Cooperation Council (GCC), Southern Common Market (MERCOSUR), North American Free Trade Agreement (NAFTA), Southern African Development Community (SADC), South Asian Free Trade Area (SAFTA), Central American Integration System (SICA), Trans-Pacific Strategic Economic Partnership (TPP).

Bibliography

Amnesty International (2013) "A Missed Opportunity: Why is the EU Migration 'Task Force' Failing to Meet Its Objective to Save Lives?" Available at: http://www.sos-europe-amnesty.eu/a-missed-opportunity-why-is-the-eu-migration-task-force-failing-to-meet-its-objective-to-save-lives-news. [Accessed: 15 January 2015]

Asher, Sain and Gregory Wallace (8 September 2014) "Deportation: Its Cost – and

Human Toll", *Money*. Available at: http://money.cnn.com/2014/09/08/news/economy/deportation-by-the-numbers. [Accessed: 15 January 2015]

Barbora, S., S. Thieme, A. K. Siegmann, V. Menon and G. Gurung (2008) "Migration Matters in South Asia: Commonalities and Critiques", *Economic & Political Weekly* 43.24, pp. 57–65.

Barsky, Robert F. (1994) *Constructing a Productive Other: Discourse Theory and the Convention Refugee Hearing*. Philadelphia, PA and Amsterdam: John Benjamins.

Barsky, Robert F. (2001) *Arguing and Justifying: Assessing the Convention Refugee Choice of Moment, Motive and Host Country*. Aldershot, Sydney and Burlington, VT: Ashgate Press.

Beaver, Janice Cheryl (2006) "U.S. International Borders: Brief Facts", *CRS Report for Congress*. Available at: https://www.fas.org/sgp/crs/misc/RS21729.pdf. [Accessed: 15 January 2015]

Blinder, Scott (23 June 2014) "Deportations, Removals and Voluntary Departures from the UK", *Migration Observatory*. Available at: http://www.migrationobservatory.ox.ac.uk/briefings/deportations-removals-and-voluntary-departures-uk. [Accessed: 15 January 2015]

Chomsky, Aviva (2014) *Undocumented: How Immigration Became Illegal*. Boston: Beacon Press.

Chomsky, Noam (2006) "Globalization: Noam Chomsky Interviewed by Maria Ahmed", *Global Agenda*. Available at: http://www.chomsky.info/interviews/2006----.htm. [Accessed: 15 January 2015]

Congress (2013) "Border Security, Economic Opportunity, and Immigration Modernization Act", *United States Congress*. Available at: https://www.govtrack.us/congress/bills/113/s74. [Accessed: 15 January 2015]

Congressional Budget Office (2013) "Letter". Available at: http://www.cbo.gov/sites/default/files/cbofiles/attachments/s744aspassed.pdf. [Accessed: 15 January 2015]

Cornelius, Wayne A. (ed.) (2004) *Controlling Immigration: A Global Perspective*. Stanford, CA: Stanford University Press.

Datta, Pranati (2004) "Push-Pull Factors of Undocumented Migration from Bangladesh to West Bengal: A Perception Study", *Qualitative Report* 9.2, pp. 335–58.

Eger, Thomas and Hans-Bernd Schäfer (eds.) (2012) *Research Handbook on the Economics of European Union Law*. Cheltenham, UK and Northampton, MA: Edward Elgar.

European Commission (2014) "Task Force for the Mediterranean: Actions on Migation and Asylum". Available at: http://ec.europa.eu/dgs/home-affairs/what-is-new/news/news/2014/20140527_01_en.htm. [Accessed 15 January 2015]

European Parliament (2004) "Right of Union Citizens and Their Family Members to Move and Reside Freely within the Territory of the Member States", *European Union*. Available at: http://europa.eu/legislation_summaries/education_training_youth/lifelong_learning/l33152_en.htm. [Accessed: 15 January 2015]

European Union (2013) "Task Force for the Mediterranean: Actions on Migration and Asylum in the EU" (TFM). Available at: http://ec.europa.eu/dgs/home-affairs/what-is-new/news/news/2014/20140527_01_en.htm. [Accessed: 15 January 2015]

Global Migration Group (2010) "Statement on the Human Rights of Migrants in Irregular Situations", *Global Migration Group*. Available at: http://www.

globalrnigrationgroup.org/pdf/GMG%20Joint%20Statement%/20Adopted%20 30%20Septh202010.pdf. [Accessed: 15 January 2015]
Hardy, Lisa and Raymond Michalowski (2014) "Victimizing the Undocumented: Immigration Policy and Border Enforcement as State Crime", in Rothe and Kauzlarich (2014), pp. 3–14.
Hayter, Teresa (2000) *Open Borders: The Case against Immigration Controls*. London and Sterling, VI: Pluto Press.
Hermann, Christoph and Birgit Mahnkopf (2010) "Still a Future for the European Social Model?", *Global Labour Journal* 1.3, pp. 314–30.
Hobbs, Robert Dean (2011) *Multilingual Education Model Construction Based on Superior Cognitive Skills of Multilingual Students*. PhD dissertation. University of Phoenix, Arizona.
InfoPlease (2015) "Demographic Statistics", *Infoplease*. Available at: http://www.infoplease.com/us/census/data/demographic.html. [Accessed: 15 January 2015]
Jefferson, Thomas (1774) *A Summary View of the Rights of British America. Set Forth in Some Resolutions Intended for the Inspection of the Present Delegates of the People of Virginia. Now in Convention. By a Native, and Member of the House of Burgesses*. Williamsburg, VA: Clementina Rind.
Juss, Satvinder S. (2004) "Free Movement and the World Order", *International Journal of Refugee Law* 16.3, pp. 289–335.
Kant, Immanuel (1972) *Perpetual Peace: A Philosophical Essay*, trans. Campbell Smith. New York and London: Garland.
Kraler, Albert (2012) *Gender, Generations and the Family in International Migration*. Amsterdam: Amsterdam University Press.
Markert, Bernd, Edita Baltrėnaitė, Ewa Chudzińska, Silvia De Marco, Jean Diatta, Zahra Ghaffari, Svetlana Gorelova, Jorge Marcovecchio, Guntis Tabors, Meie Wang, Naglaa Yousef, Stefan Fraenzle and Simone Wuenschmann (2014) "Multilingual Education of Students on a Global Scale and Perspective—International Networking on the Example of Bioindication and Biomonitoring (B&B technologies)", *Environmental Science and Pollution Research* 21.8, pp. 5450–6.
McNevin, Ann (2011) *Contesting Citizenship: Irregular Migrants and New Frontiers of the Political*. New York: Columbia University Press.
Michalowski, Raymond and Lisa Hardy (2014) "Victimizing the Undocumented: Immigration Policy and Border Enforcement as State Crime" in Rothe and Kauzlarich (2014), pp. 87–109.
Nanda, Ved P. (2011) "Domestic and International Legal Responses to Emerging Migration Issues", *Journal of International & Comparative Law* 17, pp. 355–80.
Obama, Barack (2014) "Remarks by the President in Address to the Nation on Immigration", The White House: Office of the Press Secretary. Available at: https://www.whitehouse.gov/the-press-office/2014/11/20/remarks-president-address-nation-immigration (Accessed: 15 January 2015).
Orrenius, Pia (June 2014) "Enforcement and Illegal Migration: Enforcement Deters Immigration with Many Unintended Consequences", *IZA World of Labor*. Available at: http://wol.iza.org/articles/enforcement-and-illegal-migration. [Accessed: 15 January 2015]
Petersilia, Joan and Kevin R. Reitz (eds.) (2012) *The Oxford Handbook of Sentencing and Corrections*. Oxford and New York: Oxford University Press.

Pickering, Sharon (2011) *Women, Borders, and Violence: Current Issues in Asylum, Forced Migration and Trafficking*. New York: Springer.

Pillay, Navanethem (2011) "UN High Commissioner for Human Rights, Global Forum on Migration and Development/Civil Society Days", *The Global Campaign for Ratification of the Convention on Rights of Migrants*. Available at: http://www.migrantsrights.org/past_events.htm. [Accessed: 15 January 2015]

Riley, Jason L. (2008) *Let Them in: The Case for Open Borders*. London: Gotham.

Rothe, Dawn L. and David Kauzlarich (eds.) (2014) *Towards a Victimology of State Crime*. London: Routledge.

Samuels, Fiona and Sanju Wagle (June 2011) *Population Mobility and HIV and AIDS: Review of Laws, Policies and Treaties between Bangladesh, Nepal and India*. London: Overseas Development Institute Background Note. Available at: http://www.odi.org/publications/5733-hiv-aids-migration-emphasis-bangladesh-nepal-india. [Accessed: 15 January 2015]

Skutnabb-Kangas, Tove and Kathleen Heugh (eds.) (2011) *Multilingual Education and Sustainable Diversity Work: From Periphery to Center*. Abingdon, Oxon: Routledge.

Thieme, Susan (2006) *Social Networks and Migration: Far West Nepalese Labour Migrants in Delhi*. Munich: LIT Verlag Münster.

Ungar, Rick (17 December 2014) "Federal Judge Declares Obama Immigration Executive Order Unconstitutional; Problem is Nobody Asked for His Opinion", *Forbes Magazine*. Available at: http://www.forbes.com/sites/rickungar/2014/12/17/federal-judge-declares-obama-immigration-executive-order-unconstitutional-problem-is-nobody-asked-for-his-opinion/1. [Accessed: 15 January 2015]

United Nations (s.d.) *The Universal Declaration of Human Rights: History of the Document*. Available at: http://www.un.org/en/documents/udhr/history.shtml. [Accessed: 15 January 2015]

Vaughan, Jessica (2015) "Deportation Numbers Unwrapped: Raw Statistics Reveal the Real Story of ICE Enforcement in Decline". Washington: Center for Immigration Studies. Available at: http://cis.org/ICE-Illegal-Immigrant-Deportations. [Accessed: 15 January 2015]

Zanfrini, Laura, Winfried Kluth, Vardan Gevorgyan, Tzenē Kavounidē, Irina Ivakhnyuk, Marnia Belhadj, Rosa Aparicio, José Marîa Ruiz de Huidobro De Carlos and Colin Manchip (2008) *Policies on Irregular Migrants*. Strasbourg: Council of Europe Publishing.

Index

For Product Safety Concerns and Information please contact our EU
representative GPSR@taylorandfrancis.com
Taylor & Francis Verlag GmbH, Kaufingerstraße 24, 80331 München, Germany

www.ingramcontent.com/pod-product-compliance
Ingram Content Group UK Ltd.
Pitfield, Milton Keynes, MK11 3LW, UK
UKHW022129190926
475702UK00013B/1713
* 9 7 8 1 1 3 8 6 3 4 9 9 2 *